CAMBRIDGE International Examinations

IGCSE
Accou
Catherine Co

CAMBRIDGE
UNIVERSITY PRESS

CAMBRIDGE UNIVERSITY PRESS
Cambridge, New York, Melbourne, Madrid, Cape Town, Singapore, São Paulo

Cambridge University Press
The Water Club, Beach Road, Granger Bay, Cape Town 8005, South Africa

www.cambridge.org
Information on this title: www.cambridge.org/9780521893466

©Cambridge University Press 2002

This book is in copyright. Subject to statutory exception
and to the provisions of relevant collective licensing agreements,
no reproduction of any part may take place without
the written permission of Cambridge University Press.

First published 2002
Reprinted 2003, 2005, 2006

Printed in the United Kingdom at the University Press, Cambridge

ISBN-13   978-0-521-89346-6 paperback
ISBN-10   0-521-89346-1 paperback

. . . .

Cambridge University Press has no responsibility for the persistence or
accuracy of URLS for external or third-party Internet websites referred
to in this book, and does not guarantee that any content on such
websites is, or will remain, accurate or appropriate.

Introduction

The aim of this book is to provide an up-to-date text covering the Cambridge International Examinations International General Certificate in Secondary Education Accounting syllabus.

The syllabus can be studied at two levels – Core Curriculum and Extended Curriculum. Candidates expected to obtain Grades C–G should follow the Core Curriculum and only enter for Papers 1 and 2 of the examination. Those candidates likely to obtain Grade C or higher should also enter for Paper 3 of the examination. Paper 1 is in the form of Multiple Choice questions and Papers 2 and 3 consist of structured questions. It is recommended that students obtain an up-to-date syllabus, so they can see which topics are included in each part of the Curriculum.

This book covers all the IGCSE Accounting Curriculum. However, the topics are not covered in the order in which they appear in the Curriculum. They have been presented in what the author's long teaching experience has shown to be a suitable order for an accounting student commencing a course at this level. The table on the next page shows the chapter(s) of the book in which each section of the Curriculum may be found.

Chapers, 1–15, 17 and 19 are concerned with the accounts of businesses involved in trading – the buying and selling of goods without changing them in any way. The accounts of manufacturing businesses are considered in Chapter 18. The accounts of clubs and societies are considered in Chapter 16.

Each chapter is complete in itself and contains appropriate examples. The Review Questions at the end of each chapter are taken from past examination papers wherever possible. Answers to questions marked with an asterisk (*) are given at the end of the book.

It is always advisable to show all calculations when answering accounting questions. In the examination, all the structured questions are answered on the actual examination paper, but space is provided for calculations.

In common with most accounting textbooks, dates used in the examples throughout this book are expressed as 20–0, 20–1, 20–2 and so on. Actual dates are used in examination papers. Those Review Questions taken from past papers show the dates as they appeared on the actual examination paper.

Where to find each section of the syllabus

Chapter	Syllabus Section 1				Syllabus Section 2							Syllabus Section 3				Syllabus Section 4			Syllabus Section 5					Syllabus Section 6				Syllabus Section 7			
	1	2	3	4	1	2	3	4	5	6	7	1	2	3	4	1	2	3	1	2	3	4	5	1	2	3	4	1	2	3	4
1	√	√	√	√																											
2													√	√																	
3															√																
4													√	√	√																
5													√																		
6												√	√	√																	
7			√	√																				√				√			
8					√	√	√	√	√	√	√								√	√											
9																				√			√	√							
10																					√			√							
11																						√		√							
12																		√													
13																	√						√								
14																√															
15																										√		√			
16																											√				
17																									√						
18																											√				
19														√										√							
20	√			√																				√				√	√	√	√

iv Accounting: IGCSE

Contents

Introduction iii
Chapter   1   Introduction to accounting 1
             2   Double entry bookkeeping – Part A 6
             3   The Trial Balance 20
             4   Double entry bookkeeping – Part B 29
             5   Petty cash book 41
             6   Business documents and books of prime entry......... 48
             7   Final Accounts 63
             8   Accounting rules 80
             9   Accruals and prepayments 86
           10   Depreciation and disposal of fixed asssets 103
           11   Bad debts and provision for doubtful debts........... 120
           12   Bank reconciliation statements 134
           13   Journal entries and correction of errors 145
           14   Control accounts..................................... 159
           15   Incomplete records................................... 167
           16   Accounts of clubs and societies 184
           17   Partnership accounts 198
           18   Accounts of manufacturing businesses 213
           19   Departmental accounts 223
           20   Analysis and interpretation 229

Answers to review questions...................................... 248
Examination papers 271
Index 291

CHAPTER 1: Introduction to accounting

The need for business accounts

Bookkeeping and accounting are both concerned with the financial records of a business. The detailed recording of all the financial transactions of a business is known as **bookkeeping**. **Accounting** makes use of these records to prepare periodic financial statements, which can be used to assess the performance of the business.

It is impossible, even in a small business, to remember the full details of everything that takes place, so it is necessary to make a record of every transaction which affects the business. Every business is different, so the records maintained will vary because of the different information which is required, but the basis of all the accounting systems is **double entry bookkeeping**.

The main aim of the owner of a business is for the business to make a profit. Periodically, a **Trading and Profit and Loss Account** is prepared which shows the calculation of the profit earned by the business. Where a business makes a profit, the owner can receive a proper return on the money invested in the business and funds are available for expanding the business, replacing equipment, and so on. Where a business makes a loss, it may eventually result in the business being closed down as the owner's investment in the business falls, and the business is not able to obtain up-to-date equipment and keep pace with competitors.

The owner of a business also needs to know the financial position of the business, and so, periodically, a **Balance Sheet** is prepared. This summarises the position of a business, in monetary terms, on a certain date. The Balance Sheet shows what the business owns, known as **assets**, and what the business owes, known as **liabilities**.

The Trading and Profit and Loss Account and the Balance Sheet collectively are often referred to as **final accounts**. Whilst these provide valuable information, they can only record the financial aspects of the business. Non-monetary factors can play an important part in the success of a business, but these cannot be recorded in the accounting records (see Chapter 8). It is also important to bear in mind that, whilst most of the information recorded in the accounts is based on facts, some figures have to be based on **estimates** (for example how much an asset has lost in value through depreciation).

The progress of a business can be measured by comparing the final accounts of one year with those of previous years, and with those of similar businesses. Various accounting ratios can be calculated to measure the relationship between figures within the final accounts, and these ratios can also be used for comparison purposes.

All the terms mentioned above are explained in detail in following chapters.

The Balance Sheet equation

A person starting a business usually provides the funds or resources necessary to set up the business. This is known as **capital**. So the resources, or **assets**, in the business will be equal to the resources or capital provided by the owner of the business. This means that **assets = capital**.

Other people may also supply the business with assets. These amounts owing by the business are **liabilities**. Applying the same formula as above, the assets in the business will be equal to the resources provided by the owner (the capital) plus the resources provided by other people (the liabilities). This means that **assets = capital + liabilities**. Capital is also known as owner's equilty, therefore we say: assets = owner's equilty + liabilities and the abbreviated accounting equation is A = OE + L. This is known as the Balance Sheet equation. The two sides of the equation will **always** be equal. The individual amounts of assets, liabilities and capital may change, but the total assets will always equal the total of the capital plus the liabilities.

The accounting equation may be expressed in the form of a **Balance Sheet**, which is a statement showing the financial position of a business on a certain date. It lists the assets, the liabilities and the capital. **Assets** consist of everything that the business owns, plus any money owing to the business. **Liabilities** consist of anything the business owes. **Capital** is a form of liability as it is the amount the business owes to the owner of the business. It is important to remember that the accounting records are the records of the business, not the records of the owner of the business.

A Balance Sheet must always have a heading, which should include the date on which the Balance Sheet applied. It is also usual to show the name under which the business trades (this may be the name of the owner if the business trades under that name).

The Balance Sheet will be affected every time the business makes some change to the assets, liabilities and capital.

■ Example

20–2 June 1 James Jones set up a business to trade under the name of Jones Stores. He opened a business bank account and paid in $50 000 as capital.
2 The business bought premises for $30 000 and paid by cheque.
3 The business bought a stock of goods costing $4 500 on credit.
4 The business sold goods, which had cost $500, on credit.

Prepare the Balance Sheet of Jones Stores, as it would appear at the close of business on each of the dates given above.

Jones Stores

Balance Sheet as at 1 June 20–2

Assets	$	Liabilities	$
Bank	50 000	Capital	50 000
	50 000		50 000

The assets of the business are equal to the liabilities of the business.

Jones Stores

Balance Sheet as at 2 June 20–2

Assets	$	Liabilities	$
Premises	30 000	Capital	50 000
Bank	20 000		
	50 000		50 000

The asset of bank has been reduced as money has been spent in obtaining a new asset. The individual assets have changed, but the total of the assets remains the same.

Jones Stores

Balance Sheet as at 3 June 20–2

Assets	$	Liabilities	$
Premises	30 000	Capital	50 000
Stock	4 500	Creditors	4 500
Bank	20 000		
	54 500		50 000

Buying goods on credit means that the business is supplied with the goods but does not pay for them immediately. The business has obtained a new asset in the form of stock of goods, but has also acquired a liability, as it now owes the supplier of the goods (known as a **creditor**).

Jones Stores

Balance Sheet as at 4 June 20–2

Assets	$	Liabilities	$
Premises	30 000	Capital	50 000
Stock	4 000	Creditors	4 500
Debtors	500		
Bank	20 000		
	54 500		50 000

The asset of stock has been reduced but a new asset has been obtained in the form of money owed to the business by a customer (known as a **debtor**).

In order to keep the example simple, the goods were sold to the customer at the price the business paid for them. It is obvious that, in practice, they must be sold at a price above cost price to enable the business to earn a profit.

A Balance Sheet can be displayed in different ways, and it is usual for the assets and liabilities to be divided up into different classes. Balance Sheets will be explained in more detail in Chapter 7.

In the above example, a new Balance Sheet was prepared after every transaction. This is obviously impossible in practice, as, in one single hour, there can be several changes to the business's assets and liabilities. A system of **double entry bookkeeping** has been developed where all the day-to-day transactions are recorded. (This is dealt with in detail in chapters 2 and 4.) A Balance Sheet is only prepared periodically – usually at the close of business on the last day of the financial year of the business. A financial year does not necessarily run from 1 January to 31 December. A business may be started on any date. The final accounts will be prepared for twelve-month periods from that date, which are known as financial years.

Review questions

1. (a) Explain the meaning of the terms –
    (i) assets
    (ii) liabilities
    (iii) capital
   (b) State whether **each** of the following items is an asset or a liability:
    Office equipment Loan from ABC
    Creditor   Cash
    Machinery   Expenses owing

*2. Redraft the following Balance Sheet to correct any mistakes.

Farad

Balance Sheet for the year ended 31 March 20–6

Assets	$	Liabilities	$
Loan from bank	20 000	Capital	65 000
Cash	2 600	Fixtures and fittings	22 00
Machinery	34 000	Debtors	13 400
Creditors	15 400		
Stock	28 400		
	100 400		100 400

3. Rachel had the following items in her Balance Sheet at 30 September 20–5.

| Capital | $20 000 | Equipment | $12 900 | Bank | $2 200 |
| Creditors | $2 900 | Stock | $4 700 | Debtor | $3 100 |

During the first week of October Rachel had the following transactions:
(a) Received $2 500 by cheque from the debtors.
(b) Paid $1 000 by cheque to creditors.
(c) Bought further stock costing $900 on credit.
(d) Bought further equipment and paid $500 by cheque.

Draw up Rachel's Balance Sheet as at 7 October 20–5 after the above transactions have been completed.

Chapter 1 – Introduction to accounting

CHAPTER 2
Double entry bookkeeping – Part A

Introduction

Chapter 1 explained that, as it is impractical to produce a new Balance Sheet after every transaction, day-to-day transactions are recorded using the **double entry system**. In the example given in Chapter 1 it was shown that every transaction affected the Balance Sheet in **two** ways. This dual aspect of a **giving** and a **receiving** is recorded in the day-to-day records.

The business will keep a separate **ledger account** for each debtor and creditor with whom it has dealings, a separate ledger account for each type of asset, expense, liability, and so on. Every transaction concerning a particular person, asset, expense, etc. is recorded in the appropriate account.

The ledger can be in the form of a bound book (in which case one ledger account will appear on each page) or a file of separate sheets of paper, with an account on each. Where accounts are maintained using a computer, a ledger will consist of a computer file, which is divided into separate accounts. A typical ledger account is shown below.

Account name

Debit   Credit

Date	Details	Folio	$	Date	Details	Folio	$

The account is divided into two sides by the centre line. The left-hand side is the **debit** side (usually abbreviated to **Dr.**) and the right-hand side is the **credit** side (usually abbreviated to **Cr.**). On each side there are columns in which to record the date, details and amount of each transaction. The **folio** column is used for cross-referencing the accounts.

Because there is a giving and receiving in every transaction, **two** entries are made – a debit in one account and a credit in another account. The **debit** entry is made in the account which **gains** the value, which can be **assets** gained by the business or **expenses** paid by the business. The **credit** entry is made in the account which **gives** the value, which can be **liabilities** incurred by the business or **income** received by the business.

■ Example

20–2 March 1 Abdul set up a business. He opened a business bank account and paid in $40 000 as capital.
2 Bought business premises for $20 000 and paid by cheque.

Enter the transactions in the ledger of the business.

Abdul

Bank account Page 1

	Date	Details	Folio	$	Date	Details	Folio	$	
(a)	20–2 Mar 1	Capital	2	40 000	20–2 Mar 2	Premises	3	20 000	(b)

Capital account Page 2

Date	Details	Folio	$	Date	Details	Folio	$	
				20–2 Mar 1	Bank	1	40 000	(a)

Premises account Page 3

	Date	Details	Folio	$	Date	Details	Folio	$
(b)	20–2 Mar 2	Bank	1	20 000				

Notes: 1. The first transaction has been labelled (a) for reference purposes. The bank account was debited to show value being received and the capital account was credited to show value being given.
2. The second transaction has been labelled (b) for reference purposes. The premises account was debited to show value being received and the bank account was credited to show value being given.
3. In each case the details column of each account shows the name of the account where the opposite half of the double entry is made, and the folio number gives the page on which that account will be found.

Care must be taken to ensure that a **double entry** is made for a transaction, before going on to enter the next item. Examination questions give a list of items to enter into the accounts, but, in practice, information for entering in the accounts is obtained from **business documents**. These are explained in Chapter 6.

Assets and liabilities, expenses and incomes

Every type of asset, liability, expense and income has its own ledger account. In practice, each ledger account has its own page or sheet. This is obviously not possible in exercises, so it is usual to show several accounts on one page.

■ **Example**

20–2 March 1 Abdul set up a business. He opened a business bank account and paid in $40 000 as capital.
2 Bought business premises for $20 000 and paid by cheque.
3 Paid $950 for insurance by cheque.
4 Part of the premises was rented out to another business and a cheque for $200 rent was received.
5 Bought equipment and paid by cheque, $8 000.
6 Paid for repairs to premises by cheque, $70.
7 Received a loan of $5 000 from ABC Ltd. which was paid into the bank.

Enter the transactions in the ledger of the business.

Abdul

Bank account   Page 1

Date	Details	Folio	$	Date	Details	Folio	$
20–2				20–2			
Mar 1	Capital	2	40 000	Mar 2	Premises	3	20 000
4	Rent received	5	200	3	Insurance	4	950
7	ABC Ltd. Loan	8	5 000	5	Equipment	6	8 000
				6	Repairs	7	70

Capital account
Page 2

Date	Details	Folio	$	Date	Details	Folio	$
				20–2 Mar 1	Bank	1	40 000

Premises account
Page 3

Date	Details	Folio	$	Date	Details	Folio	$
20–2 Mar 2	Bank	1	20 000				

Insurance account
Page 4

Date	Details	Folio	$	Date	Details	Folio	$
20–2 Mar 3	Bank	1	950				

Rent Received account
Page 5

Date	Details	Folio	$	Date	Details	Folio	$
				20–2 Mar 4	Bank	1	200

Equipment account
Page 6

Date	Details	Folio	$	Date	Details	Folio	$
20–2 Mar 5	Bank	1	8 000				

Repairs account
Page 7

Date	Details	Folio	$	Date	Details	Folio	$
20–2 Mar 6	Bank	1	70				

ABC Ltd. Loan account
Page 8

Date	Details	Folio	$	Date	Details	Folio	$
				20–2 Mar 7	Bank	1	5 000

Note: Repairs to premises do not increase the value of the asset. They are a running expense and are entered into an expense account.

Balancing accounts

Where any accounts of assets and liabilities have several entries recorded in them, it is usual to **balance** these accounts at the end of each month. The balance shows the amount remaining in that account, and is the difference between the two sides of the account. The procedure may be summarised as –

(a) On a separate piece of paper, or on a calculator, add up each side of the account. Find the difference between the two sides of the account.
(b) (i) Enter this difference on the next available line on the side of the account which has the smallest total.
  (ii) Insert the date of balancing in the date column. This is usually the last day of the month.
  (iii) Insert the description 'Balance' in the details column.
  (iv) Insert 'c/d' in the folio column to indicate that the balance is going to be carried down.
(c) Total each side of the account by adding up and showing the amount in total lines (a single line above the figure, and either a single or a double line below the figure). These totals must be on the same level.
(d) Make a double entry for the balance carried down.
  (i) On the line below the totals of the account enter the amount of the balance on the opposite side of the account from where the words 'Balance c/d' appeared.
  (ii) Insert the date. This is usually the first day of the next month.
  (iii) Insert the description 'Balance' in the details column.
  (iv) Insert 'b/d' in the folio column to indicate that the balance has been brought down from the previous month.

■ Example

Balance the bank account which appeared in Abdul's ledger at the end of his first week of trading.

The entries already appearing in the bank account have been taken from the previous example.

Abdul

Bank account   Page 1

Date	Details	Folio	$	Date	Details	Folio	$
20–2				20–2			
Mar 1	Capital	2	40 000	Mar 2	Premises	3	20 000
4	Rent received	5	200	3	Insurance	4	950
7	ABC Ltd. Loan	8	5 000	5	Equipment	6	8 000
				6	Repairs	7	70
				7	Balance	c/d	16 180
			45 200				45 200
20–2							
Mar 8	Balance	b/d	16 180				

Note: The debit side totalled $45 200 and the credit side totalled $29 020, so the balance (the difference between the two sides) was $16 180.

Sales, purchases, and returns

Two accounts are needed to record the purchase of goods in which the business trades, and the later sale of those goods. These must be kept separate, as the goods will come in at cost price and usually go out at a higher price, which enables the business to earn a profit. Instead of a 'Goods account' there is a **'Purchases account'** and a **'Sales account'**. A Stock account is only used at the end of each financial year to record the value of the stock at that date.

Purchases

Whenever a business purchases goods, the purchases account will be debited. If the goods were paid for at the time of purchase, the double entry will be made by crediting the bank account, if payment was made by cheque, or crediting the cash account, if payment was made in cash.

If the business does not pay for the goods at the time of purchase, this is known as **buying on credit**. In this case, the credit entry will be made in the account of the supplier (to show the value coming from that account). Until the account is paid, the supplier is a **trade creditor** of the business. When payment is made to the supplier, his/her account is debited (to show value going into that account) and the bank account or cash account is credited (to show value coming out of that account).

■ **Example** 20–2 March 10 Abdul purchased goods, $950, and paid by cheque.
12 Abdul purchased goods, $1 000, on credit from East & Co.
16 Abdul paid the amount due to East & Co. by cheque.

Record the above in Abdul's ledger.

Abdul

Bank account Page 1

Date	Details	Folio	$	Date	Details	Folio	$
				20–2 Mar 10	Purchases	9	950
				16	East & Co.	10	1 000

Purchases account Page 9

Date	Details	Folio	$	Date	Details	Folio	$
20–2 Mar 10	Bank	1	950				
12	East & Co.	10	1 000				

East & Co. account Page 10

Date	Details	Folio	$	Date	Details	Folio	$
20–2 Mar 16	Bank	1	1 000	20–2 Mar 12	Purchases	9	1 000
			1 000				1 000

Note: East & Co.'s account has been totalled as both sides equal $1 000, so the account is 'in balance' and is closed.

Sales

Whenever a business sells goods, the sales account is credited. If the goods were paid for at the time of sale, the double entry will be made by debiting the bank account, if a cheque was received, or the cash account, if cash was received.

If the customer does not pay for the goods at the time of sale, this is known as **selling on credit**. In this case, the debit entry will be made in the account of the customer (to show value going into that account). Until the account is paid, the customer is a **trade debtor** of the business. When

■ **Example**

20–2 March 17 Abdul sold goods, $650, on credit to North.
20 Abdul sold goods, $180, for cash.
21 North gave Abdul $500 in cash, on account.

Record the above in Abdul's ledger. Balance North's account and bring down the balance.

Abdul

Sales account — Page 11

Date	Details	Folio	$	Date	Details	Folio	$
				20–2 Mar 17	North	12	650
				20	Cash	13	180

North account — Page 12

Date	Details	Folio	$	Date	Details	Folio	$
20–2 Mar 17	Sales	11	650	20–2 Mar 21	Cash	13	500
				21	Balance	c/d	150
			650				650
20–2 Mar 22	Balance	b/d	150				

Cash account — Page 13

Date	Details	Folio	$	Date	Details	Folio	$
20–2 Mar 20	Sales	11	180				
21	North	12	500				

Notes: 1. The term 'on account' is used to indicate that only part of the amount owing is being paid at that point. The balance will be paid at a later date.
2. On 22 March North is a debtor as he owes Abdul $150.

Returns

It can happen that goods purchased are not satisfactory – they may be damaged, faulty, or not what was ordered. These will be returned to the supplier and are known as **purchases returns** or **returns outward**. Instead of crediting the purchases account to record the value going out, it is usual to credit a separate account, the purchases returns account (or returns outward account). The debit entry will be made in the account of the supplier (to show the value coming into that account). This entry will reduce the amount owing to the supplier.

Where goods sold by a business prove to be unsatisfactory, a customer may return them to the business. These are known as **sales returns** or **returns inward**. When a customer returns goods, the sales returns account (or returns inward account) is debited, to show value coming into that account. The account of the customer is credited (to show value going out of that account). This entry will reduce the amount owing by the customer.

■ Example

20–2 March 22 Abdul purchased goods, $690, on credit from Western.
          23 Abdul sold goods, $830, on credit to Southern.
          25 Abdul returned damaged goods, $75, to Western.
          27 Southern returned goods, which were not as ordered, $43, to Abdul.
          28 Abdul paid, by cheque, the balance owing to Western.

Record the above in Abdul's ledger. Total the account of Western and balance the account of Southern on 28 March.

Abdul

Purchases account Page 9

Date	Details	Folio	$	Date	Details	Folio	$
20–2 Mar 22	Western	14	690				

Western account Page 14

Date	Details	Folio	$	Date	Details	Folio	$
20–2 Mar 25	Purchases returns	16	75	20–2 Mar 22	Purchases	9	690
28	Bank	1	615				
			690				690

Sales account — Page 11

Date	Details	Folio	$	Date	Details	Folio	$
				20–2 Mar 23	Southern	15	830

Southern account — Page 15

Date	Details	Folio	$	Date	Details	Folio	$
20–2 Mar 23	Sales	11	830	20–2 Mar 27	Sales returns	17	43
			830	28	Balance	c/d	787
							830
20–2 Mar 29	Balance	b/d	787				

Purchases Returns account — Page 16

Date	Details	Folio	$	Date	Details	Folio	$
				20–2 Mar 25	Western	14	75

Sales Returns account — Page 17

Date	Details	Folio	$	Date	Details	Folio	$
20–2 Mar 27	Southern	15	43				

Bank account — Page 1

Date	Details	Folio	$	Date	Details	Folio	$
				20–2 Mar 28	Western	14	615

Carriage inwards and carriage outwards

Both carriage inwards and carriage outwards relate to the cost of transporting goods. It is important that they are treated separately in the accounts as carriage inwards is part of the cost of purchasing goods, whereas carriage outwards is a selling expense.

Carriage inwards occurs when a business has to pay for purchased goods to be delivered to its premises. This cost is debited to a carriage inwards account. **Carriage outwards** occurs when a business pays for sold goods to be delivered to its customers' premises. This cost is debited to a carriage outwards account.

In each case a credit entry will be made in the cash account or bank account if payment was made, or the account of the supplier of the service if no payment was made at the time.

Drawings

'**Drawings**' is the term used when the owner of a business takes any value from the business for his/her own use. This may be in the form of money, goods, or even fixed assets. To avoid the capital account having a large number of entries, a drawings account is used to record all amounts withdrawn by the owner. At the end of the financial year the total of the drawings account is transferred to the capital account, and so reduces the amount the business owes the owner.

Whenever the owner makes drawings, the drawings account is debited (to show value going into that account). If money is withdrawn, the cash account or the bank account is credited (to show value going out of that account). If a fixed asset is withdrawn, the appropriate fixed asset account is credited (to show value going out of the account). If the owner of the business withdraws goods for his/her own use, the purchases account is credited with the cost of these goods (to show value going out of the account). The business originally purchased these goods with the intention of selling them to customers. The amount of goods available for sale to customers has been reduced as the owner has removed some of those goods, so the purchases account must record this reduction.

Running balance accounts

The traditional form of presentation has been used for all ledger accounts prepared in this Chapter. These are often referred to as '**T' accounts** because of their shape (a debit side and a credit side and a line down the centre).

A modern alternative is known as the **running balance format**. This style of presentation is used in computerised accounting systems, for example, the preparation of bank statements. Instead of appearing on different sides of the account, the debit and credit transactions are recorded in adjoining columns. The third column, the balance column, is updated after every transaction (hence the term 'running balance'). The advantage of this form of presentation is that the balance of the account is shown after every transaction. Where the accounts are prepared manually, the greater number of calculations may lead to an increase in errors.

■ **Example**

20–2 March 1 Abdul set up a business. He opened a business bank account and paid in $40 000 as capital.
2 Bought business premises for $20 000 and paid by cheque.
3 Paid $950 for insurance by cheque.
4 Part of the premises were rented out to another business and a cheque for $200 rent was received.
5 Bought equipment and paid by cheque, $8 000.
6 Paid for repairs to premises by cheque, $70.
7 Received a loan of $5 000 from ABC Ltd. which was paid into the bank.

Write up the Bank account in Abdul's ledger using the running balance format.

Bank account Page 1

Date	Details	Folio	Debit	Credit	Balance
			$	$	$
20–2					
Mar 1	Capital	2	40 000		40 000 Dr.
2	Premises	3		20 000	20 000 Dr.
3	Insurance	4		950	19 050 Dr.
4	Rent received	5	200		19 250 Dr.
5	Equipment	6		8 000	11 250 Dr.
6	Repairs	7		70	11 180 Dr.
7	ABC Ltd. Loan	8	5 000		16 180 Dr.

The traditional 'T' format is used throughout this book. Whenever a ledger account is required, either form of presentation is acceptable.

Examination questions often require only one account to be presented, instead of a set of double entry records. This is simply because of the limited time available.

Review questions

1. (a) Name the system which records the two aspects of all business transactions.

[IGCSE 1997]

(b) Explain what is meant by Trade Creditors.

[IGCSE 1997]

(c) Which one of the following describes a credit transaction?
Payment is made: before goods are received
when goods are received
after goods are received.

[IGCSE 1998]

(d) Ann, a sole trader, took goods from the business for her own use. Name the two ledger accounts in Ann's ledger in which this is recorded.

[IGCSE 2000]

2. Ester made the following transactions. State which account would be debited and which account would be credited in **each** case.
   (a) Goods for resale were purchased on credit from Moses.
   (b) Cost of delivering these goods to Ester's premises was paid in cash.
   (c) Equipment was purchased on credit from Machines Ltd.
   (d) Ester took cash from the business for her own use.
   (e) Unsatisfactory goods were returned to Moses.
   (f) Repairs to equipment were paid by cheque.
   (g) A cash loan was made to Ester's son David.
   (h) A cheque was received from the sale of surplus equipment.

3. Joe King is a self-employed builder. ABC Ltd. are builders' merchants, who supply sand, bricks and other materials to Joe King on credit terms. These goods are used by Joe in the day-to-day running of his business. Joe King's transactions for March 1995 included the following:
   March 10 Bought sand and bricks from ABC Ltd. on credit for $2 000.
         12 Returned unwanted bricks to ABC Ltd., value $600.
         18 Paid ABC Ltd. by cheque $1 000.
   (a) From the information given, write up the ledger account of ABC Ltd. in Joe King's books, showing the balance at 18 March 1995.
   (b) Is ABC Ltd. a debtor or a creditor of King?

[IGCSE 1995]

*4. On 1 August 20–5 Barry Bandara decided to set up a business, which would trade under the name of Bandara Bargains. The following are the transactions of the business for the month of August 20–5:
   20–5 August   1 Capital of $25 000 was paid into a business bank account.
              2 Paid rent of premises by cheque, $400.
              5 Bought goods, $1 850, and paid by cheque.
              9 Bought goods, $2 600, on credit from John Kamati.
             13 Sold goods, $260 for cash.
             18 Returned unsatisfactory goods, $140, to John Kamati.
             21 Paid advertising expenses, $90, in cash.
             25 Received commission, $50, in cash from Hangula & Co.
             28 Paid the amount owing to John Kamati by cheque.
             29 Barry Bandara withdrew $100 from the bank for personal use.

Enter the transactions in the ledger of Bandara Bargains for the month of August 20–5. Balance the Bank account and the Cash account at the end of the month.

5. George Metwali set up a business on 1 November 20–8, to trade under the name of Metwali Stores. The following are the transactions for the first month of trading:

20–8 November
- 1 Capital of $30 000 was paid into a business bank account.
- 2 Purchased premises, $20 000 and paid by cheque.
- 4 Purchased goods, $1 900, and paid by cheque.
- 7 Sold goods, $1 250, on credit to E. Helmuth.
- 11 E. Helmuth returned goods, $120, which were damaged.
- 15 Sold goods, $90, for cash.
- 15 Paid $5 in cash for the goods to be delivered to the customer.
- 19 Purchased office stationery, $15, and paid in cash.
- 24 George Metwali took goods, costing $20, for personal use.
- 29 E. Helmuth sent a cheque for $700, on account.

Enter the above transactions in the ledger of Metwali Stores for the month of November 20–8. Balance the Bank account, Cash account, and E. Helmuth account at the end of the month.

6. The following account appears in the ledger of Elisabeth Eaves. Explain **each** item in the account, and also state where the double entry for each item will be found.

Jenny Jones account

Date	Details	Folio	$	Date	Details	Folio	$
20–6				20–6			
Jan 4	Sales		260	Jan 6	Returns		15
21	Sales		330	19	Bank		245
				31	Balance	c/d	330
			590				590
20–6							
Feb 1	Balance	b/d	330				

CHAPTER 3: The Trial Balance

A trial balance is a list of the balances of accounts contained in the ledger. It is prepared on a certain date, and this date must be included as part of the heading of the trial balance. The name of each account is shown and whether the balance of the account is debit or credit. A trial balance is *not* part of the double entry system.

Purpose of a trial balance

A trial balance is drawn up periodically to check the arithmetical accuracy of the double entry bookkeeping. The trial balance can assist in locating errors. It is, however, important to remember that it only indicates that the total debits equal the total credits – it does not prove the complete accuracy of the bookkeeping.

A trial balance is also a convenient list from which to prepare final accounts.

Preparation of a trial balance

Where the ledger accounts are balanced monthly, a trial balance may be prepared at the end of each month. Those ledger accounts which remain open at the month-end are listed. The difference, or balance, on each account is entered in either the debit column or the credit column. If the ledger account has a debit balance (where the debit side of the account shows a greater amount than the credit side) the amount is entered in the debit column of the trial balance. If the ledger account has a credit balance (where the credit side of the account shows a greater amount than the debit side) the amount is entered in the credit column of the trial balance. The two columns are then totalled. If they agree, it proves the arithmetical accuracy of the double entry bookkeeping.

■ **Example**   20–2 March 1   Abdul set up a business.

The transactions for his first week of trading were recorded in his ledger as shown on pages 8–10 in Chapter 2.

Prepare a Trial Balance of Abdul as at 7 March 20–2.

Abdul

Trial Balance as at 7 March 20–2

	Folio	Debit $	Credit $
Bank	1	16 180	
Capital	2		40 000
Premises	3	20 000	
Insurance	4	950	
Rent received	5		200
Equipment	6	8 000	
Repairs	7	70	
ABC Ltd. Loan	8		5 000
		45 200	45 200

Notes: 1. It is usual to find 'Debit' and 'Credit' abbreviated to 'Dr.' and 'Cr.'.
2. Questions do not always show the folio numbers of the accounts.

In practice, a trial balance is always prepared from actual accounts. In examination questions, a trial balance may be required from a given list of balances, or a trial balance containing errors may require correction. In these cases, it is necessary to know which ledger account has a debit balance and which has a credit balance. Certain types of accounts always have a debit balance and certain types of account always have a credit balance.

Debit balances may be summarised as **assets** and **expenditures**, and **credit** balances may be summarised as **liabilities** and **income**. The following lists expand this basic definition.

Debit balances	**Credit balances**
Assets e.g. cash, stock, premises, debtors, etc.	Liabilities e.g. loans, creditors, etc.
Expenses e.g. rent, insurance, wages, etc.	Income e.g. commission received, rent received, etc.
Drawings	Capital
Purchases	Sales
Sales returns	Purchases returns

Notes: The bank account can have either a debit balance (if there is money in the bank) or a credit balance (if there is a bank overdraft).

■ Example

The following Trial Balance, prepared by an inexperienced bookkeeper, does not balance as it contains several errors.

MacDonald & Co.
Trial Balance for the year ending 30 November 20–5

	Debit $	Credit $
Capital		30 000
Bank overdraft	7 000	
Cash	400	
Debtors		8 600
Creditors	9 500	
Stock	3 500	
Purchases		32 420
Sales	43 400	
Sales returns		2 300
Purchases returns	1 640	
Machinery	12 100	
Equipment		4 200
Wages	13 800	
Rent		3 200
Drawings		8 000
Sundry expenses	3 020	
	94 360	88 720

Prepare a corrected Trial Balance of MacDonald & Co. as at 30 November 20–5.

The first step is to study each item and decide whether the figure is in the correct column or whether it requires amending. Once this has been done, a new trial balance can be prepared, under the correct heading.

MacDonald & Co.
Trial Balance as at 30 November 20–5

	Debit $	Credit $
Capital		30 000
Bank overdraft		7 000
Cash	400	
Debtors	8 600	
Creditors		9 500
Stock	3 500	
Purchases	32 420	
Sales		43 400
Sales returns	2 300	
Purchases returns		1 640
Machinery	12 100	
Equipment	4 200	
Wages	13 800	
Rent	3 200	
Drawings	8 000	
Sundry expenses	3 020	
	91 540	91 540

The trial balance and errors
If the trial balance does not balance
If the totals of a trial balance fail to agree, the probable cause of the error may be –
(a) An error of addition, which may be –
 (i) an error of addition in the trial balance
 (ii) an error of addition in an account
(b) An error of double entry, which may be caused by –
 (i) making only a single entry, rather then a double entry
 (ii) entering different amounts in the accounts concerned.

The basic steps for locating an error may be summarised as follows.
(a) Check the addition of the trial balance.
(b) Check the calculation of the balances of the accounts.
(c) Check that each balance has been entered in the correct column of the trial balance.
(d) Check that the amount of each account balance has been correctly entered in the trial balance.
(e) Check that no balances have been omitted from the trial balance.
(f) Look for a transaction with an amount equal to the difference in the trial balance and check the double entry.

(g) Look for a transaction with an amount equal to half the difference on the trial balance and check the double entry. Where two debit (or two credit) entries are made instead of a double entry, the trial balance will be out of balance by twice the amount of the transaction.

(h) As a last resort it may be necessary to check the bookkeeping entries for every transaction which has taken place since the date of the last trial balance.

If the trial balance does balance

Some errors can occur which do not affect the agreement of the trial balance totals.

(a) **Error of omission** — If a transaction is completely omitted from the books there will be neither a debit entry nor a credit entry, so the trial balance will balance. For example, cash sales not entered in the books.

(b) **Error of commission** — This occurs when a transaction is entered using the correct amount and on the correct side, but in the wrong account of the same class. For example, sales on credit to A. Khan correctly credited to the sales account, but debited to M. Khan's account instead of A. Khan's.

(c) **Error of principle** — This occurs when a transaction is entered using the correct amount and on the correct side, but in the wrong class of account. For example, cash paid for machinery repairs correctly credited to the cash account, but debited to the machinery account instead of machinery repairs account.

(d) **Compensating errors** — These occur where two, or more, errors cancel each other out. For example if the sales account is added up $100 too much and the purchases account is also over-added by the same amount, there is an extra $100 on both the debit side and the credit side, so the trial balance will balance.

(e) **Error of original entry** — This occurs where an incorrect figure is used when the transaction is first entered in the accounts. The double entry will be made using this incorrect amount in both accounts. For example, if the total of an invoice is $1 010 but it is incorrectly entered in the accounts as $1 100, the trial balance will balance.

(f) **Complete reversal of entries**   This occurs where the correct amounts have been entered in the correct accounts, but the entry has been made on the wrong side of each account. For example, cash purchases debited in the cash account and credited in the purchases account. This is a reversal of the correct entry, but the trial balance will balance.

Review questions

1. (a) State what a trial balance is.
   [IGCSE 1998]
   (b) State **one** purpose of preparing a trial balance.
   [IGCSE 1999]
   (c) Complete the following sentence:
   In a trial balance, all accounts with a **debit** balance are either expense accounts or … accounts.
   [IGCSE 2000]
   (d) Name **one** type of error which would **not** affect the balancing of a trial balance.
   [IGCSE 2000]
   (e) The trial balance totals of a business do not agree. Describe **one** error which could cause this.
   [IGCSE 2000]
   (f) A sale on credit to Smith was entered in the debit side of Robinson's ledger account.
   (i) Name this type of error.
   (ii) How will this type of error affect the seller's trial balance?
   The credit total will exceed the debit total.
   The credit and debit totals will be the same.
   The debit total will exceed the credit total.
   [IGCSE 2000]

*2. The following list of balances was taken from the books of Joe Kover, a sole trader, on 30 June 1998.

	$
Stock 1 July 1997	14 000
Purchases	70 000
Trade creditors	10 000
Sales	90 000
Trade debtors	6 000
Rent paid	3 000
Balance at bank (Dr.)	5 000
Fixtures and fittings	22 000

(a) Prepare Joe's Trial Balance at 30 June 1998.
(b) State and explain one purpose of preparing a trial balance.

[IGCSE 1998]

3. Josh Magir is a sole trader who prepares his own accounts. He is not an experienced bookkeeper, but on 31 March 1996 he drew up the Trial Balance shown below.

Trial Balance as at 31 March 1996

	Debit $	Credit $
Purchases	12 500	
Sales		17 000
Debtors		4 550
Creditors	3 800	
Balance at bank (Dr.)	1 250	
Rent paid	2 000	
Sales returns		700
Stock 1 April 1995		3 000
Capital		?
	19 550	25 250

Josh has put certain balances in the wrong columns.

Prepare a corrected Trial Balance for Josh as at 31 March 1996, showing his capital account balance.

[IGCSE 1996]

4. Joe began trading on 1 April 2000 and paid $10 000 into a business bank account. He borrowed a further $5 000 from his sister, Freda, and also paid this into the bank account. A summary of Joe's transactions for the period 1 April to 30 September 2000 is given below.

	$
Bought stock on credit	6 000
Sold goods (cost price $4 000) on credit for	5 500
Paid rent of premises by cheque	1 000
Received from debtors and paid into bank	3 600
Paid trade creditors by cheque	4 700
Paid general expenses by cheque	2 000

(a) Draw up Joe's bank account for the six months ended 30 September 2000. Bring down his closing balance.
(b) Using the information given, and your answer to (a), prepare a Trial Balance for Joe as at 30 September 2000. Show your workings, which may be in the form of ledger accounts.

[IGCSE 2000]

5. At the end of April 2000 an inexperienced bookkeeper prepared the following Trial Balance for Khalid Hassan.

	Debit $	Credit $
Sales	95 300	
Purchases		51 600
Stock 1 May 1999	5 000	
Wages	18 200	
General expenses	7 300	
Repairs and maintenance		2 700
Machinery and equipment	58 550	
Motors	15 900	
Debtors		15 800
Creditors	7 300	
Cash		350
Bank overdraft	3 800	
Drawings		12 000
Capital (balancing figure)		128 900
	211 350	211 350

In addition to the obvious errors in the trial balance, the accountant also discovered the following errors, which the trial balance failed to disclose:

1. $150 for the cost of repairing a motor had been debited to the motors account.
2. $50 cash paid for general expenses had not been recorded.
3. Errors of addition had been made resulting in the sales being overcast by $100 and the wages being overcast by the same amount.
4. When an invoice for goods purchased on credit was recorded the amount was entered as $1 000 instead of $100.
5. A cheque received from a debtor for $200 had been debited to the debtor's account and credited to the bank account.

   (a) For **each** of the above items (1–5) state the type of error that was made.
   (b) Prepare an amended Trial Balance for Khalid Hassan at 30 April showing the correct capital balance.
   (c) Khalid's brother Yousef also has a business. When Yousef prepared his trial balance at 31 March 2000 he found that the credit side exceeded the debit side by $250. Describe **four** procedures that Yousef could carry out to find the errors that caused the difference on the trial balance.

[IGCSE 2000]

CHAPTER 4
Double entry bookkeeping – Part B

Division of the ledger

As a business grows, it can become difficult to record all the ledger accounts in one book, so it is necessary to divide up the ledger. This also enables the same type of accounts to be kept together.

The ledger is usually divided into –

Sales Ledger — This is also known as the **Debtors Ledger**, and is where all **personal** accounts of the credit customers (the debtors) are kept.

Purchases Ledger — This is also known as the **Creditors Ledger**, and is where all **personal** accounts of the credit suppliers (the creditors) are kept.

Nominal Ledger — This is also known as the **General Ledger**, and is where all other accounts (except cash and bank) are kept. The accounts for sales, purchases, returns, assets, liabilities, expenses and incomes all appear in this ledger. The accounts which record expenses, income and capital are known as **nominal** accounts. Those recording assets are known as **real** accounts.

Cash Books — These contain the main cash book (which is explained below) and the petty cash book (see Chapter 5).

The two-column cash book

In Chapter 2, two separate accounts, on different pages of the ledger, were used to record cash and bank transactions. In practice, these accounts are brought together into one book, the cash book. Whilst the cash book acts as a ledger account for cash and bank, and is part of the double entry bookkeeping system, it is also a **book of prime entry** (see Chapter 6).

The basic rules of double entry still apply. The only difference is that the cash account and the bank account appear side by side in the cash book.

Any money received is recorded on the debit side and entered in the appropriate column, depending on whether it was put in the cash till or put into the bank. Any money paid is recorded on the credit side, being shown in the cash column if it was paid in cash, and the bank column if it was paid by cheque. It is important to remember that there are two accounts side by side, and each account must be balanced separately.

Contra entries

Cash may be withdrawn from the bank to replenish the cash till, or surplus cash in the till may be paid into the bank. In each case, both the debit entry and the credit entry will be in the cash book. The entries are as follows:

Cash withdrawn from the bank and placed in the cash till –
Debit Cash account
Credit Bank account
Surplus cash in the cash till paid into the bank –
Debit Bank account
Credit Cash account

These entries are known as **contra entries** and a 'c' is placed in the folio column to indicate that the double entry is on the other side of the same book.

■ Example

20–9 June 1 Meena Sami started a business with a capital of $10 000 which was paid into a business bank account.
3 Purchased goods, $4 000, on credit from Wholesalers Ltd. Paid rent, $250, by cheque.
11 Sold goods, $1 500, on credit to Local Stores.
14 Withdrew £200 from the bank for office use. Paid advertising expenses, $60, in cash.
20 Paid the amount due to Wholesalers Ltd. by cheque.
22 Cash sales $750. Paid $800 cash into bank.
27 Meena took $50 cash for her personal use. Bought fixtures, $3 600, and paid by cheque.

Record the above transactions in the books of Meena Sami. Show the cash and bank accounts in a two-column cash book, and divide the ledger into sales ledger, purchases ledger, and nominal ledger. Balance the cash book at the end of the month.

Meena Sami

Sales Ledger

Local Stores account — Page 1

Date	Details	Folio	$	Date	Details	Folio	$
20–9 June 1	Sales	NL4	1 500				

Purchases Ledger

Wholesalers Ltd. account

Page 1

Date	Details	Folio	$	Date	Details	Folio	$
20–9 June 20	Bank	CB1	4 000 4 000	20–9 June 3	Purchases	NL2	4 000 4 000

Nominal Ledger

Capital account

Page 1

Date	Details	Folio	$	Date	Details	Folio	$
				20–9 June 1	Bank	CB1	10 000

Purchases account

Page 2

Date	Details	Folio	$	Date	Details	Folio	$
20–9 June 3	Wholesalers Ltd.	PL1	4 000				

Rent account

Page 3

Date	Details	Folio	$	Date	Details	Folio	$
20–9 June 3	Bank	CB1	250				

Sales account

Page 4

Date	Details	Folio	$	Date	Details	Folio	$
				20–9 June 11 22	Local Stores Cash	SL1 CB1	1 500 750

Chapter 4 – Double entry bookkeeping – Part B

Advertising Expenses account — Page 5

Date	Details	Folio	$	Date	Details	Folio	$
20–9 June 14	Cash	CB1	60				

Drawings account — Page 6

Date	Details	Folio	$	Date	Details	Folio	$
20–9 June 27	Cash	CB1	50				

Fixtures account — Page 7

Date	Details	Folio	$	Date	Details	Folio	$
20–9 June 27	Bank	CB1	3 600				

Meena Sami

Cash Book — Page 1

Date	Details	Folio	Cash $	Bank $	Date	Details	Folio	Cash $	Bank $
20–9					20–9				
June 1	Capital	NL1		10 000	June 3	Rent	NL3		250
14	Bank	c	200		14	Cash	c		200
22	Sales	NL4	750		14	Advertising	NL5	60	
22	Cash	c		800	20	Wholesalers Ltd.	PL1		4 000
					22	Bank	c	800	
					27	Drawings	NL6	50	
					27	Fixtures	NL7		3 600
					30	Balance	c/d	40	2 750
			950	10 800				950	10 800
20–9 July 1	Balance	b/d	40	2 750					

Notes: PL = Purchases Ledger NL = Nominal Ledger
SL = Sales Ledger c = Contra entry

Bank overdraft

The bank may allow a business to **overdraw**, which means that the business may pay out more from the bank than was paid in. This overdraft will be a liability of the business, as it is money owed to the bank. The bank account in the cash book is balanced in the usual way (refer to pages 10–11). The credit side will show the larger amount, so the balance carried down will appear on the debit side, and the balance brought down will appear on the credit side.

■ **Example**

20–9 June 1 Meena Sami started a business.
Assume that all the transactions were the same as the previous example, except that the cheque paid on 27 June for fixtures was for $6 600 (instead of $3 600).

Prepare Meena Sami's two-column cash book for June 20–9. Balance the cash book and bring down the balances on 1 July 20–9.

Meena Sami

Cash Book — Page 1

Date	Details	Folio	Cash $	Bank $	Date	Details	Folio	Cash $	Bank $
20–9					20–9				
June 1	Capital	NL1		10 000	June 3	Rent	NL3		250
14	Bank	c	200		14	Cash	c		200
22	Sales	NL4	750		14	Advertising	NL5	60	
22	Cash	c		800	20	Wholesalers Ltd.	PL1		4 000
30	Balance	c/d		250	22	Bank	c	800	
					27	Drawings	NL6	50	
					27	Fixtures	NL7		6 600
					30	Balance	c/d	40	
			950	11 050				950	11 050
20–9					20–9				
July 1	Balance	b/d	40		July 1	Balance	b/d		250

The three-column cash book

Cash discounts

It is common to find a third column on each side of a cash book where **cash discount** can be recorded. Cash discount is an allowance given for payment by a customer within a time limit set by the supplier. **Discount allowed** is when the business allows its customers (debtors) a discount when they pay their accounts within the time limit set by the business. **Discount received** is when the business receives a discount when it pays its suppliers (creditors) within the time limit they set.

Cash discount encourages customers to pay their debts quickly. Whilst the supplier receives slightly less money, this money is available for use elsewhere in the business. Payment does not have to be made in cash to obtain a cash discount – it is the time of payment, not the manner of payment, which determines whether cash discount is available. Cash discount is usually stated in percentage terms. It appears on an invoice as a note, but not an actual deduction from the amount due. This is because the discount will only be given if the amount is paid within the set time limit. Discount allowed is an expense as it is the cost of collecting debts promptly, and discount received is an income as it is benefit received from paying debts promptly.

When cash discount is taken, a double entry must be made in the accounts. At the time discount is allowed or received, an entry is made in the personal account of the debtor or creditor to show that this amount is no longer outstanding. Any discount allowed is listed in the discount allowed column on the debit side of the cash book, and any discount received is listed in the discount received column on the credit side of the cash book. These are **not** part of the double entry. At the end of the period, usually monthly, the discount columns are totalled. The total of the discount allowed column is debited to the discount allowed account in the nominal ledger: this is the double entry for all the individual credit entries in the personal accounts of debtors. The total of the discount received column is credited to the discount received account in the nominal ledger: this is the double entry for all the individual debit entries in the personal accounts of creditors.

Dishonoured cheques

A dishonoured cheque is a cheque that a business has received from a debtor and which the debtor's bank refuses to pay. This may be because of an error on the cheque e.g. amount in words differing from amount in figures, no signature, etc. It may be because the debtor has not enough money in his/her account and has not arranged an overdraft. The cheque is usually returned to the business that paid it into the bank. The business must make a double entry to show the return of the cheque by debiting the debtor's account and crediting the bank account.

■ Example

20–9 July 1 Meena Sami had a cash balance of $40 and a bank overdraft of $250.
    5 Sold goods, $2 000, on credit to Abu.
     Cash sales $590.
     Paid $600 cash into bank.
    11 Bought goods, $1 800, on credit from Wholesalers Ltd.
     Bought goods, $500 on credit from Goodbuys.
    16 Abu paid the amount due by cheque less a cash discount of $2\frac{1}{2}\%$.
    19 Sold goods, $900, on credit to Abu.

23 Paid the amount due to Wholesalers Ltd. by cheque less a cash discount of 2%.
Paid the amount due to Goodbuys by cheque less a cash discount of 3%.
27 Abu paid $900 by cheque.
30 Abu's cheque was dishonoured and was returned by the bank.

Record the above transactions in the books of Meena Sami. Balance the cash book and the personal accounts at the end of July 20–9.

Meena Sami

Sales Ledger

Abu account   Page 2

Date	Details	Folio	$	Date	Details	Folio	$
20–9				20–9			
July 5	Sales	NL4	2 000	July 16	Bank	CB2	1 950
19	Sales	NL4	900		Discount	CB2	50
30	Bank (dis-			27	Bank	CB2	900
	honoured			31	Balance	c/d	900
	cheque)	CB2	900				
			3 800				3 800
20–9							
Aug 1	Balance	b/d	900				

Purchases Ledger

Wholesalers Ltd. account   Page 1

Date	Details	Folio	$	Date	Details	Folio	$
20–9				20–9			
July 23	Bank	CB1	1 764	July 11	Purchases	NL2	1 800
	Discount	CB1	36				
			1 800				1 800

Goodbuys account   Page 2

Date	Details	Folio	$	Date	Details	Folio	$
20–9 July 23	Bank Discount	CB1 CB1	485 15 500	20–9 July 11	Purchases	NL2	500 500

Nominal Ledger

Sales account   Page 4

Date	Details	Folio	$	Date	Details	Folio	$
				20–9 July 1 1 19	Abu Cash Abu	SL1 CB2 SL2	2 000 590 900

Purchases account   Page 2

Date	Details	Folio	$	Date	Details	Folio	$
20–9 July 11 11	Wholesalers Ltd. Goodbuys	PL1 PL2	1 800 500				

Discount Allowed account   Page 8

Date	Details	Folio	$	Date	Details	Folio	$
20–9 July 31	Total for month	CB2	50				

Discount Received account   Page 9

Date	Details	Folio	$	Date	Details	Folio	$
				20–9 July 31	Total for month	CB2	51

Meena Sami

Cash Book

Page 2

Date	Details	Folio	Discount Allowed	Cash	Bank	Date	Details	Folio	Discount Received	Cash	Bank
			$	$	$				$	$	$
20–9						20–9					
July 1	Balance	b/d		40		July 1	Balance	b/d			250
5	Sales	NL4		590		5	Bank	c		600	
5	Cash	c			600	23	Wholesalers Ltd.	PL1	36		1 764
16	Abu	SL2	50		1 950	23	Goodbuys	PL2	15		485
27	Abu	SL2			900	30	Abu (dishonoured cheque)	SL2			900
						31	Balance	c/d		30	51
			50	630	3 450				51	630	3 450
20–9			NL8						NL9		
Aug 1	Balance	b/d		30	51						

Review questions

1. (a) What is a dishonoured cheque?
   (b) What is cash discount?

   [IGCSE 1995]

   (c) A business sold goods to a customer for $2 000, offering a $2\frac{1}{2}$% discount for payment within 28 days.
      (i) Name this type of discount.
      (ii) The customer paid within 28 days. How much discount did he deduct?

   [IGCSE 1997]

   (d) When using a three-column cash book, to which account is the debit total of the discount column transferred?

   [IGCSE 1995]

2. (a) Explain how the ledger of a business may be divided.
   (b) In the books of John Bull, state in which ledger **each** of the following accounts would appear:
      (i) Purchases account
      (ii) A. Rose (a customer) account
      (iii) John Bull Capital account
      (iv) Sales returns account
      (v) T. Thorn (a supplier) account
      (vi) Rent received account

3. Rafael Maia maintains a two-column cash book. At 31 March 1998, the balances in his cash book were –

	$
Cash column	300 (debit)
Bank column	11 000 (debit)

Rafael had the following transactions in April 1998:

April 3 Received and banked a cheque for $840 from V. Hussain, a debtor.
    4 Received cash from sales, $1 000. This was not banked.
    7 Paid A. Korn, a creditor, by cheque, $2 640.
  10 Paid $800 of his cash into the bank.
  14 Paid wages by cash, $400.
  23 Paid electricity by cheque, $600.
  25 Received and banked a cheque for $70. This was a refund of an insurance premium.
  27 Cashed a cheque for $400 at the bank and placed the cash in the office cash box.
  30 Paid wages by cheque, $500.

(a) Write up Rafael Maia's two-column cash book for April 1998 and balance the cash and bank columns at 30 April 1998.
(b) (i) Explain why Rafael Maia may sometimes have a credit balance on the bank columns of his cash book.
    (ii) State, with reasons, if it is possible for Rafael Maia to have a credit balance on the cash columns of the cash book.

[IGCSE 1998]

*4. Josiah Mangombe is a sole trader who records all his cash and bank transactions in a three-column cash book.

Balances at 1 September 1996 were:

	$
Bank overdraft	1 800
Cash in hand	400

Josiah's transactions for the month of September 1996 were as follows:

September 3 Received and banked cheque for $95 from A. Brown in settlement of his account after deducting cash discount of 5%.
    7 Cash sales paid directly into bank $300.
  12 Josiah paid further capital into bank $5 000. Paid cheques in settlement of accounts owing to J. Smith $500 and C. Jones $200, in each case deducting $2\frac{1}{2}\%$ cash discount.
  15 Paid wages in cash $200.
      Cash sales (not banked) $176.
  21 Paid salaries by cheque $650.
      Paid motor expenses in cash $210.
  23 Cash sales (not banked) $307.

25 Received and banked a cheque for $780 from AZ Ltd. in settlement of their account of $800 after deducting cash discount.

30 Josiah's drawings, by cheque, $800.

(a) Record the above transactions in Josiah's three-column cash book. Bring down the cash and bank balances at 1 October 1996.
(b) Total the discount columns and show how the relevant discount accounts would appear in the nominal ledger at 30 September 1996.
(c) Explain why only the totals of discount received and discount allowed are entered in these accounts.

[IGCSE 1996]

5. Walter Fischer started a business on 1 August 20–5. The following are the transactions for his first month of trading. Enter the transactions in the books of Walter Fischer. Balance the cash book and the personal accounts at the end of the month. Take out a Trial Balance as at 31 August 20–5.

20–5 August 1 Walter Fischer put capital of $45 000 into a business bank account.
2 Paid rent of premises, $310, by cheque.
6 Bought goods, $2 500, on credit from Haser & Co.
Cash sales $750.
8 Paid $600 cash into the bank.
13 Sold goods, $1 400, on credit to Z. Zigon.
18 Settled Haser & Co.'s account by cheque, less 2% cash discount.
Bought further goods, $1 950, on credit from Haser & Co.
21 Bought stationery, $14, and paid in cash.
Walter took cash, $25, for his own use.
26 Received a cheque from Z. Zigon to settle his account, after he deducted $2\frac{1}{2}$% cash discount.
29 Sold goods, $1 020, on credit to Z. Zigon.

6. 20–8 February 1 J. Fernando started a business with a capital of $33 000 which was placed in a business bank account.
2 Purchased a motor vehicle and paid by cheque, $8 500.
4 Bought goods, $1 700, on credit from N. Navaro.
Bought goods, $2 200, on credit from B. Balbo.
9 Sold goods, $900, on credit to A. Ziege.
Sold goods, $800, on credit to Josef & Co.
15 Withdrew cash from bank for office use $250.
18 Paid for motor expenses, $20, in cash.
Paid B. Balbo a cheque for $2 145, after deducting cash discount of $2\frac{1}{2}$%.

20 Paid N. Navaro a cheque for $1 690 in full settlement. Purchased further goods, $1 850, on credit from N.Navaro.
25 Josef & Co. paid their account by cheque, after deducting a cash discount of $2^1/_2$%.
28 J. Fernando took goods, $50, for his own use.

Enter the above transactions in the books of J. Fernando.
Balance the cash book and the personal accounts on 28 February 20–8.
Extract a Trial Balance as at 28 February 20–8.

CHAPTER 5
Petty cash book

A petty cash book is used to record low-value cash payments such as postages, travelling expenses and window cleaning. Like the cash book, the petty cash book serves two purposes. It is a book of prime entry as it lists transactions for transferring to the ledger accounts at a later stage. It also acts as a ledger account for petty cash transactions, and so is part of the double entry system.

If all the small cash payments were recorded individually in the main cash book they would take up a lot of space. In addition, each of these items would need to be posted to the ledger, which would mean a very large number of entries.

The petty cash book is often the responsibility of a junior member of staff, known as the petty cashier. Keeping the petty cash book is often regarded as useful training for junior members of staff. By delegating this routine task, the chief cashier is able to concentrate on more important aspects of the accounting records. Periodically, the chief cashier should check the work of the petty cashier.

When paying out cash, the petty cashier should obtain a **petty cash voucher**. This voucher is presented by the person receiving the cash. It should show details of the expenditure and be signed to indicate that the money has been received from the petty cashier. At the end of the period, the petty cashier can check the cash spent against these vouchers.

The imprest system of petty cash

The imprest system is used for most petty cash books. The petty cashier starts each period (e.g. week, month etc.) with a certain amount of money – the **imprest amount** or **float**. Payments are made out of this amount during the period and recorded in the petty cash book. At the end of the period, when the petty cash book is balanced, the chief cashier will give the petty cashier enough cash to restore the balance remaining to the imprest amount. Thus the amount with which the petty cashier starts each new period is always equal to the imprest amount.

■ **Example**

Henri maintains a petty cash book with an imprest of $100.

20–3		$
1 January	Amount of imprest	100
1–31 January	Total paid out of petty cash	91
31 January	Balance of petty cash	9
1 February	Imprest restored	91
1 February	Balance of petty cash	100

If it is found that the imprest amount is insufficient, it may be increased to a higher amount.

The layout of a petty cash book

A petty cash book resembles a ledger account which has several extra columns on the credit side, as shown below.

Petty Cash Book

Debit | | | | | | | | | | | Credit

Date	Details	Folio	Total Received	Date	Details	Voucher	Total Paid	Analysis Columns		
			$				$	$	$	$

The folio column on the credit side is replaced by a column for recording the petty cash voucher number.

The **analysis columns** are used to break down the payments into different categories. These columns show the total petty cash spent on each main type of expense. The totals of these columns are posted to the ledger (see below).

In practice, the number of analysis columns will depend on the main types of expense which are usually paid out of petty cash. In examinations, guidance will be given regarding the columns required.

Writing up a petty cash book

Applying the usual rules of double entry, the petty cash book is debited with amounts received. The credit entry will be in the main cash book, or the account where the cash came from, e.g. account of a debtor.

Any money paid out is entered on the credit side under the total paid column, and is also shown in the column for that particular expense, e.g. postages, travelling expenses etc.

The entries made at the end of the period may be summarised as –
(a) Add up the total paid column.
(b) Total each of the analysis columns. If these totals are added across horizontally, they should agree with the figure in the total paid column.

(c) Balance the petty cash book and carry down the balance. The analysis columns are complete, so the total received and the total paid columns are balanced in the same way as an ordinary ledger account.
(d) Debit the petty cash book with the amount received to restore the imprest.
(e) Complete the double entry for the payments from the petty cash book by **debiting** the relevant expense accounts in the nominal ledger with the **total** of each analysis column. Indicate that this has been completed by writing the relevant ledger account folio number below the total of each analysis column.

■ Example

Henri keeps an analysed petty cash book using the imprest system. The imprest amount is $100. His transactions for the month of January 20–3 were –

	$	Voucher number
January 1 Balance	100	
4 Bought postage stamps	5	1
7 Bought fuel for motor vehicle	22	2
11 Bought computer copy paper	12	3
13 Paid for parcel postage	4	4
19 Bought fuel for motor vehicle	25	5
24 Bought ink cartridge for computer	13	6
28 Paid window cleaner	10	7

(a) Enter the transactions in Henri's petty cash book for the month of January 20–3. The petty cash book should have **four** analysis columns – postages, office expenses, motor expenses, and cleaning.
(b) Balance the book on 31 January and carry down the balance. Show the restoration of the imprest on 1 February.
(c) Post the totals of the analysis columns to the appropriate accounts in the nominal ledger.

Henri

Petty Cash Book
Page 1

Date	Details	Folio	Total Received	Date	Details	Vo	Total Paid	Postages	Office Expenses	Motor	Cleaning
			$				$	$	$	$	$
20–3				20–3							
Jan 1	Balance	b/d	100	Jan 4	Postage stamps	1	5	5			
				7	Motor fuel	2	22			22	
				11	Copy paper	3	12		12		
				13	Parcel post	4	4	4			
				19	Motor fuel	5	25			25	
				24	Ink cartridge	6	13		13		
				28	Window cleaner	7	10				10
							91	9	25	47	10
				31	Balance	c/d	9	NL14	NL28	NL19	NL3
			100				100				
Feb 1	Balance	b/d	9								
	Cash		91								

Henri

Nominal Ledger

Postages account
Page 14

Date	Details	Folio	$	Date	Details	Folio	$
20–3							
Jan 31	Petty cash	PCB1	9				

Office Expenses account
Page 28

Date	Details	Folio	$	Date	Details	Folio	$
20–3							
Jan 31	Petty cash	PCB1	25				

Motor Expenses account — Page 19

Date	Details	Folio	$	Date	Details	Folio	$
20–3 Jan 31	Petty cash	PCB1	47				

Cleaning account — Page 3

Date	Details	Folio	$	Date	Details	Folio	$
20–3 Jan 31	Petty cash	PCB1	10				

Where the amount involved is small, a business may pay creditors from petty cash. In this case, one of the analysis columns will be headed 'Ledger accounts'. The entries are recorded in the petty cash book in the usual way, and the analysis column totalled at the end of the period. Instead of posting the total to an expense account, each individual item is debited to the purchase ledger account of the creditor concerned.

Review questions

1. (a) (i) Name a suitable book that Ella can use to record small cash payments.
      (ii) State and explain **two** advantages of using the book you have named in (i).

      [IGCSE 1999]

   (b) (i) Explain what is meant by the imprest petty cash system.
       (ii) State **two** advantages of using analysis columns in a petty cash book.

       [IGCSE 1995]

* 2. Katie, a sole trader, keeps a petty cash book using the imprest system. The imprest amount is $90. Her transactions for the month of May 20–6 were –

		$	Voucher number
May 1	Balance	90	
3	Paid L. James, a creditor	15	1
9	Bought postage stamps	4	2
15	Bought stationery	7	3
21	Paid T. Giles, a creditor	9	4
24	Bought postage stamps	2	5
29	Paid part-time assistant's wages	40	6

Chapter 5 – Petty cash book

(a) Enter the transactions in Katie's petty cash book for the month of May 20–6. The petty cash book should have **four** analysis columns – stationery, postages, wages, and ledger accounts.
(b) Balance the book on 31 May and carry down the balance. Show the restoration of the imprest on 1 June.
(c) Open ledger accounts to complete the double entry for –
   (i) the petty cash analysis columns headed stationery, postages and wages
   (ii) the transactions dated 3 and 21 May 20–6.

3. Frederick Bortoli is a sole trader who keeps an analysed petty cash book on the imprest system. The imprest amount is $200. His transactions for the month of April 1996 were as follows:

		$
April 1	Petty cash in hand	28
1	Petty cash restored to imprest amount	
6	Bought office stationery	14
12	Paid travelling expenses	24
14	Paid cleaner's wages	40
16	Bought postage stamps	18
18	Bought typing paper	28
21	Paid cleaner's wages	40
25	Bought postage stamps	6
28	Paid travelling expenses	8

(a) Write up Frederick's petty cash book to record his transactions. The book should have analysis columns for –
   (i) stationery
   (ii) cleaning
   (iii) travel expenses
   (iv) postage
(b) Balance the petty cash book on 30 April 1996 and carry down the balance.
(c) Make the entry on 1 May 1996 to restore the petty cash imprest amount.

[IGCSE 1996]

4. (a) Explain what is meant by the imprest system in relation to petty cash books.
   (b) Sidon Zakari is a sole trader who keeps an analysed petty cash book using the imprest system. The imprest amount is $250. His transactions for the month of October 2000 were as follows –

		$
Oct 1	Balance brought down	32
1	Petty cash restored to imprest amount	
4	Bought office stationery	19
7	Paid travelling expenses	24
12	Received cash from member of staff for personal telephone calls	3

15	Bought postage stamps	6
21	Paid to Gideon Solumga, a creditor	25
28	Paid cleaner	110

Draw up a petty cash book for the month of October 2000 with an analysis column for each of the following –
(i) postages and stationery
(ii) travelling expenses
(iii) cleaning expenses
(iv) ledger accounts.

Enter the above transactions. Balance the book on 31 October 2000 and carry down the balance. Make the entry on 1 November 2000 to restore the petty cash to the imprest amount.

(c) Explain how the double entry is completed for items recorded in the analysis columns of a petty cash book.

[IGCSE 2000]

CHAPTER 6
Business documents and books of prime entry

Business documents

Invoice

When goods are sold on credit, the supplier will issue an invoice. The form of invoice varies from business to business, but they all show the same basic information – the name of the supplier, the name of the customer, the date, and full details, quantities, and prices of the goods supplied. The original (top copy) of the invoice is sent to the customer, who uses it to record his credit purchases. A copy of the invoice is retained by the seller, who uses it to record his credit sales.

Sometimes a deduction is shown on an invoice for **Trade Discount**. This reduction in the price of the goods may be given to other businesses within the same trade. These businesses will not be prepared to pay the full retail price, as they will need to be able to make a profit on the goods they sell. Trade discount may also be used to encourage customers to buy in large quantities and the percentage rate may vary according to the quantity purchased. It is important to remember that **Cash Discount** is *not* deducted from an invoice, as this is only available if the invoice is paid within the period set by the seller.

■ **Example**

Andy Capp is the owner of a do-it-yourself store. On 2 June 20–4 he purchased goods on credit from Deal Timber Ltd. Andy received the following invoice from Deal Timber.

```
                    DEAL TIMBER LTD.

                 NORTH ROAD, SOUTHBOURNE
                    TELE: 0801 654321

                         INVOICE

                                        No: INV 4731
   To: Andy Capp                        Date: 2 June 20–4
       Do-it-yourself Stores
       Short Street
       Longford
```

Quantity	Description	Unit Price	Total Amount
		$	$
20 metres	Floorboards	1.20	24.00
4	Doors	40.00	160.00
			184.00
	Less 25% Trade discount		46.00
			138.00
	Terms: 2% Cash discount if paid by 31 July 20–4		

Debit Note

When goods are received they should be checked to see that they correspond exactly with what was ordered – in quality, quantity, and price – and that they are in good condition. The purchaser may send a debit note to the supplier to report any faults, shortages or overcharges. As with invoices, the form of a debit note may vary from business to business.

Example

On 7 June 20–4 Andy Capp returned damaged goods to Deal Timber Ltd. Andy sent the following debit note to Deal Timber Ltd.

Tele: 0919 12486	**ANDY CAPP**	Do-it-yourself Stores Short Street Longford
	DEBIT NOTE	
To: Deal Timber Ltd. North Road Southbourne		No: 130 Date: 7 June 20–4

	Price	Amount
	$	$
The following items have been returned-		
2 Doors	40.00	80.00
Less 25% Trade discount		20.00
		60.00
Reason for return: Damaged Please issue a Credit Note		

The debit note does not always show the price of the goods. Where the price is included, it is the price that the customer was actually charged for those goods, i.e. the price after trade discount.

A debit note (instead of an additional invoice) may also be issued by a supplier where there is an under-charge on an invoice.

Credit Note

When goods are returned, or there has been an over-charge, a supplier may issue a credit note. This reduces the amount owed by the customer. Again the form of the document may vary, but all contain the same basic information. Credit notes are often printed in red, so that they are not confused with invoices.

The original (top copy) of the credit note is sent to the customer, who uses it to record his/her purchases returns. A copy of the credit note is retained by the seller, who uses it to record his/her sales returns. Where goods were sold subject to a trade discount, this must also be shown as a deduction on a credit note. This is necessary so that the credit is equal to the price actually charged for those goods originally.

■ **Example** On 7 June 20–4 Andy Capp returned damaged goods, together with a debit note, to Deal Timber Ltd. The following credit note was issued by Deal Timber Ltd. to Andy Capp on 9 June 20–4.

DEAL TIMBER LTD.

NORTH ROAD, SOUTHBOURNE
TELE: 0801 654321

CREDIT NOTE

No: CR 358
Date: 9 June 20–4

To: Andy Capp
    Do-it-yourself Stores
    Short Street
    Longford

Quantity	Description	Unit Price	Total Amount
		$	$
2	Doors	40.00	80.00
	Less 25% Trade		
	discount		20.00
			60.00
	Reason for credit –		
	Damaged goods		

Statement of Account

It is usual for a supplier to issue a monthly statement of account to the customer. Whilst the actual form of a statement may vary, it is basically a summary of the transactions during the month. It shows the balance due (if any) at the start of the period, invoices and credit notes issued, payments received, and the balance due at the end of the period.

A statement of account acts as a reminder to the customer of the amount due. The customer can also check the statement against his records to ensure that no errors have been made either by himself/herself or by the supplier.

■ **Example** Deal Timber Ltd. issue monthly statements of account to all their customers. The following statement of account was issued to Andy Capp at 30 June 20–4.

DEAL TIMBER LTD.

NORTH ROAD, SOUTHBOURNE
TELE: 0801 654321

STATEMENT

To: Andy Capp   Date: 30 June 20–4
    Do-it-yourself Stores
    Short Street
    Longford

Date	Reference No.	Debit	Credit	Balance
		$	$	$
20–4				
June 2	INV 4731	138.00		138.00
9	CR 358		60.00	78.00

The last amount in the balance column is the amount due.

Terms: 2% Cash discount if paid by 31 July 20–4.

Books of prime entry

It was explained in Chapter 4 that the ledger is often divided up as the business grows. Similarly, it is often more efficient for a business to record transactions in books of prime entry (sometimes called **books of original entry** or **subsidiary books**) *before* they are entered in the ledger. Where there are a lot of transactions of the same type, e.g. credit sales, a book of prime entry may be kept. This is basically a listing device and so keeps a lot of detail out of the ledger.

The books of prime entry are –
Sales journal
Purchases journal
Sales returns journal
Purchases returns journal
Cash book (see Chapter 4)
Petty cash book (see Chapter 5)
Journal (see Chapter 13)

Sales Journal

The sales journal is sometimes referred to as the **sales book**, or the **sales day book**. It is a list of dates on which credit sales were made, the names of the customers and the amounts of the sales. The sales journal is written up from the copies of the sales invoices sent to customers.

A debit entry is made in the personal account of the customer in the sales ledger (the relevant account number being noted in the folio column of the sales journal). **At the end of the month**, the **total** of the sales journal is credited to the sales account in the nominal ledger. This single figure forms the double entry for all the individual debit entries in the personal accounts.

Sales Returns Journal

The sales returns journal is sometimes referred to as the **sales returns book**, or the **returns inwards book** (or **journal**). It is written up from the copies of the credit notes sent to customers. Like the sales journal, it is a list of dates, names and amounts.

A credit entry is made in the personal account of the customer in the sales ledger (the relevant account number being noted in the folio column of the sales returns journal). **At the end of the month**, the **total** of the sales returns journal is debited to the sales returns account in the nominal ledger. This single figure forms the double entry for all the individual credit entries in the personal accounts.

■ **Example**

On 2 June 20–4 Deal Timber Ltd. sold goods on credit to Andy Capp. The invoice, shown earlier, had a total of $138, after the deduction of trade discount. In addition, goods, $412, were sold on credit to The Joinery Co. on 11 June, and goods, $584, were sold on credit to A. Woods on 23 June. Andy Capp returned goods and the credit note for $60, shown earlier, was issued on 9 June. On 17 June, The Joinery Co. was issued with a credit note for $10 because of an over-charge.

Make the necessary entries in the books of Deal Timber Ltd. for the month of June 20–4.

Deal Timber Ltd.

Sales Journal

Page 1

Date	Name	Invoice Number	Folio	Amount
				$
20–4				
June 2	Andy Capp	INV 4731	SL1	138
11	The Joinery Co.	INV 4732	SL2	412
23	A. Woods	INV 4733	SL3	584
30	Transferred to sales account		NL1	1 134

Sales Returns Journal

Page 1

Date	Name	Credit Note Number	Folio	Amount
				$
20–4				
June 9	Andy Capp	CR 358	SL1	60
17	The Joinery Co.	CR 359	SL2	10
30	Transferred to sales returns account		NL2	70

Sales Ledger

Andy Capp account

Page 1

Date	Details	Folio	$	Date	Details	Folio	$
20–2				20–4			
June 2	Sales	SJ1	138	June 9	Sales returns	SRJ1	60

The Joinery Co. account

Page 2

Date	Details	Folio	$	Date	Details	Folio	$
20–4				20–4			
June 11	Sales	SJ1	412	June 17	Sales returns	SRJ1	10

A. Woods account Page 3

Date	Details	Folio	$	Date	Details	Folio	$
20–4 June 23	Sales	SJ1	584				

Nominal Ledger

Sales account Page 1

Date	Details	Folio	$	Date	Details	Folio	$
				20–4 June 30	Credit sales for month	SJ1	1 134

Sales Returns account Page 2

Date	Details	Folio	$	Date	Details	Folio	$
20–4 June 30	Returns for month	SRJ1	70				

Purchases Journal

The purchases journal is sometimes referred to as the **purchases book**, or the **purchases day book**. It is a list of dates on which credit purchases were made, the names of the suppliers and the amounts of the purchases. The purchases journal is written up from the invoices received from suppliers.

A credit entry is made in the personal account of the supplier in the purchases ledger (the relevant account number being noted in the folio column of the purchases journal). **At the end of the month**, the **total** of the purchases journal is debited to the purchases account in the nominal ledger. This single figure forms the double entry for all the individual credit entries in the personal accounts.

Purchases Returns Journal

The purchases returns journal is sometimes referred to as the **purchases returns book**, or the **returns outwards book** (or **journal**). It is written up from the credit notes received from suppliers. Like the purchases journal, it is a list of dates, names and amounts. A debit entry is made in the personal account of the supplier in the purchases ledger (the relevant account number being noted in the folio column of the purchases returns journal).

At the end of the month, the **total** of the purchases returns journal is credited to the purchases returns account in the nominal ledger. This single figure forms the double entry for all the individual debit entries in the personal accounts.

■ **Example**

On 2 June 20–4 Andy Capp purchased goods on credit from Deal Timber Ltd. The invoice, shown earlier, had a total of $138, after the deduction of trade discount. In addition, Andy Capp purchased goods, $387, on credit from Beech & Co. on 16 June (Invoice number 926). Goods were returned to Deal Timber Ltd. who issued the credit note shown earlier, for $60, on 9 June. On 20 June Andy Capp returned goods to Beech & Co. and received a credit note (CR 44) for $52.

Make the necessary entries in the books of Andy Capp for the month of June 20–4.

Andy Capp

Purchases Journal — Page 1

Date	Name	Invoice Number	Folio	Amount
				$
20–4				
June 2	Deal Timber Ltd.	INV 4731	PL1	138
16	Beech & Co.	INV 926	PL2	387
30	Transferred to purchases account		NL1	525

Purchases Returns Journal — Page 1

Date	Name	Credit Note Number	Folio	Amount
				$
20–4				
June 9	Deal Timber Ltd.	CR 358	PL1	60
20	Beech & Co.	CR 44	PL2	52
30	Transferred to purchases returns account		NL2	112

Purchases Ledger

Deal Timber Ltd. account — Page 1

Date	Details	Folio	$	Date	Details	Folio	$
20–4 June 9	Purchases returns	PRJ1	60	20–4 June 2	Purchases	PJ1	138

Beech & Co. account — Page 2

Date	Details	Folio	$	Date	Details	Folio	$
20–4 June 20	Purchases returns	PRJ1	52	20–4 June 16	Purchases	PJ1	387

Nominal Ledger

Purchases account — Page 1

Date	Details	Folio	$	Date	Details	Folio	$
20–4 June 30	Credit purchases for month	PJ1	525				

Purchases Returns account — Page 2

Date	Details	Folio	$	Date	Details	Folio	$
				20–4 June 30	Returns for month	PRJ1	112

It is important to remember that trade discount, unlike cash discount, is **not** entered in the books, of either the purchaser or the seller, as part of the double entry system.

Review questions

1. (a) State one reason why a supplier issues a credit note.
   [IGCSE 1999]
   (b) Why does a supplier send a monthly statement of account to a customer?
   To calculate the profit made on sales to the customer.
   To show the amount owing to or by the customer at the end of the month.
   To show the full details of every invoice and credit note.
   To show how much credit is available to the customer at the end of the month.
   [IGCSE 2000]
   (c) State which type of discount is **not** recorded in the ledger accounts.
   [IGCSE 1997]
   (d) Name **one** book of prime entry.
   [IGCSE 2000]
   (e) Name the document used by a business to record purchases on credit in its purchases book.
   [IGCSE 1997]
   (f) Complete the following sentence:
   The total of the sales returns journal is transferred to the …… side of the …… account in the …… ledger.

2. Explain the difference between –
   (a) Trade discount and cash discount
   (b) Credit note and debit note.

3. Andy Mann is a wholesaler. He supplies goods on credit to Sam who has a general retail store. Sam's account in Andy's ledger is shown below.
   (a) Calculate the balance on Sam's account on 28 March and enter the amount in the appropriate column above.

Sam

Date	Details	Debit	Credit	Balance
		$	$	$
1998				
Mar 1	Balance			1 000 Dr.
4	Sales	450		1 450
10	Sales returns		50	1 400
21	Bank		975	
	Discount		25	400
28	Sales	300		

58 Accounting: IGCSE

(b) State whether Sam was a debtor or creditor of Andy Mann's on 28 March.
(c) Andy keeps a sales ledger and a purchase ledger. State in which of these ledgers Sam's account would appear.
(d) (i) Explain what is meant by 'Discount' (on 21 March) in Sam's account.
(ii) Calculate the percentage **rate** claimed by Sam. Show your workings.
(e) The table below shows three entries from Sam's account. Complete the table to show for each entry
(i) the name of the business document on which the entry in Andy's ledger is based;
(ii) the name of the person (Andy or Sam) who sent the document.

Date	Transaction	Name of business document	Name of person sending document
Mar 4	Sales		
10	Sales returns		
21	Bank		

[IGCSE 1998]

*4. Study the invoice shown below and answer the questions that follow.

SALES INVOICE
KUOMI INTERNATIONAL

INVOICE

Head office
Palmeiras Estate
Quintas Velhas

Invoice No: 25701
Date: 15/9/96
Tel: 0012-746928

Description	Quantity	Price $	Total $
Lighting Units	4	50.00 each	(i)
Wooden Cases	24	10.00 each	240.00
		Total	(ii)

Allied Factors
20–24 High Street
Fartown

A/c No: AF 3740

Chapter 6 – Business documents and books of prime entry

(a) What is the name of the business sending the invoice?
(b) Calculate the missing amounts at (i) and (ii) and enter these in the boxes. Show your workings.
(c) State in which book of original entry this invoice would be entered:
   (i) by the business sending the invoice;
   (ii) by the business receiving the invoice.
(d) Two of the lighting units were received damaged, and were returned on 20 September. The supplier could not replace them and sent a document to reduce the charge. Name this document.
(e) After the damaged units were returned how much was owing to the seller from this transaction? Show your workings.
(f) The amount owing was unpaid on 30 September. In the seller's books is the business owing the amount a debtor or a creditor?

[IGCSE 1996]

5. Johnny Ipinge owns a food store. On 13 July 1997 he received the credit note shown below from Amalgamated Distributors Ltd.

AMALGAMATED DISTRIBUTORS LTD.

CREDIT NOTE

Newton House   C/N. J1/461
Springfield, OXTON

Date	Description/Details	Quantity/Price	Amount $
10 July 1997	Cases of tinned fruit – damaged in transit and returned	4 cases @ $160 per case	(i)

Add Carriage on above goods   70.00

To: Johnny Ipinge
   Family Stores   (ii)
   High Road
   OXTON

(a) Calculate the missing amounts at (i) and (ii) on the credit note and enter these in the boxes. Show your workings.

(b) State **one** other reason, apart from damaged goods being returned, why a supplier might issue a credit note to a customer.

(c) The following transactions for July have not yet been entered in Johnny's books:

1997

    1 July Invoice received from Amalgamated Distributors Ltd. for goods supplied on credit, $2 680.

  13 July Credit note received from Amalgamated Distributors Ltd. for goods returned on 10 July as in (a).

  29 July Johnny paid the net amount owing to Amalgamated Distributors Ltd. by cheque, deducting $2\frac{1}{2}\%$ cash discount.

Write up the ledger account of Amalgamated Distributors Ltd. in Johnny's books to record the above transactions.

(d) In the books of **Amalgamated Distributors Ltd.**, in which ledger account will the discount deducted by Johnny on 29 July be shown?

[IGCSE 1997]

6. On 2 May 2000 Marianne Jones received the document shown below from her supplier, Zen Wholesale.

ZEN WHOLESALE

Riverside Warehouse
New Street
South Town

Tel: 0796-151023

Date 2000	Details	Debit	Credit	Balance
		$	$	$
1 April	Balance b/f	1 000		1 000 (DR)
12 April	Sales	300		1 300 (DR)
19 April	Sales Returns		50	1 250 (DR)
30 April	Bank		975	
	Discount		25	

Ms M. Jones
High Street
South Town

A/c No: J/2657

Date: 30 April 2000

Chapter 6 – Business documents and books of prime entry

(a) Name the above document.
(b) Calculate the balance due from Marianne Jones to Zen Wholesale on 30 April 2000. Show your workings.
(c) (i) For the transactions on 12 and 19 April, write in the spaces below the **name of the document** sent by Zen Wholesale to Marianne.
1. 12 April: Zen Wholesale sent …… to Marianne.
2. 19 April: Zen Wholesale sent …… to Marianne.
(ii) Complete the boxes below to show the ledger account entries recording the transactions on 12 and 19 April **in the books of Zen Wholesale**.

Date of Transaction	Ledger account to be debited (DR.)		Ledger account to be credited (CR.)	
2000	Account name	Amount $	Account name	Amount $
April 12				
April 19				

(iii) Calculate the **percentage rate** of discount allowed to Marianne on 24 April. Show your workings.
(d) Zen Wholesale's accounts for the year ended 30 April 2000 were finalised on that date. State where, within Zen Wholesale's Balance Sheet, the amount due from Marianne is shown.

[IGCSE 2000]

Final Accounts

At the end of a financial period, usually a year, final accounts are prepared. These consist of a Trading Account, a Profit and Loss Account, and a Balance Sheet. They show the calculation of the profit earned (or the loss incurred) during the period and the financial position of the business at the end of the period.

Final accounts are usually prepared from a trial balance. Every item in a trial balance appears **once** in the final accounts. To ensure that nothing is overlooked, it is useful to place a tick (√) against each item as it is used. Sometimes there are notes to a trial balance giving information on adjustments to be made to certain figures, or information on items which are not yet recorded in the books. These notes appear **twice** in the final accounts. To ensure that this is done, it is useful to place a tick (√) against the notes each time they are used.

Example Trial Balance

The following trial balance was extracted from the books of Maria Nowka as at 31 July 20–6. This trial balance will be used in the following examples to prepare a set of final accounts.

Maria Nowka

Trial Balance as at 31 July 20–6

	Debit $	Credit $
Sales		186 000
Purchases	143 000	
Stock 1 August 20–5	32 000	
Sales returns	1 800	
Purchases returns		4 000
Carriage inwards	5 000	
Discount received		3 500
Loan interest	1 800	
Wages	15 400	
Heat & light	2 500	
General expenses	4 200	
Premises	65 000	
Fixtures & equipment	29 000	
Loan from ABC Ltd.		25 000
Creditors		23 000
Debtors	28 000	
Bank	25 500	
Cash	100	
Capital		120 000
Drawings	8 200	
	361 500	361 500

Additional information

1. Stock on 31 July 20–6 was valued at $26 000.
2. Maria had taken goods costing $200 for her own use during the year. No record of this has been made in the accounting records.

Trading Account

As the name implies, this account deals with trading - buying and selling. The account shows the calculation of the profit earned on the goods sold, i.e. the difference between the selling price and the cost price. This is known as the **Gross Profit**. The basic formula is –

   Sales – Cost of Goods Sold = Gross Profit

The sales figure is the total of the goods actually sold, which is the sales less any **sales returns**.

To calculate the profit on what has been sold, the cost of those goods must be deducted from the sales revenue. This is not necessarily the total cost of goods purchased, as some of the goods purchased may still be in stock (unsold). The basic formula to calculate the cost of sales is –

Opening stock + Purchases – Closing Stock

The purchases figure may have to be reduced if there have been **purchase returns**, in order to get the cost of goods actually purchased.

The owner of a business may take **goods for his own use**. Where this has been entered in the books, the total purchases will have been reduced by the cost of these goods. If this transaction has not been recorded, the purchases figure must be reduced in order to show the actual cost of the goods available for sale.

If **carriage inwards** has been paid on any goods purchased, this must be added to the cost of the actual goods in order to take into account the total cost of the goods.

A Trading Account must always have a heading, which should state the period of time covered by the account, and it is also usual to include the name under which the business trades. The sales revenue is shown on the credit side of a Trading Account and the cost of goods sold is shown on the debit side. The difference between the two sides, the gross profit, appears on the debit side, so that the two sides of the account balance.

■ **Example**

From the trial balance and its accompanying notes, shown earlier, prepare the Trading Account of Maria Nowka for the year ended 31 July 20–6.

Maria Nowka
Trading Account for the year ended 31 July 20–6

	$	$		$	$
Opening stock		32 000	Sales	186 000	
Purchases	143 000		Less Sales returns	1 800	184 200
Less Purchases returns	4 000				
	139 000				
Less Goods for own use	200				
	138 800				
Carriage inwards	5 000	143 800			
		175 800			
Less Closing stock		26 000			
Cost of goods sold		149 800			
Gross Profit c/d		34 400			
		184 200			184 200

As the items are entered in the Trading Account they should be ticked off in the trial balance and its accompanying notes. The abbreviation 'c/d' has been shown by the gross profit, as this is carried down to the Profit and Loss Account.

The Trading Account has been presented in the traditional 2-sided format similar to a traditional ledger account. This is known as the **horizontal** format or 'T' format. In practice, most businesses prepare their final accounts in **vertical** format. The same information is shown, but is presented in a different way. The account is not divided into a debit and a credit side. Instead it resembles an arithmetic calculation, i.e. Sales – Cost of goods sold = Gross Profit.

In examination questions either method of presentation is acceptable. However, candidates following the extended curriculum are expected to understand final accounts in vertical format.

■ **Example**

Prepare the Trading Account of Maria Nowka for the year ended 31 July 20–6 using the vertical method of presentation.

Maria Nowka

Trading Account for the year ended 31 July 20–6

	$	$	$
Sales		186 000	
Less Sales returns		1 800	184 200
Less Cost of goods sold –			
Opening stock		32 000	
Purchases	143 000		
Less Purchases returns	4 000		
	139 000		
Less Goods for own use	200		
	138 800		
Carriage inwards	5 000	143 800	
		175 800	
Less Closing stock		26 000	149 800
Gross Profit			34 400

Profit and Loss Account

As the name implies, this account deals with profits and losses, gains and expenses. The account shows the calculation of the final, or true, profit. This is the profit the business has earned after taking into consideration all the running expenses and any other items of income. This is known as the **Net Profit**. The basic formula is –

Gross Profit + Other Income – Expenses = Net Profit

A Profit and Loss Account must always have a heading, which should state the period of time covered by the account, and it is also usual to include the name under which the business trades. The gross profit (calculated in the Trading Account) is brought down on the credit side of the Profit and Loss Account, and any other gains are also shown on the credit side. The expenses of running the business are shown on the debit side. The difference between the two sides, the balancing figure, is the net profit or the net loss. If the income exceeds the expenses there is a net profit and this will appear on the debit side of the account. If the expenses exceed the income there is a net loss and this will appear on the credit side of the account.

■ **Example**

From the trial balance and the Trading Account, shown earlier, prepare the Profit and Loss Account of Maria Nowka for the year ended 31 July 20–6.

Maria Nowka

Profit and Loss Account for the year ended 31 July 20–6

	$		$
Loan interest	1 800	Gross Profit b/d	34 400
Wages	15 400	Discount received	3 500
Heat & light	2 500		
General expenses	4 200		
Net Profit	14 000		
	37 900		37 900

As the items are entered in the Profit and Loss Account they should be ticked off in the trial balance (and the accompanying notes where applicable).

The Profit and Loss Account has been presented in the traditional **horizontal** format. As with the Trading Account, the Profit and Loss Account can be presented in the **vertical** format. It shows the arithmetic calculation: Gross Profit + Other income – Expenses = Net Profit. A consistent format should be followed for a set of final accounts. The Trading Account, Profit and Loss Account and Balance Sheet should all be prepared in the same format – either horizontal or vertical.

■ **Example**

Prepare the Profit and Loss Account of Maria Nowka for the year ended 31 July 20–6 using the vertical method of presentation.

Maria Nowka
Profit and Loss Account for the year ended 31 July 20–6

	$	$
Gross Profit		34 400
Add Discount received		3 500
		37 900
Less Loan interest	1 800	
Wages	15 400	
Heat & light	2 500	
General expenses	4 200	23 900
Net Profit		14 000

In practice, the Trading Account and the Profit and Loss Account are usually shown as a combined account under one heading, instead of being shown as two separate accounts. The combined account will be used from this point onwards. Using the horizontal method, there is one heading for the two combined accounts, and the profit and loss items follow immediately below the totals of the Trading Account. Using the vertical method, there is one heading for the two combined accounts, and the words 'Gross Profit' are written only once.

The Trading and Profit and Loss Accounts are part of the double entry bookkeeping system. Each item recorded must have a corresponding double entry. Items appearing as credit entries in the Trading and Profit and Loss Account will have a debit entry in the appropriate ledger account, and vice versa. It is important to remember that where an item is deducted on the debit side (e.g. purchases returns) this is equal to showing it on the credit side. Similarly, if an item is deducted on the credit side (e.g. sales returns) this is equal to showing it on the debit side.

■ **Example** From the Trading Account and the Profit and Loss Account, shown earlier, prepare the following accounts in Maria Nowka's ledger, showing how each account is closed on 31 July 20–6: Sales account, Sales returns account, Discount received account, Loan interest account.

Maria Nowka

Sales account

Date	Details	Folio	$	Date	Details	Folio	$
20–6 July 31	Trading		186 000 186 000	20–6 July 31	Total to date		186 000 186 000

Sales Returns account

Date	Details	Folio	$	Date	Details	Folio	$
20–6 July 31	Total to date		1 800 1 800	20–6 July 31	Trading		1 800 1 800

Discount Received account

Date	Details	Folio	$	Date	Details	Folio	$
20–6 July 31	Profit and Loss		3 500 3 500	20–6 July 31	Total to date		3 500 3 500

Loan Interest account

Date	Details	Folio	$	Date	Details	Folio	$
20–6 July 31	Total to date		1 800 1 800	20–6 July 31	Profit and Loss		1 800 1 800

Two entries are required in the stock account. The opening stock is transferred out of the stock account (credit) and in to the Trading Account (debit). The closing stock is then debited in the stock account and a corresponding credit entry is made in the Trading Account.

■ **Example**

From the Trading Account, shown earlier, prepare the Stock account in Maria Nowka's ledger on 31 July 20–6.

Maria Nowka

Stock account

Date	Details	Folio	$	Date	Details	Folio	$
20–5 Aug 1	Balance	b/d	32 000 32 000	20–6 July 31	Trading		32 000 32 000
20–6 July 31	Trading		26 000				

If the business has earned a net profit, the double entry is a credit in the capital account. This is the return on the owner's investment, and increases the amount owed to the owner. If the business made a net loss, the double entry is a debit in the capital account, as this reduces the amount due to the owner.

Balance Sheet

This is not an account, but is a statement of the financial position of the business on a certain date. It shows what the business owns, and amounts owing to the business – the **assets**, and what the business owes – the **liabilities**, and the **capital**. A Balance Sheet must always have a heading, which should include the date on which the Balance Sheet applied. It is also usual to show the name under which the business trades. Some elementary Balance Sheets were prepared in Chapter 1. There are different kinds of assets and liabilities, and, in practice, it is usual to group the assets and liabilities into these different categories.

Assets

There are two kinds of assets –

1. **Fixed Assets**
   These are long-term assets, which were acquired for use in the business, not for resale. They enable the business to earn revenue.

   Examples: premises, machinery, fixtures

In the Balance Sheet they are usually listed in increasing order of liquidity, which means the most permanent assets are listed first. A typical order may be –
- Premises
- Machinery
- Fixtures
- Motor vehicles

2. **Current Assets**

   These are short-term assets which are constantly changing. If not in the form of cash already, they can usually be turned into cash more easily than is possible with fixed assets.

   Examples: stock, debtors, bank

   In the Balance Sheet they are usually listed in increasing order of liquidity, which means the assets furthest away from cash are listed first. A typical order may be –
   - Stock
   - Debtors
   - Bank
   - Cash

Liabilities

There are two kinds of liabilities –

1. **Long-term Liabilities**

   These are amounts owed by the business which do not have to be repaid within the next 12 months.

   Examples: bank loan, loan or mortgage

2. **Current Liabilities**

   These are amounts owed by the business which are due for repayment within the next 12 months. Current liabilities arise from the normal trading activities, so they are constantly changing.

   Examples: creditors, bank overdraft

Example

From the Trial Balance and its accompanying notes, and the Profit and Loss Account, shown earlier, prepare the Balance Sheet of Maria Nowka as at 31 July 20–6.

Maria Nowka
Balance Sheet as at 31 July 20–6

	$	$		$
Fixed assets			**Capital**	
Premises		65 000	Opening balance	120 000
Fixtures & equipment		29 000	Plus Net Profit	14 000
		94 000		134 000
Current assets			Less Drawings	
Stock	26 000		(8 200 + 200)	8 400
Debtors	28 000			125 600
Bank	25 500		**Long-term liabilities**	
Cash	100	79 600	Loan – ABC Ltd.	25 000
			Current liabilities	
			Creditors	23 000
		173 600		173 600

Notes: 1. The drawings have been increased because of the goods taken for personal use, which had not been recorded.
2. The balance on the capital account, owing to Maria Nowka, has been increased by the net profit, and reduced by the amount of drawings.

As the items are entered in the Balance Sheet they should be ticked off in the trial balance and its accompanying notes. Once the Balance Sheet is completed, all the items in the trial balance should have been used once in the final accounts, and the notes to the trial balance should have been used twice.

The Balance Sheet has been presented in a traditional two-sided format, with the assets on the left and the liabilities on the right. It is equally correct to show the assets on the right and the liabilities on the left. A Balance Sheet can also be presented in vertical format, where the items are not divided between the left-hand side and the right-hand side. Instead, the resources used in the business (the assets) are listed, and then where those resources have come from (the liabilities and capital) are listed.

■ **Example** Prepare the Balance Sheet of Maria Nowka as at 31 July 20–6 using the vertical method of presentation.

Maria Nowka
Balance Sheet as at 31 July 20–6

	$	$	$
Fixed assets			
Premises			65 000
Fixtures & equipment			29 000
			94 000
Current assets			
Stock		26 000	
Debtors		28 000	
Bank		25 500	
Cash		100	
		79 600	
Less Current liabilities			
Creditors		23 000	
Working capital			56 600
			150 600
Less Long-term liabilities			
Loan – ABC Ltd.			25 000
			125 600
Financed by			
Capital			
Opening balance			120 000
Plus Net Profit			14 000
			134 000
Less Drawings (8200 + 200)			8 400
			125 600

Notes:
1. As there is only one current liability, the amount is shown in the centre money column. Where there are several current liabilities, the separate amounts should be shown in the first column and the total in the centre column.
2. The long-term liabilities could be shown as an addition to the capital. The method used in the above Balance Sheet is preferable, as it shows clearly the resources provided by the owner.
3. The vertical format has an advantage over the horizontal format as it shows the **Working Capital**. This is very important to a business (see Chapter 20).

The Balance Sheet is **not** part of the double entry system. It is a list of the balances of those accounts remaining open after the preparation of the Trading and Profit and Loss Account, i.e. it is a list of the assets, liabilities and capital.

After the preparation of the Profit and Loss Account, a double entry is made in the capital account for the net profit (or net loss). The drawings account is transferred to the capital account. This means that the balance on the capital account is equal to the amount owed to the owner.

■ **Example**

Using the information given earlier, show how the Capital account would appear in Maria Nowka's ledger on 31 July 20–6.

Maria Nowka

Capital account

Date	Details	Folio	$	Date	Details	Folio	$
20–6 July 31	Drawings Balance	c/d	8 400 125 600 __134 000__	20–5 Aug 1 20–6 July 31 20–6 Aug 1	Balance Net Profit Balance	b/d b/d	120 000 14 000 __134 000__ 125 600

Review questions

1. (a) State one example of a current liability.
   [IGCSE 2000]
   (b) State one example of a fixed asset.
   [IGCSE 1999]
   (c) State what is meant by gross profit.
   [IGCSE 1999]
   (d) What is the result when the expenses of a business exceed its gross profit?
   [IGCSE 1995]
   (e) Complete the following sentences:
      1. The balance on the carriage inwards account is added to the …… in the …… Account.
      2. The balance on the carriage outwards account is entered in the …… Account.
   [IGCSE 1999]
   (f) State which of the following entries in a business's trial balance will be shown in the Profit and Loss Account:
   Bank loan, Bank account, Bank charges, Bank overdraft.
   [IGCSE 2000]

(g) At the end of its financial year, a business has a credit balance of $2 650 on the discount received account. To which final account will this balance be transferred?

[IGCSE 1997]

(h) State how net profit affects a sole trader's capital.

[IGCSE 1996]

2. The trading results of Mohammed Riyas for the year ended 31 October 20–3 are shown below.

Trading and Profit and Loss Account for the year ended 31 October 20–3

		$	$
Sales			100 000
Cost of goods sold –			
(i) _____ 1 November 20–2		13 000	
Purchases		65 000	
		78 000	
Stock 31 October 20–3	(ii)	_____	
			68 000
Gross Profit			32 000
Discount (iii) _____			1 500
			33 500
Wages		19 000	
Rent	(iv)	_____	
Insurance		1 900	
General expenses		9 800	34 800
			(1 300)
(v) _____			

Enter the missing words and figures in the boxes (i) to (v) on the Trading and Profit and Loss Account.

3. The Balance Sheet of Nepembe Stores is shown below. There are some words and figures missing.

Balance Sheet as at 1 March 20–4

	$	$	$
(i) [____] assets			150 000
Current assets			
Stock		44 000	
Debtors	(ii) [____]		
		73 000	
Less Current liabilities			
Creditors	18 000		
Bank overdraft	(iii) [____]		
		22 000	51 000
			201 000
(iv) [____]			
Financed by			
Capital			
Balance at 28 February 20–3			180 000
Add Net (v) [____]			43 000
			223 000
Less Drawings		(vi) [____]	
			201 000

Enter the missing words and figures in the boxes (i) to (vi) on the Balance Sheet.

4. The following Balance Sheet has been prepared by an inexperienced bookkeeper. Redraft the Balance Sheet, under the correct heading, correcting any errors and dividing the assets and liabilities into suitable categories.

M. El Sayed

Balance Sheet for the year ended 31 August 20–8

Liabilities	$	Assets	$
Capital	30 000	Cash	370
Debtors	6 120	Motor vehicles	7 080
Loan from YZ (repayable in 5 years)	7 000	Creditors	4 520
Net Profit	10 100	Premises	21 500
		Stock	9 400
		Drawings	4 200
		Equipment	6 100
		Bank overdraft	3 150
	53 220		56 320

5. The following Trial Balance was extracted from the books of Robbie MacDuff as at 30 June 20–9. Prepare the Trading and Profit and Loss Account for the year ended 30 June 20–9, and a Balance Sheet as at 30 June 20–9.

	Debit $	Credit $
Stock 1 July 20–8	31 000	
Purchases	238 000	
Sales		305 000
Purchases returns		500
Carriage inwards	3 000	
Carriage outwards	1 500	
Wages and salaries	32 500	
Rent and rates	4 200	
Rent received		1 100
Fixtures & fittings	23 000	
Debtors	20 500	
Creditors		13 100
Capital		70 000
Drawings	16 500	
Cash	500	
Bank	19 000	
	389 700	389 700

Stock at 30 June 20–9 was valued at $18 800.

*6. The following Trial Balance was extracted from the books of Al Haffar Stores on 31 October 20–1, **after** the preparation of the Trading Account for the year ended 31 October 20–1.

	Debit $	Credit $
Gross profit		67 500
Salaries and wages	27 100	
Packing and postages	1 850	
Rent and rates	7 510	
Loan interest	1 000	
Insurance	1 430	
Motor expenses	10 110	
Commission received		7 500
Debtors	8 200	
Creditors		15 100
Stock 31 October 20–1	21 140	
Buildings	29 000	
Machinery	11 000	
Motor vehicles	16 100	
Loan from Finance Co.		10 000
Capital		64 000
Drawings	15 300	
Cash	260	
Bank	14 100	
	164 100	164 100

Prepare the Profit and Loss Account of Al Haffar Stores for the year ended 31 October 20–1 and a Balance Sheet as at 31 October 20–1.

78 Accounting: IGCSE

7. The following figures have been extracted from the books of Dawood Traders at 31 December 20–5.

	$		$
Capital	22 500	Bank overdraft	10 500
Cash	600	Debtors	12 900
Creditors	17 250	Purchases	33 000
Sales	50 100	Sales returns	3 540
Purchases returns	2 460	Equipment	7 200
Wages	20 700	Rent and rates	4 800
Drawings	12 000	Discount allowed	420
Sundry expenses	4 290	Discount received	660
Stock 1 January 20–5	4 020	Stock 31 December 20–5	7 500

Prepare (a) A Trial Balance as at 31 December 20–5.
(b) A Trading and Profit and Loss Account for the year ended 31 December 20–5.
(c) A Balance Sheet as at 31 December 20–5.

8. (a) Explain the difference between
   (i) carriage inwards and carriage outwards
   (ii) discount allowed and discount received.

The following accounts were drawn up for Jasper Cato, who has a furniture shop, by his bookkeeper who only had a limited knowledge of preparing final accounts.

Final Accounts as at 30 September 2000

	$		$
Purchases	25 200	Sales	37 600
Stock 1 October 1999	4 500	Returns outward	900
Stock 30 September 2000	6 000	Discount received	280
Profit on goods c/d	3 080		
	38 780		38 780
Carriage inwards	1 200	Profit on goods b/d	3 080
Returns inward	1 600	Discount allowed	160
Administration expenses	7 230	Carriage outwards	1 480
Sundry expenses	170	Loss for year c/d	5 480
	10 200		10 200
Loss for year b/d	5 480	Capital 1 October 1999	27 000
Capital left	21 520		
	27 000		27 000

(b) Redraft the accounts under the correct heading to show the correct gross profit (or loss) and the net profit (or loss) for the year.

[IGCSE 2000]

CHAPTER 8 Accounting rules

It is important that everyone who is involved in preparing accounting records applies the same basic rules. It would be impossible for other people to fully understand the financial position of a business where the accountant had made his own rules regarding how various items were recorded. A comparison of the financial results of different businesses is meaningless if they have followed different procedures for their accounting records.

A generally accepted set of accounting rules has been developed, so that everyone follows the same procedures and applies the same criteria. The main accounting rules are summarised in this chapter. Some of these have already been applied in the practical accounting covered in previous chapters.

Concepts and conventions

Concepts are basically rules, which set down how the financial activities of a business are recorded. Like any other set of rules, concepts can be interpreted in different ways. **Conventions** may be regarded as the generally accepted methods by which the rules (concepts) are applied to given situations.

The main accounting rules, and how they are applied to the accounting records, are explained below.

Business entity

For accounting purposes, the business is treated as completely separate from the owner of that business. The accounting records are the records from the viewpoint of the business – the assets of the *business*, the money spent by the *business*, and so on. The owner's personal assets, the owner's personal spending etc. do **not** appear in the accounting records of the business.

The only time that the owner's personal transactions appear in the accounting records of the business is when the business is also affected. This can occur when the owner introduces capital into the business and when he/she makes drawings from the business. In the books of the business, capital introduced will appear as a credit in the capital account, showing the funds coming *from* the owner, who thus becomes a 'creditor' of the business. Drawings are debited to the owner's account in the books of the business, showing the amount going *to* the owner, and so reducing the indebtedness of the business to the owner.

Going concern

Accounting always assumes that the business will continue to operate for an indefinite period of time. The final accounts of a business are prepared on the basis that there is no intention to close down the business, or to reduce the size of the business by any significant amount. Applying this concept, the fixed assets of a business appear in the Balance Sheet at book value, that is, at cost less depreciation to date (see Chapter10), and stock appears at the lower of cost or net realisable value (see later in this chapter).

Where it is expected that the business will cease to trade in the near future, the value of the assets in the Balance Sheet will have to be adjusted. In these circumstances the expected sale values of the fixed assets are more meaningful than the book values.

Duality

In accounting, all entries are made on the basis that for every transaction there are two aspects – a giving and a receiving. For every outgoing there is a benefit received. The term **double entry** is used to describe how the dual aspect of all transactions is recorded.

Money measurement

The accounts of a business only record the information which can be expressed in monetary terms. Measuring items in terms of money is objective and does not rely on personal opinions. It can be understood by everyone and is an acceptable way of establishing the value of transactions. This means that the accounts cannot possibly give a full picture of the state of the business. There are many aspects of a business which do not appear in the accounting records because they cannot be measured in terms of money. The value of a good manager, a loyal workforce and high staff morale are of great benefit to a business. They cannot be included in the accounts, however, as a money value cannot be placed on them. The fact that the business is expected to suffer as a result of increased competition or the introduction of rival products cannot be recorded in the accounts as these possible effects cannot be measured in monetary terms.

Realisation

It is important that a profit is only recorded when it has actually been earned. Profit is *not* regarded as being earned when a customer places an order for goods. At the other extreme, profit is *not* regarded as being earned when the customer actually pays for the goods or services.

In accounting, profit is regarded as being earned at the time the goods or services pass to the customer. This is when the legal title passes to the buyer, who then has an obligation, or liability, to pay for those goods or services.

Consistency

In some areas of accounting, a choice of method is available, e.g. depreciation. The accounting method which is likely to give the most realistic outcome should be selected. Once a certain method is chosen it should be applied consistently from year to year. Changing to a different method would lead to profits being distorted and would make comparison of the financial results of different years impossible.

A business can, of course, change the method used, but should not do so without careful consideration. Where a change is made, the effects of this should be noted in the final accounts.

Matching

This is sometimes known as the **accruals concept**. The costs and expenses of making sales are deducted from the sales revenue in order to calculate the profit. Under the realisation concept, profit is earned when the ownership of goods passes to the customer, not when the goods are paid for. The matching concept extends this principle, so that profit is calculated by matching the revenue of the period against the costs of the same period.

The figures shown in the Trading and Profit and Loss Account should relate to the period of time covered by that account, irrespective of the actual amount paid or received. It is, therefore, necessary to adjust the items of income and expense for amounts **prepaid** or **accrued** (as explained in Chapter 9).

This concept is also applied to **capital expenditure**, which is explained later in this chapter.

Prudence

This concept is sometimes known as **conservatism**. The following phrase is often used to describe this concept: "never anticipate a profit, but provide for all possible losses".

Applying this concept ensures that the accounts present a realistic picture of the state of the business. The accountant should be cautious and always avoid overstating profit, overvaluing assets and understating liabilities. Profits should only be recognised when it is reasonably certain that they will be realised, and all known liabilities should be provided for. If it seems likely that a proportion of the debtors will not pay their accounts, this expected loss should be anticipated by making a **provision for doubtful debts** (see Chapter11). The concept of prudence is also applied to **stock valuation**, as explained later in this chapter.

The term "prudence prevails" is often used, as this concept overrides (overrules) all the other concepts. In a situation where applying one of the other concepts would go against prudence, then the concept of prudence is applied in preference to the other concept. For example, under the realisation concept, profit is regarded as being earned when the goods pass to the customer: after the debt has been owing for some time, the prudence concept may override this and the debt may be written off.

Capital and revenue expenditure and receipts

Capital expenditure is money spent by a business on the purchase of fixed assets, which are to be used in the business and which are not intended for resale. This also includes adding value to existing fixed assets by extension or improvement. It is important to remember that capital expenditure includes the costs of delivering and installing fixed assets, and also any legal costs incurred in the purchase of land and buildings.

Revenue expenditure is money spent on running a business on a day-to-day basis. This includes all the expenses of administration, selling and distribution, the costs of maintaining the fixed assets, and the purchase of stock intended for resale.

Revenue expenditure appears in the Trading and Profit and Loss Account where the costs of the period are **matched** against the revenue of the same period. Capital expenditure appears in the fixed assets section of the Balance Sheet. It is incorrect to charge the cost of a fixed asset against the profits of one accounting period, because the benefit lasts for several years. The capital expenditure is matched against the revenue it helps to earn by an annual depreciation charge (see Chapter10).

If capital and revenue expenditure are not treated correctly the net profit will be over- or under-stated and the Balance Sheet, whilst still balancing, will also be incorrect. If the cost of a machine purchased for use in the business were included as purchases of goods for resale, both the gross profit and the net profit would be understated. In the Balance Sheet, the fixed assets would be undervalued, and the balance on the capital account would be understated because of the reduced net profit.

Revenue receipts are sales or other items of income such as rent received and discount received. These are recorded in the Trading and Profit and Loss Account.

A capital receipt occurs when a fixed asset is sold. In the same way that capital expenditure is not included in the Trading and Profit and Loss Account, capital receipts are also excluded. Only any profit or loss made on the sale of the fixed asset will appear in the Profit and Loss Account (refer to disposals of fixed assets in Chapter10).

Stock valuation

A business must value its stock at the end of each financial year. The closing stock of one year becomes the opening stock of the following year. Both stocks appear in the Trading Account, and so affect the calculation of both the gross profit and the net profit. In the Balance Sheet, closing stock appears as a current asset and the net profit is added to the capital. The value placed on the stock should never be over-valued as this can result in both the net profit and the current assets being overstated.

Applying the **concept of prudence**, stock must always be valued at **the lower of cost or net realisable value.**

The cost of stock is what it cost the business to buy the goods, plus all the costs incurred in bringing the goods to their present condition and location, for example, carriage inwards. The net realisable value is what the business estimates will be received when the stock is sold, less any further costs to complete goods and less all costs which are expected to be incurred in selling the goods. Usually the cost of the stock will be the lower figure. It can happen that the stock gets damaged or becomes old, or goes out of fashion, in which case the net realisable value will be the lower figure.

Review questions

1. (a) Name the accounting concept referred to in the following statement:
   "If in doubt, overstate losses and understate profits."
   [IGCSE 1999]
   (b) Explain what is meant by the concept of business entity.
   (c) It is not possible to record all aspects of a business in money terms. Name **two** such aspects of a business.
   [IGCSE 1997]
   (d) To-day a man tells the owner of a clothing shop that he will buy a coat tomorrow.
       (i) Explain why the owner of the shop should not yet record this as a sale.
       (ii) State which concept you have applied in (i).
   [IGCSE 1999]

2. (a) Frederick owns a factory making cardboard boxes. State **one** example of capital expenditure and **one** example of revenue expenditure for his business.
   [IGCSE 2000]
   (b) For **each** item state whether it is capital or revenue expenditure:
   Computer operator's salary
   Computer maintenance contract
   Purchase of new computer
   [IGCSE 1999]
   (c) Repairs to one of the machines owned by a partnership have been carried out at a cost of $2 000. The partners suggest that the cost of the repairs should be added to the original cost of the machine in the Balance Sheet. Comment on the partners' suggested treatment of the cost of the repairs.
   [IGCSE 1999]

*3. (a) (i) Explain what capital expenditure and revenue expenditure are.
       (ii) Explain why it is important to distinguish between them.
    (b) For each of the following items of expenditure state whether it is capital expenditure or revenue expenditure. Give a reason for each answer.

84 Accounting: IGCSE

    (i) The purchase of a new delivery van
    (ii) Repairs and servicing for the van
    (iii) Petrol used on the van's journeys
    (iv) Wages paid to the firm's workmen for building a garage for the van
    (v) Fitting four new tyres to the van

  (c) In error, a firm's machinery account includes $2 000 paid for machinery repairs. Explain how this affects the firm's
    (i) Profit and Loss Account
    (ii) Balance Sheet.
    [IGCSE 1995]

4. (a) State the effect on the gross profit of a business if closing stock is under-valued.
    [IGCSE 1999]
  (b) A business over-values its closing stock by $3 000. Complete the following sentence to show how this affects its net profit:
    "Net profit is …… by $ ……"
    [IGCSE 2000]

5. (a) Stock valuation is often described as being at the lower of cost or net realisable value. Explain the meaning of
    (i) cost,
    (ii) net realisable value.
  (b) State which accounting concept is applied when stock is valued.
  (c) Jane Hall is a sole trader whose year-end is 31 October. According to the stock records the value of her stock at 31 October 2000 was $4 800. The following items were then discovered:
    1. One stock sheet was under-cast by $100.
    2. The total at the bottom of one stock sheet of $267 had been carried forward to the next page as $276.
    3. The stock figure includes $190 goods sent to Jane on approval. No invoice has been received for these goods and Jane intends to return them to the supplier.
    4. On 5 September 2000, Jane sent goods with a selling price of $450 to Ben Newton on sale or return. Jane's gross profit is 20% of the selling price. On 31 October Ben returned half of the goods to Jane. The goods were not received by Jane until 1 November.

    Calculate the correct valuation of stock at 31 October 2000.
  (d) Using your answer to (c) state how the adjustment to the stock will affect the following:
    (i) gross profit for the year ended 31 October 2000
    (ii) net profit for the year ended 31 October 2000
    (iii) net profit for the year ending 31 October 2001
  (e) Explain why the totals of the Balance Sheet prepared at 31 October 2000 agreed, even though the stock was incorrect.
    [IGCSE 2000]

CHAPTER 9: Accruals and prepayments

The final accounts prepared up to this point have not really been true to life. In practice, adjustments often have to be made to the accounting records at the end of the financial year in order that the year-end accounts show a realistic view of the financial position of the business. These year-end adjustments must now be considered. This chapter will concentrate on accruals and prepayments and the following chapters will cover depreciation of fixed assets and provision for doubtful debts.

A Trading and Profit and Loss Account relates to a specified period of time, which should be indicated in the heading of the account. Only costs and revenues which relate to that period of time should be included in the account. It is necessary to make adjustments for items which relate to the year in question but which have not actually been paid or received. Adjustments must also be made for items which have been paid or received during the year in question but which relate to a different period of time. This is an application of the **matching concept.**

A Balance Sheet shows the financial position of a business on a certain date. To show the true position it is necessary to include any outstanding costs and revenues and also to include any items which are paid in advance for a future period.

Accrued and prepaid expenses

Accruals

An accrual is an amount due in an accounting period, which is unpaid at the end of that period. If an expense is **accrued** it means that a benefit or service received during an accounting period remains unpaid at the end of that period.

When expenses are paid during the financial year they are debited to the relevant expense account. At the end of the year the expense is transferred to the Profit and Loss Account. It is important to apply the **matching concept** and transfer to Profit and Loss Account the expense relating to that particular period – whether or not the amount has actually been paid. Any amount due but unpaid must be added to the amount paid and the total transferred to the Profit and Loss Account. The accrual will be brought down as a credit balance on the expense account. This will appear in the Balance Sheet as a current liability, as it is an amount owing by the business which should be paid in the near future.

The entries may be summarised as –
(a) Debit Expense account } when the expense is paid.
    Credit Cash book
(b) Debit the Expense account with any outstanding amount at the end of the year and carry down as a credit balance.
(c) Credit the Expense account and debit the Profit and Loss Account with the difference on the Expense account (this represents the expense for the year).
(d) Enter the credit balance on the Expense account as a current liability in the Balance Sheet.

■ Example

Zola's financial year ends on 31 December.

He rents a workshop at an annual rent of $2 400, payable in four quarterly instalments of $600. During 20–8, Zola paid rent by cheque on 1 January, 1 April and 1 July. The rent due on 1 October remained unpaid on 31 December 20–8.

(a) Write up the Rent account in Zola's ledger for the year ended 31 December 20–8.
(b) Prepare a relevant extract from Zola's Profit and Loss Account for the year ended 31 December 20–8.
(c) Prepare a relevant extract from Zola's Balance Sheet as at 31 December 20–8.

Zola

(a) Rent account

Date	Details	Folio	$	Date	Details	Folio	$
20–8				20–8			
Jan 1	Bank		600	Dec 31	Profit and Loss		2 400
Apr 1	Bank		600				
July 1	Bank		600				
Dec 31	Balance	c/d	600				
			2 400				2 400
				20–9			
				Jan 1	Balance	b/d	600

(b) **Extract from Profit and Loss Account for the year ended 31 December 20–8**

	$
Expenses – Rent	2 400

(c) **Extract from Balance Sheet as at 31 December 20–8**

	$
Current liabilities	
Accrual – Rent	600

Chapter 9 – Accruals and prepayments

Where there are several expenses owing at the end of the year it is usual to show the total amount of the accruals in one figure in the Balance Sheet instead of itemising all the individual amounts.

Prepayments

A prepayment is when a payment is paid in advance of the period to which it relates. If an expense is **prepaid** it means that an amount is paid during an accounting period for a benefit or service to be received in a future period.

The **matching concept** must be applied to ensure that only the expense for the particular period is entered in the Profit and Loss Account. The amount paid in advance must be deducted from the total amount paid and only the amount relating to the particular period transferred to the Profit and Loss Account. The prepayment will be brought down as a debit balance on the expense account. This will appear in the Balance Sheet as a current asset as it is a short-term benefit the business has paid for but not used up.

The entries may be summarised as –

(a) Debit Expense account } when the expense is paid.
    Credit Cash book
(b) Credit the Expense account with any amount prepaid at the end of the year and carry down as a debit balance.
(c) Credit the Expense account and debit the Profit and Loss Account with the difference on the Expense account (this represents the expense for the year).
(d) Enter the debit balance on the Expense account as a current asset in the Balance Sheet.

■ **Example**

Zola's financial year ends on 31 December.

On 1 October 20–8 he purchased a new motor vehicle and paid one year's motor vehicle insurance of $400 by cheque.

(a) Write up the Motor Vehicle Insurance account in Zola's ledger for the year ended 31 December 20–8.
(b) Prepare a relevant extract from Zola's Profit and Loss Account for the year ended 31 December 20–8.
(c) Prepare a relevant extract from Zola's Balance Sheet as at 31 December 20–8.

Zola

(a) Motor Vehicle Insurance account

Date	Details	Folio	$	Date	Details	Folio	$
20–8				20–8			
Oct 1	Bank		400	Dec 31	Profit and Loss		100
					Balance	c/d	300
			400				400
20–9							
Jan 1	Balance	b/d	300				

(b) **Extract from Profit and Loss Account for the year ended 31 December 20–8**

	$
Expenses – Motor vehicle insurance	100

(c) **Extract from Balance Sheet as at 31 December 20–8**

	$
Current assets	
Prepayment – Motor vehicle insurance	300

Where there are several expenses prepaid at the end of the year it is usual to show the total amount of the prepayments in one figure in the Balance Sheet instead of itemising all the individual amounts.

A prepayment can also take place when items such as stationery, packing materials and postage stamps are not fully used up within the financial year. Such stocks are really a form of prepayment and are treated in the same way as expenses prepaid. These stocks must not be included in the stock of goods for resale.

■ **Example**

Zola's financial year ends on 31 December.

All goods sold are packed in cardboard boxes before being sent to customers. During 20–8 Zola purchased packing material, $75, on 2 January, and $96 on 5 September, paying in cash. On 31 December 20–8 the stock of packing materials was valued at $38.

Write up the Packing Material account in Zola's ledger for the year ended 31 December 20–8.

Zola

Packing Material account

Date	Details	Folio	$	Date	Details	Folio	$
20–8				20–8			
Jan 2	Cash		75	Dec 31	Profit and Loss		133
Sept 5	Cash		96		Balance	c/d	38
			171				171
20–9							
Jan 1	Balance	b/d	38				

The stock of packing material (amount prepaid) at 31 December 20–8 will appear as a current asset in Zola's Balance Sheet at that date.

Accrued and prepaid income

Accruals

If an item of income is accrued it means that a person receiving a benefit or service provided by the business during an accounting period has not paid for this at the end of the business's financial year.

When income is received during the financial year it is credited to the relevant income account. At the end of the year, the income transferred to the Profit and Loss Account must relate to that particular period. Just as the **matching concept** is applied to expenses, it is also applied to income. Any amount due but not received is added to the amount received and the total transferred to the Profit and Loss Account. The accrued income will be brought down as a debit balance on the income account. This will appear in the Balance Sheet as a current asset as it is an amount owing to the business which should be received in the near future.

The entries may be summarised as –
(a) Debit Cash book } when the income is received.
    Credit Income account
(b) Credit the Income account with any outstanding amount at the end of the year and carry down as a debit balance.
(c) Debit the Income account and credit the Profit and Loss Account with the difference on the Income account (this represents the income for the year).
(d) Enter the debit balance on the Income account as a current asset in the Balance Sheet.

■ **Example**

Zola's financial year ends on 31 December.

He acts as an agent for Super Suits and receives commission on all orders he takes on behalf of Super Suits. The commission is paid in arrears at the end of each four-month period.

Zola received a cheque from Super Suits for $250 on 5 May 20–8 and a cheque for $210 on 4 September 20–8. At 31 December 20–8 Super Suits owed commission to Zola amounting to $235 for the period 1 September to 31 December 20–8.

(a) Write up the Commission Received account in Zola's ledger for the year ended 31 December 20–8.
(b) Prepare a relevant extract from Zola's Profit and Loss Account for the year ended 31 December 20–8.
(c) Prepare a relevant extract from Zola's Balance Sheet as at 31 December 20–8.

Zola

(a) **Commission Received account**

Date	Details	Folio	$	Date	Details	Folio	$
20–8				20–8			
Dec 31	Profit and Loss		695	May 5	Bank		250
				Sept 4	Bank		210
				Dec 31	Balance	c/d	235
			695				695
20–9							
Jan 1	Balance	b/d	235				

(b) **Extract from Profit and Loss Account for the year ended 31 December 20–8**

	$
Gross Profit	xxx
Add Commission received	695

(c) **Extract from Balance Sheet as at 31 December 20–8**

	$
Current assets	
Debtor for commission	235

Prepayments

If an item of income is prepaid, or paid in advance, it means that a person has paid for a benefit or service, but at the end of the business's financial year this has not yet been provided by the business.

The **matching concept** must be applied. The amount received in advance must be deducted from the total amount received and only the amount for the particular period transferred to the Profit and Loss Account. The prepaid income will be brought down as a credit balance on the income account. This will appear as a current liability in the Balance Sheet as the business has a liability to provide something in the next financial year for which it has already received payment.

The entries may be summarised as –
(a) Debit Cash book
    Credit Income account } when the income is received.
(b) Debit the Income account with any amount received in advance at the end of the year and carry down as a credit balance.
(c) Debit the Income account and credit the Profit and Loss Account with the difference on the Income account (this represents the income for the year).
(d) Enter the credit balance on the Income account as a current liability in the Balance Sheet.

■ **Example**

Zola's financial year ends on 31 December.

He sub-lets part of his workshop to his brother, at an annual rent of $1 000, payable in two equal instalments on 1 January and 1 July each year. Zola received cheques from his brother, for $500 each, on 1 January, 1 July and 31 December 20–8.
(a) Write up the Rent Received account in Zola's ledger for the year ended 31 December 20–8.
(b) Prepare a relevant extract from Zola's Profit and Loss Account for the year ended 31 December 20–8.
(c) Prepare a relevant extract from Zola's Balance Sheet as at 31 December 20–8.

Zola

(a) **Rent Received account**

Date	Details	Folio	$	Date	Details	Folio	$
20–8				20–8			
Dec 31	Profit and Loss		1 000	Jan 1	Bank		500
	Balance	c/d	500	July 1	Bank		500
				Dec 31	Bank		500
			1 500				1 500
				20–9			
				Jan 1	Balance	b/d	500

(b) **Extract from Profit and Loss Account for the year ended 31 December 20–8**

	$
Gross Profit	xxx
Add Rent received	1 000

(c) **Extract from Balance Sheet as at 31 December 20–8**

	$
Current liabilities	
Income prepaid	500

Opening balances on expense and income accounts

The closing balance of an account at the end of one financial year becomes the opening balance of the account for the next financial year. Any accrual or prepayment at the end of the financial year will appear as a balance on the relevant account, and will be carried down to the following financial year. This opening balance must be taken into consideration when the expense or income relating to the following year is calculated.

Expenses

■ **Example 1**

Zola's financial year ends on 31 December.

He rents a workshop at an annual rent of $2 400, payable in four quarterly instalments of $600. On 1 January 20–9 Zola's Rent account showed a credit balance of $600 for rent due on 1 October 20–8. During 20–9 Zola paid rent by cheque as follows – $1 200 on 2 January, $600 on 1 April, $600 on 1 July and $600 on 1 October.

Write up the Rent account in Zola's ledger for the year ended 31 December 20–9.

Zola

Rent account

Date	Details	Folio	$	Date	Details	Folio	$
20–9				20–9			
Jan 2	Bank		1 200	Jan 1	Balance	b/d	600
Apr 1	Bank		600	Dec 31	Profit and Loss		2 400
July 1	Bank		600				
Oct 1	Balance		600				
			3 000				3 000

The $2 400 transferred to the Profit and Loss Account for the year ended 31 December 20–9 is the rent which relates to that period of time. This is the amount paid less the amount relating to the previous financial year.

■ **Example 2**

Zola's financial year ends on 31 December.

On 1 January 20–9 Zola's Motor Vehicle Insurance account showed a debit balance of $300. On 1 October 20–9 he paid one year's motor vehicle insurance of $440 by cheque.

Write up the Motor Vehicle Insurance account in Zola's ledger for the year ended 31 December 20–9.

Zola

Motor Vehicle Insurance account

Date	Details	Folio	$	Date	Details	Folio	$
20–9				20–9			
Jan 1	Balance	b/d	300	Dec 31	Profit and Loss		410
Oct 1	Bank		440		Balance	c/d	330
			740				740
20–0							
Jan 1	Balance	b/d	330				

The $410 transferred to the Profit and Loss Account for the year ended 31 December 20–9 is the insurance which relates to that period of time. This is the amount paid, $440, less the amount which relates to the next financial year, $330, plus the amount paid in the last financial year which relates to this financial year, $300.

The insurance prepaid of $330 at 31 December 20–9 will appear as a current asset in Zola's Balance Sheet at that date.

Income

■ **Example 1**

Zola's financial year ends on 31 December.
On 1 January 20–9 his Commission Received account showed a debit balance of $235. During 20–9 he received commission amounting to $1 050, by cheque. On 31 December 20–9 Super Suits owed Zola commission amounting to $248 for the four months ending 31 December 20–9.
Write up the Commission Received account in Zola's ledger for the year ended 31 December 20–9.

Zola

Commission Received account

Date	Details	Folio	$	Date	Details	Folio	$
20–9				20–9			
Jan 1	Balance	b/d	235	Dec 31	Bank		1 050*
Dec 31	Profit and Loss		1 063		Balance	c/d	248
			1 298				1 298
20–0							
Jan 1	Balance	b/d	248				

*A date of 31 December is shown as no individual dates are given in the question.
The $1 063 transferred to the Profit and Loss Account for the year ended 31 December 20–9 is the commission which relates to that period of time. This is the amount received, $1 050, less the amount which relates to the previous financial year, $235, plus the amount not yet received for this financial year, $248.

■ **Example 2**

Zola's financial year ends on 31 December.
He sub-lets part of his workshop to his brother, at an annual rent of $1 000, payable in two equal instalments on 1 January and 1 July each year. From 1 January 20–0 the annual rent was increased to $1 200.
On 1 January 20–9 Zola's Rent Received account showed a credit balance of $500. In 20–9 Zola received a cheque from his brother for $500 on 1 July, and a cheque for $600 on 31 December.
Write up the Rent Received account in Zola's ledger for the year ended 31 December 20–9.

Zola

Rent Received account

Date	Details	Folio	$	Date	Details	Folio	$
20–9 Dec 31	Profit and Loss Balance	c/d	1 000 600	20–9 Jan 1 July 1 Dec 31	Balance Bank Bank	b/d	500 500 600
			1 600				1 600
				20–0 Jan 1	Balance	b/d	600

The $1 000 transferred to the Profit and Loss Account for the year ended 31 December 20–9 is the rent which relates to that period of time. This is the amount received, $1 100, less the amount which relates to the next financial year, $600, plus the amount paid in the last financial year which relates to this financial year, $500.

Final accounts are usually prepared from a trial balance drawn up at the end of the financial year. The figures appearing in a trial balance represent the difference between the debit side and the credit side on each account on a certain date. Any information regarding accruals and prepayments will be provided as a footnote to the trial balance. It is important to remember that any footnotes to a trial balance must be entered twice in the final accounts. Accruals and prepayments will be used in the Profit and Loss Account and will also appear in the Balance Sheet.

To calculate how much should be included in the Profit and Loss Account for a particular expense the following procedure should be followed –

Accrued expenses
Amount paid during the year
Add amount accrued at end of year
Less amount accrued at start of year

Prepaid expenses
Amount paid during the year
Add amount prepaid at start of year
Less amount prepaid at end of year

To calculate how much should be included in the Profit and Loss Account for a particular item of income the following procedure should be followed –

Accrued income
Amount received during the year
Add amount accrued at end of year
Less amount accrued at start of year

Prepaid expenses
Amount received during the year
Add amount prepaid at start of year
Less amount prepaid at end of year

In examinations, calculations should always be shown so that where a figure is only partially correct, some marks may be awarded. When doing adjustments of items of expense and income, the steps in the calculation may be shown in brackets after the appropriate figure in the Profit and Loss Account.

■ Example

Zola's financial year ends on 31 December.
The Trial Balance on 31 December 20–9 included –

	Debit $
Motor vehicle insurance	740

At 31 December 20–9 motor vehicle insurance was prepaid by $330.

Prepare a relevant extract from Zola's Profit and Loss Account for the year ended 31 December 20–9.

Zola

Extract from Profit and Loss Account for the year ended 31 December 20–9

	$
Expenses – Motor vehicle insurance (740 – 330)	410

Review questions

1. (a) Where is an accrued expense found in a Balance Sheet?
   [IGCSE 1995]
   (b) State where the expenses prepaid by a business are shown within its Balance Sheet.
   [IGCSE 2000]
   (c) A business paid $1 200 for electricity during the year ended 31 December 1997, and owed a further $300 on that date.
      (i) Calculate the amount charged in the Profit and Loss Account for electricity for the year ended 31 December. Show your workings.
      (ii) Under which heading in the business Balance Sheet at 31 December would the amount owing for electricity be shown?
         Fixed assets
         Current assets
         Current liabilities
   [IGCSE 1998]

(d) On 1 May 1998 Martha, a sole trader, owed $1 000 for rent of her premises. She paid rent of $6 000 in the year ended 30 April 1999. On that date, rent due but unpaid was $1 500.
   Calculate the amount charged for rent in Martha's Profit and Loss Account for the year ended 30 April 1999. Show your workings.
[IGCSE 1999]

2. On 30 September Joe owed $500 for rent of his premises. He has made no entries for this in his books.
   (a) State how the adjustment required for rent is shown in Joe's Profit and Loss Account for the six months ended 30 September 2000.
   (b) State how the adjustment required for rent is shown in Joe's Balance Sheet as at 30 September 2000.
   (c) Explain how the matching concept is observed by the adjustments made for rent in Joe's accounts.
[IGCSE 2000]

3. Marianne makes up her annual accounts to 31 October. On 1 November 1997, balances on her ledger accounts included the following –

	$
Insurance (prepaid)	800
Rent (accrued)	650

During the year ended 31 October 1998, the following transactions took place:
(a) An insurance premium of $4 000 was paid on 1 February 1998. This payment is for 12 months to 31 January 1999.
(b) Payments were made for rent as follows –

	$
4 November 1997	650
12 February 1998	900
5 May 1998	900
15 August 1998	900

At 31 October 1998 $1 000 was owing but unpaid.

Starting with the ledger account balances on 1 November 1997, record the above transactions in the appropriate accounts. Balance the ledger accounts at 31 October 1998, showing the amounts transferred to the Profit and Loss Account for the year ended 31 October 1998.
[IGCSE 1998]

4. In the year to 30 September 1997, Cato had the following transactions:

1996		$
October 20	Paid cash for office stationery	200
December 15	Purchased office stationery on credit from Smithson	380
1997		
January 4	Returned office stationery to Smithson	45
August 30	Purchased office stationery on credit from Clifford & Co.	235
September 3	Purchased office stationery and paid by cheque	110

Write up Cato's Stationery account for the year to 30 September 1997. Show the amount to be transferred to the Profit and Loss Account.

[IGCSE 1997]

*5. The following information is taken from the books of Van Wyk & Co. as at 31 May 20–4:

	Debit $	Credit $
Sales		60 900
Purchases	46 500	
Stock 1 June 20–3	6 300	
Sales returns	300	
Purchases returns		200
Carriage inwards	200	
Repairs	550	
Motor vehicle expenses	680	
Insurance	280	
Wages	4 630	
Office expenses	470	
Commission received		1 900

Additional information

1. On 31 May 20–4

	$
stock was valued at	6 800
insurance prepaid amounts to	20
motor vehicle expenses accrued amount to	120
commission receivable due amounts to	200

2. The office expenses include office stationery. At 31 May 20–4 the stock of unused stationery was valued at $10.

Prepare the Trading and Profit and Loss Account of Van Wyk & Co. for the year ended 31 May 20–4.

6. (a) (i) Explain the difference between prepaid and accrued expenses.
 (ii) Explain how prepaid and accrued expenses affect the expenditure in the Profit and Loss Account.
 (iii) Explain how prepaid and accrued expenses should be entered in the Balance Sheet.
 (b) The following balances appeared in the ledger of Paul Silva at 1 February 1999.

	$
Rates (debit balance)	220
Motor expenses (credit balance)	170

On 10 April 1999 Paul paid $1 800 by cheque for rates. This was for the year ended 31 March 2000.
 During the year ended 31 January 2000 Paul paid a total of $2 050 for motor expenses. At 31 January 2000 he owed the garage an amount of $290 for motor repairs.

Write up the ledger accounts for Rates and Motor Expenses for the year ended 31 January 2000. Show the amounts transferred to the Profit and Loss Account and the balances brought down on 1 February 2000.
 (c) Paul's Profit and Loss Account for the year ended 31 January 2000 has not been adjusted for $75 rent receivable prepaid. State how his capital will be affected when this error is corrected.

[IGCSE 2000]

7. Explain **each** entry in the following accounts that appear in the ledger of Lucie.

Electricity account

Date	Details	Folio	$	Date	Details	Folio	$
20–2				20–2			
June 15	Cash		45	June 1	Balance	b/d	45
Aug 26	Bank		52	20–3			
Nov 19	Bank		48	May 31	Profit and Loss		170
20–3							
Feb 13	Cash		39				
May 31	Balance	c/d	31				
			215				215
				20–3			
				June 1	Balance	b/d	31

100 Accounting: IGCSE

Rent Received account

Date	Details	Folio	$	Date	Details	Folio	$
20–2				20–2			
June 1	Balance	b/d	1 300	June 2	Bank		2 600
20–3				Sept 1	Cash		1 300
May 31	Profit and Loss		5 200	Dec 3	Bank		1 300
				20–3			
				May 31	Balance	c/d	1 300
			6 500				6 500
20–3							
June 1	Balance	b/d	1 300				

8. The following Trial Balance is taken from the books of Majeed Traders after the preparation of the Trading Account for the year ended 31 August 20–7.

Majeed Traders

Trial Balance as at 31 August 20–7

	Debit $	Credit $
Gross profit		21 550
Capital		38 000
Drawings	4 700	
Insurance	1 500	
Motor vehicle expenses	3 100	
Wages & salaries	8 700	
Discount allowed	900	
Rent	2 100	
Rent received		1 260
Land & buildings	19 500	
Fixtures & fittings	2 400	
Motor vehicles	2 000	
Debtors	12 000	
Creditors		9 500
Stock at 31 August 20–7	9 750	
Bank	3 660	
	70 310	70 310

Additional information

1. The insurance covers a period of 15 months up to 30 November 20–7.

2. Part of the property is sub-let at a rental of $90 per month. The tenant has paid rent up to 31 October 20–7.

3. On 31 August 20–7

	$
wages due amount to	410
commission receivable due amounts to	270

(a) Prepare the Profit and Loss Account of Majeed Traders for the year ended 31 August 20–7.
(b) Prepare the Balance Sheet of Majeed Traders as at 31 August 20–7.

CHAPTER 10

Depreciation and disposal of fixed assets

Depreciation and how it can arise

Depreciation is an estimate of the loss in value of a fixed asset over its expected working life. Most fixed assets lose value over time. The accounts of a business should show a fair view of the financial position so it is necessary to record this loss in value. In the Profit and Loss Account depreciation of fixed assets will appear with the other expenses and the net profit will be reduced. In the Balance Sheet the fixed assets will be shown at a value below cost price, the **written-down value**, or **book value**, which is the cost minus the amount of depreciation up to that date.

Fixed assets are purchased to enable the business to earn profits over several years. It would not, therefore, be correct to charge the total cost against the profits of one year only. Depreciation enables the cost of a fixed asset to be spread over all the years which will benefit from the use of the asset. This is an application of the **matching concept**, as the cost is matched against the sales of the years which benefit from the use of the fixed asset.

Depreciation is essentially an **estimate** of the loss in value of a fixed asset: the exact amount of depreciation can only be calculated when the asset is sold. It is also important to remember that depreciation does not involve any actual money going out of the business – it is a **non-monetary expense**. Because it is charged in the Profit and Loss Account, depreciation will reduce the net profit to a more realistic figure. This is an application of the **prudence** concept. If depreciation is not taken into account the net profit will be over-stated, which could result in the owner of the business making excessive cash drawings which the business cannot really afford. This concept is also applied in the Balance Sheet when the fixed assets are not recorded at cost, but at a more prudent figure (written-down value). Just as depreciation does not involve a monetary expense, neither does it provide a cash fund for the replacement of fixed assets.

The main causes of depreciation may be summarised as –

1. Physical deterioration — This may be through wear and tear, when a fixed asset wears out through being used or it may be through rust, rot and decay, when a fixed asset falls into a bad physical condition.
2. Economic reasons — This may be because the asset becomes obsolete, when it becomes out of date because newer and more efficient assets are available or it may become inadequate as it is no longer able to meet the needs of the business.
3. Passage of time — This arises when a fixed asset has a fixed life of a certain number of years e.g. a lease.
4. Depletion — This occurs in assets such as wells or mines when the worth of the asset falls over a period of time as value is removed from the asset.

Methods of calculating depreciation

There are several ways in which depreciation can be calculated. The aim is to match that proportion of the cost of the fixed asset to the revenue earned by it each year. This is not an easy task in reality and many factors must be considered, such as –

How long will the fixed asset last?
How much will be received when the fixed asset is sold at some point in the future?
How can the benefits gained from the use of the fixed asset be measured?

There are three main methods of depreciation –
Straight line method
Reducing balance method
Revaluation method

There are other methods which may be used, but these are outside the scope of this syllabus.

Different types of fixed assets may be depreciated using different methods and using different rates. The method chosen must be the one which spreads the cost of the asset as fairly as possible over the years which benefit from the use of the asset. Once a method has been selected, it should be applied to that asset each year. This is an application of the concept of **consistency**.

Straight line method of depreciation

This may also be called the **fixed instalment method**. Under this system the same percentage rate is used each year and the amount of the depreciation charged is the same each year. It is used for fixed assets which provide equal benefits to the business each year they are in operation. Using this method, it is possible for an asset to reach a nil value in cases where no residual value (see below) is expected.

The formula for calculating the straight line method of depreciation is –

$$\frac{\text{Cost of asset}}{\text{Number of expected years of use}}$$

■ **Example**

Amir's financial year ends on 31 December.

On 1 January 20–4 he purchased a machine for $12 000. He estimates that he will keep the machine for 4 years.

What is the annual depreciation expressed in terms of –
(a) amount
(b) percentage rate?

(a) $\dfrac{\$12\,000}{4\text{ years}} = \$3\,000$

(b) $\dfrac{\$3\,000}{\$12\,000} \times \dfrac{100}{1} = 25\%$

Sometimes it is expected that the asset will have some value at the end of its working life. This is known as the **residual value**. It is necessary to estimate the amount which may be received when the asset is sold and this must be considered when calculating the annual depreciation.

The formula used in a case where a residual value is expected is –

$$\frac{\text{Cost of asset} - \text{Residual value}}{\text{Number of expected years of use}}$$

■ **Example**

Amir's financial year ends on 31 December.

On 1 January 20–4 he purchased a machine for $12 000. He estimates that he will keep the machine for 4 years and then sell it for $2 000.

What is the annual depreciation expressed in terms of –
(a) amount
(b) percentage rate (based on the original cost)?

(a) $\dfrac{\$12\,000 - \$2\,000}{4\text{ years}} = \$2\,500$

(b) $\dfrac{\$2\,500}{\$12\,000} \times \dfrac{100}{1} = 20.83\%$

Reducing balance method of depreciation

This may also be called the **diminishing balance method.** Under this method the same percentage is used each year but, because it is calculated on a different value each year, the amount of depreciation will reduce each year. At the end of the first year the agreed percentage of depreciation is deducted from the cost of the fixed asset. In later years the same percentage is used, but it is calculated on the cost of the asset less the depreciation already charged (the reduced balance). This means that a higher amount of depreciation will be charged against profits in the early years of the life of the fixed asset. Reducing balance depreciation is used for assets which, in the early years, have lower maintenance costs but give greater benefits than in later years. As the depreciation is always calculated as a percentage of the written-down value (reduced balance) of the fixed asset, the asset will never reach a nil value in the books.

Any estimated residual value will be taken into consideration when the percentage rate is decided upon.

■ Example

Amir's financial year ends on 31 December.

On 1 January 20–4 he purchased a machine for $12 000. He estimates that he will keep the machine for 4 years and then sell it for $2 000.

Calculate the depreciation for **each** of the four years ending 31 December 20–4, 20–5, 20–6 and 20–7 using the reducing balance method at the rate of 36% per annum.

	$
Cost	12 000
Depreciation for the year ended 31 December 20–4 ($12 000 x 36%)	4 320
Book value at 1 January 20–5	7 680
Depreciation for the year ended 31 December 20–5 ($7 680 x 36%)	2 765*
Book value at 1 January 20–6	4 915
Depreciation for the year ended 31 December 20–6 ($4 915 x 36%)	1 769*
Book value at 1 January 20–7	3 146
Depreciation for the year ended 31 December 20–7 ($3 146 x 36%)	1 133*
Book value at 1 January 20–8	2 013

*The figures have been adjusted to eliminate the cents as depreciation is usually expressed in whole dollars.

Revaluation method of depreciation

Sometimes it is not possible to maintain detailed records of certain types of fixed assets. For assets such as very small items of equipment, packing cases, and hand tools it is not practical to maintain full records of each particular asset. Without full accounting records the straight line and reducing value methods of depreciation cannot be operated. In such cases the revaluation method of depreciation is used.

Under this method the assets are valued at the end of each year. This value is compared with the previous valuation (or the cost, if it is the first year of ownership of the asset) and the amount by which the asset has fallen in value is the depreciation for the year.

■ **Example**

Amir's financial year ends on 31 December.

On 1 January 20–4 he purchased a machine for $12 000. He decided to revalue the machine at the end of each financial year. On 31 December 20–4 he valued the machine at $8 500.

Calculate the depreciation for the year ended 31 December 20–4.

	$
Cost of machine 1 January 20–4	12 000
Value of machine 31 December 20–4	8 500
Depreciation for the year	3 500

Recording depreciation in the ledger

The way in which depreciation is recorded in the ledger is the same for both the **straight line** and the **reducing balance** methods. Each type of asset has two accounts, one for recording the asset itself (at cost price) and one for recording the depreciation of the asset. The account in which the depreciation is recorded is known as a provision for depreciation account. The difference between the balances on these accounts represents the written-down value (or book value) of the particular asset concerned. It is important to refer to both accounts when the value of an asset is being considered.

The asset account will always have a debit balance and the provision for depreciation account will always have a credit balance.

The entries may be summarised as –

(a) Debit Asset account
    Credit Cash book
    or
    Credit Supplier's account
    } when the asset is purchased.

(b) Debit Profit and Loss Account
    Credit Provision for Depreciation account
    } at the end of the financial year, with the depreciation for the year.

(c) Balance the Provision for Depreciation account and carry down the balance.

(d) Balance the Asset account if there have been any transactions during the year and carry down the balance

■ **Example**

Amir's financial year ends on 31 December.

On 1 January 20–4 he purchased a machine for $12 000. He estimates that he will keep the machine for 4 years and then sell it for $2 000. He decided to use the straight line method of depreciation.

Make the necessary entries in Amir's ledger for **each** of the years ending 31 December 20–4, 20–5, 20–6 and 20–7.

Before any entries are made it is necessary to calculate the annual depreciation. This was done in an earlier example when a figure of $2 500 was calculated.

Amir

Machinery account

Date	Details	Folio	$	Date	Details	Folio	$
20–4 Jan 1	Bank		12 000				

Provision for Depreciation of Machinery account

Date	Details	Folio	$	Date	Details	Folio	$
20–4 Dec 31	Balance	c/d	2 500 2 500	20–4 Dec 31	Profit and Loss		2 500 2 500
20–5 Dec 31	Balance	c/d	5 000 5 000	20–5 Jan 1 Dec 31	Balance Profit and Loss	b/d	2 500 2 500 5 000
20–6 Dec 31	Balance	c/d	7 500 7 500	20–6 Jan 1 Dec 31	Balance Profit and Loss	b/d	5 000 2 500 7 500
20–7 Dec 31	Balance	c/d	10 000 10 000	20–7 Jan 1 Dec 31	Balance Profit and Loss	b/d	7 500 2 500 10 000
				20–8 Jan 1	Balance	b/d	10 000

The entries would be exactly the same where the **reducing balance** was used, except the amounts of depreciation would be decreasing each year, as illustrated in a previous calculation. This would result in the amount transferred to Profit and Loss Account being a different amount each year.

■ **Example** Amir's financial year ends on 31 December.

On 1 January 20–4 he purchased a machine for $12 000. He estimates that he will keep the machine for 4 years and then sell it for $2 000. He decided to use the reducing balance method at the rate of 36% per annum.

How much would be transferred to Amir's Profit and Loss Account for **each** of the four years ending 31 December 20–4, 20–5, 20–6 and 20–7?

The calculations have been shown in a previous example. The amounts transferred to Profit and Loss Account would be –

		$
Year ended 31 December	20–4	4 320
	20–5	2 765
	20–6	1 769
	20–7	1 133

Where the **revaluation method** is used there is no need to maintain a provision for depreciation account. Only one account is required in which both the cost and the depreciation are recorded. The entries may be summarised as –

(a) Debit Asset account
   Credit Cash book
   or
   Credit Supplier's account
   } when the asset is purchased.

(b) Credit the Asset account with the value of the asset at the end of the year and carry down as a debit balance.

(c) Transfer the difference on the account to the Profit and Loss Account as this represents the depreciation for the year.

■ **Example** Amir's financial year ends on 31 December.

On 1 January 20–4 he purchased a machine for $12 000. He decided to revalue the machine at the end of each financial year. On 31 December 20–4 he valued the machine at $8 500.

Prepare the Machinery account in Amir's ledger for the year ended 31 December 20–4.

Amir

Machinery account

Date	Details	Folio	$	Date	Details	Folio	$
20–4 Jan 1	Bank		12 000	20–4 Dec 31	Balance Profit and Loss	c/d	8 500 3 500
			12 000				12 000
20–5 Jan 1	Balance	b/d	8 500				

Chapter 10 – Depreciation and disposal of fixed assets 109

Entries for depreciation in final accounts

Entries in the Profit and Loss Account

The depreciation for the year on each type of fixed asset is debited to the Profit and Loss Account with all the other expenses and losses for the financial year. This results in a reduction of the net profit. It is usual for the depreciation on the various types of fixed asset to be listed after the monetary expenses.

Where the organisation is a manufacturing business, some of the depreciation charges may be shown in the Manufacturing account instead of the Profit and Loss Account (see Chapter 18).

Entries in the Balance Sheet

The Balance Sheet should show the written-down value (book value) for each type of fixed asset. It is preferable to show the cost price of each type of asset and deduct the total depreciation written off up to the date of the Balance Sheet.

■ Example

Amir's financial year ends on 31 December.

On 1 January 20–4 he purchased a machine for $12 000. He estimates that he will keep the machine for 4 years and then sell it for $2 000.

He decided to use the straight line method of depreciation of $2 500 per annum.

Prepare a relevant extract from Amir's Balance Sheet as at 31 December 20–4 and 31 December 20–5.

Amir

Extract from Balance Sheet as at 31 December 20–4

Fixed assets	$ Cost	$ Depreciation to date	$ Net book value
Machinery	12 000	2 500	9 500

Extract from Balance Sheet as at 31 December 20–5

Fixed assets	$ Cost	$ Depreciation to date	$ Net book value
Machinery	12 000	5 000	7 000

Final accounts are usually prepared from a trial balance drawn up at the end of the financial year. The balances on asset accounts will appear in the debit column and the balances on provision for depreciation accounts will appear in the credit column. Any depreciation to be charged for the financial year in question will be detailed in a footnote to the trial balance. This depreciation for the year must be debited to the Profit and Loss Account. The Balance Sheet must record the total depreciation written off up to the date of the Balance Sheet, so it is necessary to add the depreciation for the year to the provision for depreciation shown in the trial balance.

■ Example

An extract from Amir's Trial Balance as at 31 December 20–6 shows –

	Debit $	Credit $
Machinery	12 000	
Provision for depreciation of machinery		5 000

Amir is depreciating his machinery using the straight line method at $2 500 per annum.

Prepare –
(a) a relevant extract from Amir's Profit and Loss Account for the year ended 31 December 20–6
(b) a relevant extract from Amir's Balance Sheet as at 31 December 20–6.

Amir

Extract from Profit and Loss Account for the year ended 31 December 20–6

	$
Expenses – Depreciation of machinery	2 500

Extract from Balance Sheet as at 31 December 20–6

Fixed assets	$ Cost	$ Depreciation to date	$ Net book value
Machinery	12 000	7 500	4 500

Disposal of fixed assets

When a fixed asset reaches the end of its useful life, or when it is no longer needed by the business, it will be sold. It is important that sales of fixed assets are not treated in the same way as sales of stock in trade. When fixed assets are purchased this is known as **capital expenditure** and the asset is recorded in a fixed asset account rather than the purchases account. When fixed assets are sold this is known as a **capital receipt** and the transaction is recorded in a special account, a disposal of fixed asset account, rather than the sales account.

When a fixed asset is sold it must be eliminated from the books of account. The cost of the asset and the depreciation to date on the asset are transferred from the appropriate accounts to the disposal account. The amount received for the fixed asset is also entered in the account. Any difference on the account is the profit or loss on sale – in other words the under- or over-provision of depreciation. It is only when the asset is sold that the actual amount of depreciation is known; until this time the depreciation is only an estimate. The disposal account will be closed by transferring the difference on the account (the profit or loss on sale) to the Profit and Loss Account.

Similar entries are required when a fixed asset is disposed of but not actually sold. It may be that an asset is handed to a supplier in part-exchange for another fixed asset: it may be that the asset is scrapped and has no value whatsoever.

The entries for disposal of a fixed asset may be summarised as –

(a) Debit Disposal of Fixed Asset account
    Credit Fixed Asset account
} on the date of sale, with the cost price of the asset being sold.

(b) Debit Provision for Depreciation account
    Credit Disposal of Fixed Asset account
} on the date of sale, with the depreciation already charged on the asset being sold.

(c) Debit Cash book
    or
    Debit Debtor
    Credit Disposal of Fixed Asset account
} on the date of sale, with the proceeds.

(d) Debit Profit and Loss Account
    Credit Disposal of Fixed Asset account
    or
    Debit Disposal of Fixed Asset account
    Credit Profit and Loss Account
} at the end of the financial year, with any loss on sale. / at the end of the financial year, with any profit on sale.

■ **Example** Amir's financial year ends on 31 December.

On 1 January 20–4 he purchased a machine for $12 000. On 1 January 20–7 the provision for depreciation of machinery account showed a credit balance of $7 500. Amir sold the machine on 2 January 20–7 for $3 900 cash.

Write up the following accounts in Amir's ledger for the year ended 31 December 20–7:
(a) Machinery account
(b) Provision for depreciation of machinery account
(c) Disposal of machinery account.

Amir

(a) **Machinery account**

Date	Details	Folio	$	Date	Details	Folio	$
20–4 Jan 1	Bank		12 000	20–7 Jan 2	Disposals		12 000
			12 000				12 000

(b) **Provision for Depreciation of Machinery account**

Date	Details	Folio	$	Date	Details	Folio	$
20–7 Jan 2	Disposals		7 500	20–7 Jan 1	Balance	b/d	7 500
			7 500				7 500

(c) **Disposal of Machinery account**

Date	Details	Folio	$	Date	Details	Folio	$
20–7 Jan 2	Machinery		12 000	20–7 Jan 2	Prov. for dep.		7 500
					Cash		3 900
				Dec 31	Profit and Loss		600
			12 000				12 000

It is important that the cost and the depreciation to date that relate only to the asset being sold are removed from the records.

Every business has its own policy in relation to depreciating fixed assets which are purchased part-way through a financial year. Some businesses will charge a whole year's depreciation on all fixed assets held at the end of the financial year, irrespective of the date on which the assets were purchased. Other businesses will charge depreciation only for the proportion of the financial year that the asset has been owned. Similarly, when a fixed asset is sold, there can be differing policies. Some businesses will ignore depreciation in the year of sale while other businesses will charge depreciation up to the date of sale. In practice, a policy must be established and applied consistently: in examinations, candidates are given guidance within the question.

Review questions

1. (a) A business provides annually for the depreciation of its fixed assets. State how such depreciation will be shown –
    (i) in the Profit and Loss Account
    (ii) in the Balance Sheet
    [IGCSE 1997]
   (b) Explain **one** purpose of providing for the depreciation of fixed assets.
    [IGCSE 1996]
   (c) Explain why depreciation must be charged in the Profit and Loss Account.
    [IGCSE 1996]
   (d) A business buys a machine for $15 000. The machine's useful life is estimated to be 5 years, when it will have a trade-in value of $2 000.
    (i) Using the straight line method, calculate the annual depreciation charge.
    (ii) What type of expenditure is the purchase of the machine?
    [IGCSE 1995]
   (e) JB bought a machine for $10 000 at the beginning of his financial year on 1 October 1997. It was depreciated at a rate of 20% using the reducing balance method.
      Calculate the machine's book value in JB's Balance Sheet on 30 September 1999. Show your workings.
    [IGCSE 1999]

2. The financial year of Ambondo Traders ends on 30 June.
    On 1 July 20–0 they purchased equipment, $15 000, on credit from Radwan & Co. They decided to use the reducing balance method of depreciation at a rate of 20% per annum.
   (a) Prepare the following accounts in Ambondo Traders' ledger for **each** of the years ending 30 June 20–1, 20–2 and 20–3:
    (i) Equipment account
    (ii) Provision for Depreciation of Equipment account.
   (b) Prepare a relevant extract from Ambondo Traders' Balance Sheet as at 30 June 20–3.

3. The Balance Sheet of a business on 31 October 1999 included the following figures –

Fixed assets	$ Cost	$ Depreciation to date	$ Net book value
Machinery	31 000	16 000	15 000

Depreciation of machinery was calculated at 20% on cost for the year. It was later discovered that machinery repairs costing $1 000 had been debited to the machinery account.

Prepare a revised Balance Sheet entry at 31 October 1999 to show how the above items appear in the Balance Sheet after the errors have been corrected.

[IGCSE 1999]

4. (a) Explain what is meant by –
   (i) a fixed asset
   (ii) a current liability.

The following Trial Balance has been taken from the books of C. Ircle at 30 September 1998:

	$	$
Sales		30 000
Purchases	9 250	
Discounts receivable		900
Discounts allowed	806	
Stock at 1 October 1997	5 000	
Wages	2 950	
Rent payable	6 000	
Fixtures and fittings at cost	10 000	
Provision for depreciation of fixtures and fittings at 1 October 1997		3 000
Trade debtors	4 000	
Trade creditors		2 306
Bank	2 300	
Motor vehicles at cost	11 000	
Provision for depreciation of motor vehicles at 1 October 1997		2 000
Capital		20 000
Drawings	6 900	
	58 206	58 206

Chapter 10 – Depreciation and disposal of fixed assets

You are given the following further information:
1. Stock at 30 September 1998 amounted to $7 000.
2. Rent payable of $2 000 was owing at 30 September 1998.
3. Depreciation for the year to 30 September 1998 has to be provided as follows:
   on fixtures and fittings – 20% on cost
   on motor vehicles – 25% on cost.
(b) Prepare the Trading and Profit and Loss Account of C. Ircle for the year to 30 September 1998.
(c) Prepare the Balance Sheet of C. Ircle as at 30 September 1998.

[IGCSE 1998]

5. Joseph's fixed assets include a motor vehicle bought on 1 April 1998 for $12 800. This was estimated to have a useful life of four years, when its residual value would be $2 800.
   (a) Calculate, showing your workings, the depreciation charged on the motor vehicle for the year ended 31 March 1999 –
      (i) using the straight line method
      (ii) using the reducing balance method at a rate of 30%
   (b) Joseph's net profit for the year ended 31 March 1999 was $20 000, after charging depreciation on the motor vehicle using the straight line method.
      What is Joseph's net profit if he uses the reducing balance method instead of the straight line method? Show your workings.

[IGCSE 1999]

6. A. B. Ltd. purchased a machine on 1 January 1993 at a cost of $10 000. The machine was expected to have a useful life of 4 years. It was not expected to have any scrap value at the end of its useful life.
   (a) Calculate the depreciation charge for the machine for **each** of the years ended 31 December 1993, 1994, 1995 and 1996, based on –
      (i) the straight line method
      (ii) the reducing balance method using the rate of 60%
      Show your workings.
   (b) Describe **three** ways in which the straight line method of depreciation differs from the reducing balance method.
   (c) A. B. Ltd. used the straight line method for many years. The directors have decided that the profit for the year to 31 December 1996 can be improved if they change to the reducing balance method.
      (i) State whether or not you think the directors are right to change the basis of depreciation.
      (ii) State **two** reasons for your answer to (i).

[IGCSE 1997]

7. Gerald Trillo is a sole trader. The following balances were extracted from his books at 30 April 1997:

	Debit $	Credit $
Motor vehicles at cost	16 000	
Provision for depreciation of motor vehicles		9 000
Stock at 1 May 1996	9 000	
Sales		137 000
Purchases	63 000	
Wages	42 630	
Rent & rates	7 200	
Heating & lighting	2 415	
Motor expenses	725	
Carriage inwards	700	
Sundry expenses	1 325	
Loan from father (received on 1 November 1996)		10 000

Additional information

1. Stock at 30 April 1997 was valued at $11 000.

2. Rent and rates paid in advance at 30 April 1997 amounted to $800.

3. At 30 April 1997, Trillo owed $185 for heating and lighting.

4. Interest on the father's loan is to be provided at the rate of 10% per annum.

5. Depreciation of motor vehicles is to be provided at the rate of 10% on cost.

(a) Prepare Trillo's Trading and Profit and Loss Account for the year to 30 April 1997.
(b) State the maximum amount that Trillo can withdraw without reducing his capital invested in the business.

[IGCSE 1997]

8. The Trial Balance of Natasha Efraim at 29 September 1997 included –

	Debit $	Credit $
Plant and machinery	30 000	
Provision for depreciation of plant and machinery		12 000

On 30 September 1997 Natasha sold a machine for $2 000 in cash. This machine had been bought originally for $4 000. Depreciation written off the machine up to 29 September 1997 was $2 300.
 There are no entries in Natasha's books to record the sale of this machine.

Prepare the following accounts in the ledger of Natasha for the year ending 30 September 1997:
(a) Plant and Machinery account
(b) Provision for Depreciation of Plant and Machinery account
(c) Disposal of Machinery account.
[IGCSE 1997]

*9. Balances extracted from the books of Cosey, Fann and Tootie at 30 April 1998 are given –

	$
Machinery at cost	108 000
Provision for depreciation of machinery	42 000

The following transactions took place in the year ended 30 April 1999 –

6 June 1998	Purchased a machine costing $20 000 and paid by cheque
8 October 1998	Sold a machine for $4 000, which was paid into the bank. The machine cost $11 000 when purchased on 1 June 1995.
12 December 1998	Purchased a machine on credit from Largo Alfactum for $14 000.
7 January 1999	A machine was destroyed by fire and was scrapped. It had cost $7 000 on 1 October 1996.

A full year's depreciation is provided for on machinery in the year of purchase, but no depreciation is provided for in the year of disposal.
 Depreciation is calculated on machinery owned at 30 April each year at a rate of 25% using the straight line method.

Prepare the following accounts for the year ended 30 April 1999:
(a) Machinery at cost account
(b) Provision for Depreciation of Machinery account
(c) Disposal of Machinery account.
[IGCSE 1999]

10. Sam's financial year ends on 31 March. On 1 April 1999 balances in Sam's ledger included the following –

	$
Machinery	50 000 Dr.
Provision for depreciation of machinery	14 000 Cr.

You are given the following further information:
1. On 30 June 1999 Sam sold a machine for $6 000. This machine originally cost $15 000. Depreciation written off the machine up to 31 March 1999 was $7 000.
2. On 1 October 1999 Sam bought a new machine for $25 000, paying by cheque.

Sam depreciates his machinery at 10% on the cost of machinery held at the end of each financial year and makes no depreciation charge for machinery sold during the year.

(a) Prepare the following accounts in Sam's ledger for the year ended 31 March 2000:
  (i) Machinery account
  (ii) Provision for Depreciation of Machinery account
  (iii) Disposal of Machinery account.
(b) Prepare an extract from Sam's Balance Sheet as at 31 March 2000 to show how the machinery would appear.
(c) (i) State what is meant by the accounting concept of prudence.
  (ii) Explain how Sam observes the accounting concept of prudence by providing for depreciation of his machinery.

[IGCSE 2000]

CHAPTER 11
Bad debts and provision for doubtful debts

Bad debts

A bad debt is an amount owing to a business, which will not be paid by the debtor. When businesses sell on credit, there is an obvious risk that the customer will not pay the amount owing. It is important for a business to issue invoices and month-end statements of account promptly, and to monitor the sales ledger accounts carefully. Credit customers who do not settle their account by the agreed date should be reminded by telephone calls and letters that the account is overdue. Despite requests for payment, it can happen that the customer never pays the account – he may be bankrupt or he may have disappeared. Sometimes, where the amount due is small, attempts to recover the debt can actually cost more than the debt itself.

When it is decided that all possible means to obtain payment from the debtor have failed, the debt should be **written off**. This means that the debtor's account in the sales ledger is closed and the amount due is transferred to a bad debts account in the nominal ledger. The entries may be summarised as –

(a) Debit Bad Debts account
    Credit Debtor's account } when the debt is written off.

(b) Debit Profit and Loss Account
    Credit Bad Debts account } at the end of the financial year.

Bad debts recovered

Sometimes, after a debt has been written off as a bad debt, the debtor will pay part, or all, of the amount he owed. This amount should not be credited to the debtor's account, which is now closed. The entries may be summarised as –

(a) Debit Cash book
    Credit Bad Debts Recovered account } when the amount is received.

(b) Debit Bad Debts Recovered account
    Credit Profit and Loss Account
    *or
    Credit Bad Debts account } at the end of the financial year.

*The overall effect is that the expenses for the year are reduced whichever method is used.

■ **Example** Ahmed's financial year ends on 31 March.

He offers his credit customers a cash discount of $2^1/_2$% provided the account is paid within 30 days.

On 1 May 20–0, Ahmed sold goods, $240, on credit to Khalid. On 28 May 20–0 Khalid paid the account by cheque and purchased further goods, $200, on credit.

Ahmed wrote off the account of Khalid on 31 March 20–1.

On 20 August 20–1 Khalid sent a cheque to Ahmed for the amount he owed on 28 May 20–0.

Ahmed wrote off debtors totalling $542 during the financial year ended 31 March 20–2.

Write up the following accounts in Ahmed's ledger for **each** of the years ended 31 March 20–1 and 20–2:
(a) Khalid account
(b) Bad Debts account
(c) Bad Debts Recovered account.

Ahmed

(a)

Khalid account

Date	Details	Folio	$	Date	Details	Folio	$
20–0				20–0			
May 1	Sales		240	May 28	Bank		234
28	Sales		200		Discount		6
				20–1			
				May 31	Bad debts		200
			440				440

(b)

Bad Debts account

Date	Details	Folio	$	Date	Details	Folio	$
20–1				20–1			
Mar 31	Khalid		200	Mar 31	Profit and Loss		200
			200				200
20–2				20–2			
Mar 31	Debtors written off*		542	Mar 31	Profit and Loss		542
			542				542

*"Debtors written off" is used as no individual names, dates and amounts are given in the question.

(c)

Bad Debts Recovered account

Date	Details	Folio	$	Date	Details	Folio	$
20–2 Mar 31	Profit and Loss		200 ___ 200	20–1 Aug 20	Bank (Khalid)		200 ___ 200

Provision for doubtful debts

A provision for doubtful debts is an estimate of the amount that a business will lose in a financial year because of bad debts. This is sometimes referred to as a provision for bad debts.

It is usual for a business to maintain a provision for doubtful debts as this is an application of both the **prudence** concept and **matching** concept. By providing for the debts which a business considers doubtful, the prudence concept is being applied as profits will not be overstated and the asset of debtors in the Balance Sheet will show a more realistic amount. The matching concept is being applied as the amount of the sales for the year which are unlikely to be paid are treated as an expense of that particular year.

It is necessary to make an estimate of the amount of the debts that are unlikely to be paid. This may be done in various ways –

(a) Looking at the account of each debtor and estimating which ones will not be paid.

(b) Estimating, on the basis of past experience, what percentage of the amount owing by the debtors will not be paid.

(c) Preparing an Ageing Schedule to show how long debts have been outstanding, as the longer a debt is outstanding the more likely it is that it will become a bad debt.

Creating a provision for doubtful debts

Once it has been decided that a provision for doubtful debts should be set up, the procedure may be summarised –

(a) Calculate the provision required.

(b) Debit Profit and Loss Account
Credit Provision for Doubtful Debts account } with the amount of the provision.

(c) Deduct the amount of the provision for doubtful debts from the debtors in the Balance Sheet.

■ **Example**

Sally's financial year ends on 31 October.

During the year ended 31 October 20–3 she wrote off debtors totalling $395. On 31 October 20–3 Sally decided to create a provision for doubtful debts of 3% of the debtors, who owed $17 000 at that date.

(a) Write up the following accounts in Sally's ledger for the year ended 31 October 20–3:
  (i) Bad Debts account
  (ii) Provision for Doubtful Debts account.
(b) Prepare a relevant extract from Sally's Profit and Loss Account for the year ended 31 October 20–3.
(c) Prepare a relevant extract from Sally's Balance Sheet as at 31 October 20–3.

Sally

(a) (i) **Bad Debts account**

Date	Details	Folio	$	Date	Details	Folio	$
20–3 Oct 31	Debtors written off		395	20–3 Oct 31	Profit and Loss		395
			395				395

(ii) **Provision for Doubtful Debts account**

Date	Details	Folio	$	Date	Details	Folio	$
				20–3 Oct 31	Profit and Loss		510

(b) **Extract from Profit and Loss Account for year ended 31 October 20–3**

	$
Expenses – Bad debts	395
Provision for doubtful debts	510

(c) **Extract from Balance Sheet as at 31 October 20–3**

Current assets	$	$
Debtors	17 000	
Less Provision for doubtful debts	510	16 490

Increasing a provision for doubtful debts

At the end of the next year it is necessary to reconsider the amount of the provision. The amount of debtors may have increased, or it may be felt that the original percentage rate is insufficient. In either case it will be necessary to increase the provision. The procedure may be summarised as –
(a) Calculate the extra provision required.
(b) Debit Profit and Loss Account
 Credit Provision for Doubtful Debts account } with the extra provision required.
(c) Balance the Provision for Doubtful Debts account and carry down the balance.
(d) Deduct the balance on the Provision for Doubtful Debts account from the debtors in the Balance Sheet.

Any bad debts are written off in the usual way. They are not affected by adjustments to the provision.

■ **Example**

In the previous example Sally established a provision for doubtful debts on 31 October 20–3, amounting to $510. During the year ended 31 October 20–4 Sally wrote off bad debts of $555. At 31 October 20–4 Sally's debtors amounted to $20 000 and she decided to increase the provision for doubtful debts to 4%.
(a) Write up the following accounts in Sally's ledger for the year ended 31 October 20–4:
 (i) Bad Debts account
 (ii) Provision for Doubtful Debts account.
(b) Prepare a relevant extract from Sally's Profit and Loss Account for the year ended 31 October 20–4.
(c) Prepare a relevant extract from Sally's Balance Sheet as at 31 October 20–4.

Sally

(a) (i) Bad Debts account

Date	Details	Folio	$	Date	Details	Folio	$
20–4 Oct 31	Debtors written off		555	20–4 Oct 31	Profit and Loss		555
			555				555

124 Accounting: IGCSE

(ii) **Provision for Doubtful Debts account**

Date	Details	Folio	$	Date	Details	Folio	$
20–4 Oct 31	Balance	c/d	800	20–3 Oct 31 20–4 Oct 31	Profit and Loss Profit and Loss		510* 290
			800				800
				20–4 Nov 1	Balance	b/d	800

*This item is already in the account.

(b) **Extract from Profit and Loss Account for year ended 31 October 20–4**

	$
Expenses – Bad debts	555
Increase in provision for doubtful debts	290

(c) **Extract from Balance Sheet as at 31 October 20–4**

Current assets	$	$
Debtors	20 000	
Less provision for doubtful debts	800	19 200

Reducing a provision for doubtful debts

In future years the amount owed by debtors may fall, or it may be decided that the percentage rate of the provision for doubtful debts is too high. In either case it will be necessary to decrease the provision. The procedure may be summarised as –

(a) Calculate the surplus provision no longer required.
(b) Debit Provision for Doubtful
 Debts account } with the amount no longer required.
 Credit Profit and Loss Account
(c) Balance the Provision for Doubtful Debts account and carry down the balance.
(d) Deduct the balance on the Provision for Doubtful Debts account from the debtors in the Balance Sheet.

■ **Example** In the previous example, Sally increased her provision for doubtful debts to $800 on 31 October 20–4.

During the year ended 31 October 20–5 Sally wrote off bad debts of $610. At 31 October 20–5 her debtors amounted to $19 000 and she decided to reduce the provision for doubtful debts to 3%.
(a) Write up the following accounts in Sally's ledger for the year ended 31 October 20–5:
  (i) Bad Debts account
  (ii) Provision for Doubtful Debts account.
(b) Prepare a relevant extract from Sally's Profit and Loss Account for the year ended 31 October 20–5.
(c) Prepare a relevant extract from Sally's Balance Sheet as at 31 October 20–5.

Sally

(a) (i) **Bad Debts account**

Date	Details	Folio	$	Date	Details	Folio	$
20–5 Oct 31	Debtors written off		610	20–5 Oct 31	Profit and Loss		610
			610				610

(ii) **Provision for Doubtful Debts account**

Date	Details	Folio	$	Date	Details	Folio	$
20–5 Oct 31	Profit and Loss Balance	c/d	230 570	20–4 Nov 1	Balance	b/d	800*
			800				800
				20–5 Nov 1	Balance	b/d	570

*This item is already in the account.

(b) **Extract from Profit and Loss Account for the year ended 31 October 20–5**

	$
Gross Profit	xxx
Add reduction in provision for doubtful debts	230
Expenses – Bad debts	610

126 Accounting: IGCSE

(c) **Extract from Balance Sheet as at 31 October 20–5**

	$	$
Current assets		
Debtors	19 000	
Less Provision for doubtful debts	570	18 430

Reducing the possibility of bad debts

A business must take all possible steps to reduce the possibility of bad debts, as, if the debtor does not pay the account, the business must bear the loss.

The most obvious way to avoid the possibility of bad debts is to insist upon payment in cash at the time of sale. However, this is not always practicable. Before selling on credit to a new customer, references should be obtained – one from a bank and one from a previous or present supplier. If these are satisfactory the customer should be given a credit limit – the amount outstanding from the customer should never be allowed to exceed this limit. The credit limit can be reviewed periodically and adjusted if necessary.

It is important that invoices and month-end statements of account are issued promptly to remind the debtor of the amount outstanding. The sales ledger should be closely monitored and any overdue accounts should be investigated. Obviously the debtor should not be allowed to obtain further supplies until the outstanding balance is settled. The debtor should be contacted by letter or telephone and reminded of the need to settle the account. Legal action may be threatened if it is thought appropriate. Establishing credit limits for debtors, and the later monitoring of the debtors' accounts is referred to as **credit control**.

Review questions

1. (a) Johnny writes off as a bad debt the amount owed to him by Thomas. Name **two** accounts in Johnny's ledger in which the necessary entries are made.
   [IGCSE 1998]
   (b) (i) State what is meant by a bad debt recovered.
       (ii) Name the final account to which the total of the bad debts recovered account is transferred.
   [IGCSE 1996]
   (c) State **one** reason for maintaining a provision for doubtful debts.
   [IGCSE 1998]
   (d) How is the provision for doubtful debts shown in the Balance Sheet?
   [IGCSE 1995]
2. (a) What are bad debts?
   (b) Why is it necessary to write off bad debts?

(c) Sara's financial year ends on 31 March. During the year ended 31 March 20–5 Sara wrote off the following accounts as bad debts –

31 May 20–4	Jones and Company	$34
31 August 20–4	Riva Stores	$12
30 December 20–4	Western Traders	$63

On 28 February 20–5 Smith and Son, who owed Sara $120, sent a cheque for $96, but were unable to pay the balance of the account. This was written off as a bad debt.

On 15 March 20–5 a cheque for $68 was received from ETK, who were written off as a bad debt on 1 February 20–3.

Write up the following accounts in Sara's ledger for the year ended 31 March 20–5:
(i) Bad Debts account
(ii) Bad Debts Recovered account

3. A and B are partners in a business. A wants to make a provision for doubtful debts. B says that it is unnecessary because the debts have not become bad yet.

Comment on B's statement that no provision should be made.

[IGCSE 1999]

4. Every business that sells goods on credit wishes to avoid bad debts.
   (a) Describe the steps that may be taken before a new customer is allowed credit.
   (b) How may the customer be treated if there is doubt about his credit-worthiness?

5. (a) Explain how a provision differs from a liability.
   (b) State **two** ways in which a business might decide on the amount of its provision for doubtful debts.
   (c) The following information relates to a business that makes up its accounts to 31 March:

	$
Trade debtors 1 April 1995	40 000
Trade debtors 31 March 1996	60 000
Provision for doubtful debts 1 April 1995	2 000

This provision is to be maintained at 5% of trade debtors as at 31 March 1996.
   (i) Calculate the increase required in the provision for doubtful debts as at 31 March 1996.
   (ii) Show by means of a Balance Sheet extract how trade debtors at 31 March 1996 and the provision for doubtful debts in (c) (i) would appear in the business's Balance Sheet as at 31 March 1996.

[IGCSE 1996]

6. (a) Define the terms –
    (i) asset
    (ii) liability
   (b) An inexperienced accounting student prepared the Balance Sheet of his brother's business. It contained some errors.

   Prepare X and Co.'s Balance Sheet as it should have been prepared. Place the items in the correct order.

X and Co

Balance Sheet for the year ending 31 March 1999

	$	$
Fixed assets		
Plant and machinery at cost		60 000
Current assets		
Bank	2 175	
Debtors	16 000	
Stock	5 000	
Accruals	715	23 890
		83 890
Current liabilities		
Creditors	3 440	
Drawings	15 330	
Provision for depreciation	32 000	
Provision for bad debts	400	51 170
		32 720
Capital at 1 November 1998		46 000
Net Profit	17 000	
less prepayments	1 050	15 950
		61 950
less difference on Balance Sheet		29 230
		32 720

[IGCSE 1999]

7. Maria's financial year ends on 31 July.
   On 31 July 20–1 she created a provision for doubtful debts of 5% of the debtors, who owed $13 000 on that date.
   The following debts were written off –

   | 20–1 | 30 September | Local Stores | $375 |
   | 20–2 | 31 January | Freda's Fashions | $141 |

   On 1 May 20–2 Maria received a cheque for $97 from West & Company, who had been written off as a bad debt on 30 June 20–1.

On 31 July 20–2 Maria's debtors owed $12 650. This included $150 owing by Vernon, which should now be written off as a bad debt. Maria decided to maintain the provision for doubtful debts at 5% of the debtors.

Write up the following accounts in Maria's ledger for the year ended 31 July 20–2:
(a) Bad Debts account
(b) Bad Debts Recovered account
(c) Provision for Doubtful Debts account.

*8. The following Trial Balance is taken from the books of John Mafule after the preparation of the Trading Account for the year ended 30 June 20–6.

John Mafule
Trial Balance as at 30 June 20–6

	Debit $	Credit $
Gross profit		32 400
Capital		39 600
Drawings	8 400	
Discount allowed	1 600	
Discount received		1 800
Bad debts	210	
Provision for doubtful debts		280
Debtors	6 200	
Creditors		8 400
Stock at 30 June 20-6	16 200	
Rent	10 500	
Wages	21 600	
General expenses	4 120	
Fixtures and equipment at cost	29 000	
Provision for depreciation of fixtures and equipment		8 700
Bank		2 000
Long-term loan		5 000
Loan interest	350	
	98 180	98 180

Additional information

$
1. At 30 June 20–6
   rent prepaid amounts to   500
   general expenses accrued amount to   150

2. The provision for doubtful debts is to be maintained at 5% of the debtors.

3. Fixtures and equipment are to be depreciated at 10% per annum using the straight line method.

   (a) Prepare the Profit and Loss Account of John Mafule for the year ended 30 June 20–6.
   (b) Prepare the Balance Sheet of John Mafule as at 30 June 20–6.

9. (a) Name **one** accounting concept which is being observed when a provision for doubtful debts is maintained.
   (b) Explain the difference between bad debts and a provision for doubtful debts.
   (c) State **two** ways in which a firm may decide the amount of its provision for doubtful debts.
   (d) The following relates to the business of Mary Maranga, who writes up her accounts to 31 March each year.

	$
Trade debtors 1 April 1999	40 000
Trade debtors 31 March 2000	46 000
Bad debts written off in the year ended 31 March 2000	800

   The provision for doubtful debts is maintained at $2\frac{1}{2}\%$ of the trade debtors at the end of each year.
   (i) Show the Bad Debts and the Provision for Doubtful Debts accounts in Mary Maranga's ledger for the year ended 31 March 2000. Show the amount transferred to the Profit and Loss Account and the balance brought down on 1 April 2000.
   (ii) Show the relevant extract from Mary Maranga's Balance Sheet as at 31 March 2000.
   (e) Suggest **four** ways in which Mary may reduce the possibility of bad debts.

   [IGCSE 2000]

10. The following Trial Balance is taken from the books of Susie Smith.

Susie Smith

Trial Balance as at 30 November 20–7

	Debit $	Credit $
Sales		65 000
Purchases	50 000	
Stock at 1 December 20–6	3 000	
Salaries	2 900	
General expenses	1 500	
Rent	750	
Motor vehicle expenses	2 700	
Bad debts	250	
Provision for doubtful debts		340
Commission received		500
Equipment at cost	10 000	
Provision for depreciation of equipment		1 000
Motor vehicles	6 000	
Provision for depreciation of motor vehicles		1 500
Bank	5 140	
Capital		18 600
Drawings	6 600	
Debtors	6 100	
Creditors		8 000
	94 940	94 940

Additional information

$

1. At 30 November 20–7
    stock was valued at   4 000
    motor vehicle expenses accrued amount to   150
    commission receivable due amounts to   70

2. During the year Susie took goods costing $600 for her own use. No entries have been made in the books.

3. It is decided to write off $100 owing by debtors as bad debts.

4. The provision for doubtful debts is to be maintained at 4% of the debtors (after the additional debts are written off).

5. Equipment is to be depreciated at 10% per annum using the straight line method.

6. Motor vehicles are to be depreciated at 25% per annum using the straight line method.

   (a) Prepare the Trading and Profit and Loss Account of Susie Smith for the year ended 30 November 20–7.
   (b) Prepare the Balance Sheet of Susie Smith as at 30 November 20–7.

CHAPTER 12
Bank reconciliation statements

The purpose of bank reconciliation is to explain any difference between the bank balance appearing in the cash book of a business and the balance appearing on the bank statement provided by the bank.

When goods are supplied on credit, the supplier will send regular statements to the customer, listing the transactions that have taken place and the balance owing at the end of the period. In a similar way, the bank will issue regular statements listing the transactions that have taken place in the period and the balance, which may be either positive or overdrawn, at the end of the period.

The bank statement is a copy of the account of the business as it appears in the books of the bank. This is obviously from the viewpoint of the bank. The customer's account will have a credit balance if there is money in the account, as this is the amount the bank owes the customer (a liability of the bank). Where the customer has an overdraft, the account will show a debit balance as this is the amount the customer owes the bank (an asset of the bank). The bank account in the cash book of the business is prepared from the viewpoint of the business, and therefore items will be recorded on the opposite side to that on which they appeared on the bank statement. If a business has money in the bank, the bank account will show a debit balance, as this is the amount the bank owes the business (an asset of the business). Where the business has an overdraft, the bank account will show a credit balance as this is the amount the business owes the bank (a liability of the business).

The bank statement must be compared with the bank account in the cash book. If the balances differ it is necessary to **reconcile** them, that is, explain *why* the differences have arisen.

Reasons for differences between cash book and bank statement

(a) **Items in the cash book but not in the bank statement**
These are usually due to differences in the time at which items are recorded.

These timing differences are often due to –
(i) **cheques not yet presented**, which are cheques that have been paid by the business and credited in the cash book, but which do not appear on the bank statement. It will be some time before these cheques pass through the banking system and are deducted from the business's bank account. Until these cheques

are debited by the bank, the cash book will show a lower balance than that shown on the bank statement.
(ii) **amounts not yet credited**, which are cheques and other amounts which have been paid into the bank and debited in the cash book, but which do not appear on the bank statement. These items may not be recorded by the bank for a day or so. Until these items are credited by the bank, the cash book will show a higher balance than that shown on the bank statement.

It is of course possible that there are **errors** in the cash book which do not appear on the bank statement.

(b) **Items in the bank statement but not in the cash book**
   (i) Amounts received by the bank which have been paid directly into the business's bank account. These include **standing orders** and **credit transfers** when a person has instructed their bank to pay an amount of money directly into the bank account of the business. Interest or dividend received may also be paid directly into the business's bank account.
   (ii) Amounts paid by the bank to other people. These include **credit transfers**, **standing orders** and **direct debits** which the business has instructed the bank to pay directly from the bank account of the business.
   (iii) **Bank charges** and **bank interest** which the bank has taken from the business's account to cover the costs of running the account and for any interest on loans and overdrafts the business may have.
   (iv) **Dishonoured cheques**. These are cheques paid into the bank but which have been returned as the drawer of the cheque did not have sufficient funds to cover the cheque.
   (v) Bank errors.

Procedure for bank reconciliation

The procedure may be summarised as follows –
1. Compare the bank statement with the bank account in the cash book. Remember to compare the debit of the bank account against the credit of the bank statement, and the credit of the bank account against the debit of the bank statement. Place a tick (√) against those items which appear in both records.
2. Bring the bank account in the cash book up to date by entering any items which appear on the bank statement but which have not yet been entered in the bank account. Such items may be –
   (a) Items debited on the bank statement, e.g. bank charges, standing orders paid, etc. These should be credited in the bank account in the cash book.

(b) Items credited on the bank statement, e.g. credit transfers and standing orders paid directly into the bank. These should be debited in the bank account in the cash book.
3. Correct any errors in the cash book.
4. Balance the cash book. The balance on the bank account is now the true bank balance of the business and this figure will be shown in the Balance Sheet.
5. Prepare the bank reconciliation statement –
   (a) Start with the balance shown on the bank statement.
   (b) Add on any items that have been debited in the cash book but not yet credited on the bank statement, i.e. amounts not yet credited.
   (c) Deduct any items that have been credited in the cash book but not yet debited on the bank statement, i.e. cheques not yet presented.
   (d) Make any necessary adjustments for bank errors. Add back any amounts debited in error by the bank and deduct any amounts credited in error by the bank.
   (e) The resulting figure should equal the updated bank balance shown in the cash book.

The bank reconciliation could, alternatively, begin with the updated cash book balance and end with the bank statement balance. Where this is done, it is necessary to reverse the entries described above, i.e. add instead of deduct and vice versa.

The bank reconciliation is **not** part of the double entry system. It is simply a statement proving that, on a certain date, the bank account in the cash book and the bank statement were reconciled.

Example

The bank columns of Beatrix Lang's cash book for the month of July 20–4 are given below.

Cash book (bank columns only)

Date	Details	Folio	$	Date	Details	Folio	$
20–4				20–4			
July 1	Balance		3 640	July 10	Reiser and Co.		482
17	Sales		953	26	AB Insurance		95
23	M. Wagner		215	29	G. Bierling		416
30	Zwink and Co.		110	31	Balance	c/d	4 799
31	Sales		874				
			5 792				5 792

Beatrix Lang's bank statement for the month of July 20–4 is given below.

NATIONAL BANK LTD.
Anytown Branch

Account: Beatrix Lang

Account No: 987654
Date: 31 July 20–4

Date	Details	Debit	Credit	Balance
		$	$	$
20–4				
July 1	Balance			3 640 Cr.
15	Reiser & Co.	482		3 158
17	Cash		935	4 093
19	Rent (Standing Order)	100		3 993
28	M. Wagner		215	4 208
29	Dividend		24	4 232
30	Bank charges	50		4 182

It is discovered that Beatrix has debited $953 for sales on 17 July instead of the correct amount of $935.

(a) Make any additional entries that are required in the cash book of Beatrix Lang. Calculate a new bank balance, and bring down on 1 August 20–4.

(b) Prepare a bank reconciliation statement as at 31 July 20–4.

The first thing to do is to tick off the items which appear in both records. This should leave the following items without a tick –

    In the cash book: 30 and 31 July on the debit side
                                        26 and 29 July on the credit side
    On the bank statement: 19 and 30 July in the debit column
                                        29 July in the credit column

It is then possible to answer the question.

Beatrix Lang

(a)
Cash book (bank columns only)

Date	Details	Folio	$	Date	Details	Folio	$
20–4				20–4			
July 31	Balance	b/d	4 799	July 31	Correction of		
	Dividend		24		error		18
					Rent		100
					Bank charges		50
					Balance	c/d	4 655
			4 823				4 823
20–4							
Aug 1	Balance	b/d	4 655				

Bank reconciliation statement as at 31 July 20–4

	$	$
Balance as per bank statement		4 182
Add amounts not yet credited – Zwink & Co.	110	
Sales	874	984
		5 166
Less cheques not yet presented – AB Insurance	95	
G. Bierling	416	511
Balance as per cash book		4 655

If the alternative method of presentation were used, the bank reconciliation statement would be shown as follows.

(b)
Bank reconciliation statement as at 31 July 20–4

	$	$
Balance as per cash book		4 655
Add cheques not yet presented – AB Insurance	95	
G. Bierling	416	511
		5 166
Less amounts not yet credited – Zwink & Co.	110	
Sales	874	984
Balance as per bank statement		4 182

The cash book (bank columns) may look like an ordinary ledger account, but it is important to remember that it is the bank columns in the main cash book which are being considered. Examination questions do not usually show the discount and cash columns of the cash book to avoid presenting candidates with a large amount of data.

Bank statements shown in examination questions often give the names of the payees of the cheques paid out, the names of the people from whom money was received, and so on. This is to help candidates identify the figures easily. In practice, only cheque numbers appear for cheques paid and the words "counter credit" may be shown for cheques and cash paid in at a branch of the bank.

The above example showed the procedure when both the bank account in the books of the business and the bank statement had a positive bank balance. Exactly the same procedure is followed when one or both of the records show a bank overdraft. In this case care must be taken with the arithmetic, and it is useful to show brackets around overdraft figures. The bank statement may identify an overdraft by 'Dr.' or 'O/D' after the figure in the balance column. A bank overdraft in the cash book of a business will appear as a credit balance.

■ Example

On 31 October 20–4 the bank account in Beatrix Lang's cash book showed a credit balance of $1 010. On the same date her bank statement showed a debit balance of $1 300.

Beatrix compared the two records. She found that the following items had been entered in the cash book but not on the bank statement.
1. A cheque for $316 received from O. Rutz and paid into the bank on 30 October.
2. A cheque for $393 paid to P. R. Reiser on 28 October.

The following items were found to appear only on the bank statement.
1. Payment of rent by standing order, $100.
2. Bank charges of $67.
3. Payment of $200 by credit transfer to Alsafe Alarms Co. The bank should have debited this to the account of P. Lang, not Beatrix Lang.

(a) Make any additional entries that are required in the cash book of Beatrix Lang. Calculate a new bank balance, and bring down on 1 November 20–4.
(b) Prepare a bank reconciliation statement as at 31 October 20–4.

In this question the comparison of the bank statement with the bank account in the cash book has already been completed and the differences are listed in the question.

Beatrix Lang

(a) **Cash book (bank columns only)**

Date	Details	Folio	$	Date	Details	Folio	$
20–4 Oct 31	Balance	c/d	1 177	20–4 Oct 31	Balance Rent Bank charges		1 010 100 67
			1 177				1 177
				20–4 Nov 1	Balance	b/d	1 177

(b) **Bank reconciliation statement as at 31 October 20–4**

	$
Balance as per bank statement	(1 300)
Add amounts not yet credited – O. Rutz	316
	(984)
Less cheques not yet presented – P.R. Reiser	393
	(1 377)
Add standing order debited in error	200
Balance as per cash book	(1 177)

Reasons for bank reconciliation

When a bank reconciliation is undertaken, any errors in the bank account or on the bank statement will be revealed. Errors in the bank account require correction. The bank must be notified of any errors discovered on the bank statement.

After the bank statement has been received and the bank account written up to date, the business has an accurate figure for balance at bank. Unpresented cheques can be identified and any 'stale' cheques (those over 6 months old, which will not now be paid by the bank) can be written back in the bank account. Amounts not yet credited by the bank can also be identified.

As the bank statement is an independent accounting record, reconciling this with the bank account will help identify any fraud and embezzlement.

Review questions

1. (a) Which account is updated before a bank reconciliation statement is prepared?

   [IGCSE 1995]

   (b) Explain the meaning of the terms –
   (i) cheques not yet presented
   (ii) amounts not yet credited

   (c) Johnny's cash book showed an overdrawn balance at bank of $2 200 on 31 December 20–1. He received a bank statement showing an overdrawn balance at bank of $2 310 on 31 December 20–1. The reason for the difference was bank charges of $110, which had not been entered in the cash book.

   Johnny updated his cash book. In Johnny's Balance Sheet as at 31 December 20–1 –
   (i) under what heading will 'Bank' be shown?
   (ii) what amount will be entered for 'Bank'?

*2. The following is the bank account in the cash book of a business for the month of September 1998:

			$				$
Sept	1	Balance b/f	8 300	Sept	5	Suppliers & Co.	3 090
Sept	8	Cash sales	2 100		11	Four Wheels Garage	416
	19	A. Ali	984		20	Wages	1 640
	29	Enni & Co.	627		28	Brite Lite Electrical Co.	772
	30	Cosi Bros.	42		29	Ojay Containers	100
					30	Balance c/d	6 035
			12 053				12 053
Oct	1	Balance b/d	6 035				

The bank statement for the month of September showed the following:

CRYSTAL BANK – ANYTOWN BRANCH

		Debit	Credit	Balance
		$	$	$
1998				
Sept 1	Balance			8 300
8	Cash and cheques		2 100	10 400
10	Suppliers & Co.	3 090		7 310
15	Four Wheels Garage	416		6 894
19	Cheque		984	7 878
20	Cash	1 640		6 238
30	Cheque		42	6 280
30	Bank charges	200		6 080
	Bank interest	84		5 996

(a) Make any **additional** entries that are required in the cash book and calculate the new cash book balance. Start with the cash book balance of $6 035 at 30 September.

(b) Prepare a statement to reconcile the bank statement balance to the amended cash book balance.

(c) Cosi Bros.' cheque for $42, paid into the bank on 30 September, was returned unpaid by the bank on 8 October.
   (i) State **three** reasons why Cosi Bros.' cheque may have been returned unpaid by the bank.
   (ii) State what entries should be made in the books of the business to record the return of Cosi Bros.' cheque.

(d) State **four** reasons why it is necessary to reconcile the cash book and bank statement.

[IGCSE 1998]

3. At 30 April 1997, Charles' cash book showed a debit balance of $8 224 in his bank account. His bank statement showed a credit balance of $8 926 at the same date. Charles checked his cash book entries to the bank statement.

The following items had been entered in his cash book but were not in the bank statement:
1. An amount of $1 270 paid into the bank on 29 April 1997.
2. Cheques sent to suppliers:

		$
Cheque no.	324	600
	326	1 215
	327	494

The following items had been entered in the bank statement but not in the cash book:
1. A dividend received from Ono Ltd., for $400.
2. An amount of $336 received by bank giro (credit transfer) from A. Kimber.
3. A payment of $325 made by standing order to Fire and Theft Insurance Co.
4. A cheque for $920 from Tony Broke had been returned by the bank as dishonoured.
5. Bank charges $128.
6. An amount of $300 received from Miss Teree. The bank has credited this item to Charles' account in error.

(a) Make any additional entries that are required in Charles' cash book and calculate the new cash book balance at 30 April 1997.
(b) Prepare a statement to reconcile the bank statement balance to the amended cash book balance at 30 April 1997.
(c) State **four** reasons for preparing bank reconciliation statements.

[IGCSE 1997]

4. (a) (i) State **two** items of information given in a bank statement.
   (ii) Give **two** reasons for drawing up a bank reconciliation statement.

On 31 October 2000 the cash book (bank columns) and bank statement of Sara Perez were as follows:

Cash Book (bank columns)

	$		$
Oct 24 Balance b/d	5 203	Oct 27 Paris Fashions	2 069
25 Fine fabrics	242	28 Thai Exports	240
26 Super Satins	1 150	31 Balance c/d	5 264
30 Sales	1 078		
	7 573		7 573
Nov 1 Balance b/d	5 264		

Bank statement 31 October 2000

	Debit $	Credit $	Balance $
Oct 24 Balance			5 203 Cr.
26 Fine Fabrics		242	5 445
Super Satins		1 150	6 595
27 Cheque 185673	2 069		4 526
S.O. Motor Insurance	26		4 500
28 S.O. Rent	25		4 475
31 Bank Charges	88		4 387
Dishonoured Cheque (Fine Fabrics)	242		4 145

The following errors were discovered:
A. The debit side of the bank column in the cash book had been under-cast.
B. The bank had debited a standing order for payment of rent for $25 to Sara's business account instead of her personal account.

(b) Make any additional entries that are required in the cash book of Sara Perez. Calculate a new bank balance at 31 October 2000. Bring down the balance on 1 November 2000.
(c) Prepare a bank reconciliation statement at 31 October 2000.
(d) State the bank balance that should be shown in the Balance Sheet of Sara Perez at 31 October 2000. State whether it is an asset or a liability.

[IGCSE 2000]

CHAPTER 13

Journal entries and correction of errors

The journal

The journal is a book of prime entry, but it is not part of the double entry system. It is a journal, or diary, noting the entries to be made in the ledger. The other books of prime entry, explained earlier, are sales, purchases and returns journals and cash books. Anything that does not pass through one of these should be listed in the journal before being entered in the ledger. These items may be summarised as –

 Opening entries
 Purchase and sale of fixed assets on credit
 Other transfers e.g. writing off bad debts
 Correction of errors

A journal entry shows –
 the date
 the name of the ledger account to be debited, and the amount
 the name of the ledger account to be credited, and the amount
 a narrative.

The narrative is a brief explanation of why the entry is being made. This is necessary because of the great variety of transactions which are recorded in the journal.

Opening journal entries

These are the entries necessary to open the books when a business is first started, or when an existing business first starts to keep proper accounting records. The assets are listed in the debit column, and the liabilities in the credit column, and the difference, the capital, is inserted as the balancing figure. Ledger accounts can then be opened for all the items shown in the opening journal entry.

■ **Example**

Abdel Ayoub has been in business for two years, but has not kept any accounting records. On 1 February 20–2, he provided the following information:

Assets –   machinery $12 000, motor vehicle $3 200, stock $1 900, bank $2 660, debtor: Al Tonsi $490

Liabilities – creditor: Sallam & Co. $750

Prepare an opening journal entry for Abdel Ayoub on 1 February 20–2.

Abdel Ayoub

Journal

Date	Details	Folio	Debit	Credit
			$	$
20–2				
Feb 1	Machinery	NL1	12 000	
	Motor vehicle	NL2	3 200	
	Stock	NL3	1 900	
	Bank	CB1	2 660	
	Debtor – Al Tonsi	SL1	490	
	Creditor – Sallam & Co.	PL1		750
	Capital	NL4		19 500
	Assets and liabilities to open the books		20 250	20 250

Notes:
1. It is usual to show the debit entries first.
2. It is usual to slightly indent the names of the accounts to be credited.
3. As each journal entry is complete in itself, it is usual to rule off each one.
4. The folio numbers would be entered when the items are recorded in the ledger.

Other journal entries

A journal entry is required for any transactions which do not occur regularly, and which do not pass through any other book of prime entry. The basic rules of double entry must be applied to determine the account(s) to be debited and the account(s) to be credited. In examination questions, it is often helpful to work out the entries needed by preparing working notes in the form of ledger accounts.

■ **Example**

Sussana has a hairdressing business. The following transactions took place:
20–4 May 4 Wrote off $50 owing by Elisabeth as a bad debt.
            10 Sussana took goods costing $40 for her own use.
            16 Purchased equipment, $480, on credit from Salon Supplies.

Prepare the necessary journal entries.

Sussanna

Journal

Date	Details	Folio	Debit	Credit
			$	$
20–4 May 4	Bad Debts Elisabeth Debt written off as bad	NL1 SL1	50	50
10	Drawings Purchases Goods taken for personal use	NL2 NL3	40	40
16	Equipment Salon Supplies Equipment bought on credit	NL4 NL5*	480	480

*A nominal ledger account is used to avoid confusing Salon Supplies with trade creditors.

Correction of errors

Errors not shown by a trial balance

The errors which a trial balance will not reveal may be summarised as –
  Error of omission
  Error of commission
  Error of principle
  Compensating errors
  Error of original entry
  Complete reversal of entries

These were explained in Chapter 3.
  When these errors are later discovered, they should be corrected by a journal entry.

■ **Example**

Rango Traders prepared a trial balance on 31 December 20–1. The totals of the trial balance agreed, but the following errors were discovered on 7 January 20–2.
(a) Repairs to fixtures, $125, had been debited to the fixtures account.
(b) Sales on credit to Wiese, $154, had been entered in the account of A. Wise.
(c) Cash drawings of $200 had been completely omitted from the books.
(d) The purchases account had been under-cast by $100 and the wages account had been over-cast by $100.
(e) Purchases on credit, $495, from Kotze, were entered in the books as $594.
(f) A cheque, $300, received from Botha, was debited in his account and credited in the bank account.

Prepare the necessary journal entries to correct these errors.

Notes: (a) This is an error of principle. The fixtures account must be credited with $125 and the repairs account must be debited.
(b) This is an error of commission. A. Wise account must be credited with $154 and Wiese account must be debited.
(c) This is an error of omission. The cash account must be credited with $200 and the drawings account must be debited.
(d) These are compensating errors. The purchases account must be debited with $100 and the wages account must be credited with $100.
(e) This is an error of original entry. The purchases account must be credited with $99 and Kotze account must be debited. The $99 is the difference between the two figures, and is the amount by which the entry has been overstated.
(f) This is an error of complete reversal. The bank account must be debited with $600 and Botha account must be credited. It is necessary to double the amount of the original error in order to restore both accounts to the correct amounts.

Rango Traders

Journal

	Date	Details	Folio	Debit $	Credit $
(a)	20–2 Jan 7	Repairs Fixtures Error in posting repairs to fixtures account, now corrected	NL1 NL2	125	125
(b)		Wiese A. Wise Error in posting sales to wrong personal account, now corrected	SL1 SL2	154	154
(c)		Drawings Cash Omission of cash drawings from accounts, now corrected	NL3 CB1	200	200
(d)		Purchases Wages Purchases under-cast and wages over-cast in error, now corrected	NL4 NL5	100	100
(e)		Kotze Purchases Purchases on credit of $495 wrongly entered as $594, now corrected	PL1 NL4	99	99
(f)		Bank Botha Cheque received credited to bank and debited to Botha in error, now corrected	CB1 SL2	600	600

Errors affecting the trial balance

These were explained in Chapter 3.

If a trial balance fails to agree, and the errors cannot be found immediately, the trial balance is made to balance by inserting the difference between the two sides in a **suspense account**. This is a temporary "holding" account for the difference on a trial balance. As the errors are found, they are corrected by means of a journal entry, one part of the entry (either debit or credit) being in the suspense account. When all the errors have been discovered and corrected the suspense account will automatically close.

If necessary, draft final accounts may be prepared before all the errors are found. In this case, the balance on the suspense account will appear in the Balance Sheet as an asset, if the balance on the account is debit, or as a liability if the balance on the account is credit.

■ **Example**

Marcel's trial balance, prepared on 31 October 20–6, failed to agree. The difference of $380 was a shortage on the credit side, and was posted to a suspense account. The following errors were discovered on 4 November 20–6.

(a) The sales account was under-cast by $1 000.
(b) Cash purchases, $140, had been recorded only in the cash account.
(c) Purchases on credit from Pierre, $460, had been correctly entered in the purchases account, but credited to Pierre's account as $480.
(d) Payment by cheque, $230, to Nicole was correctly entered in the bank account but was also credited to Nicole's account.

Give the journal entries to correct the above errors.

Write up the Suspense account as it would appear after all the corrections had been made.

Notes: (a) The sales account must be credited with $1 000 and the suspense account debited.
(b) The purchases account must be debited with $140 and the suspense account credited.
(c) Pierre's account must be debited with $20 and the suspense account must be credited.
(d) Nicole's account must be debited with $460 and the suspense account credited. It is necessary to double the amount of the original error to restore Nicole's account to the correct amount.

Marcel

Journal

	Date	Details	Folio	Debit $	Credit $
(a)	20–6 Nov 4	Suspense Sales Sales account under-cast, now corrected	NL1 NL2	1 000	1 000
(b)		Purchases Suspense Cash purchases omitted from purchases account, now corrected	NL3 NL1	140	140
(c)		Pierre Suspense Purchases, $460, incorrectly entered as $480 in Pierre's account, now corrected	PL1 NL1	20	20
(d)		Nicole Suspense Payment to Nicole, $230, posted in error to credit of Nicole account, now corrected	PL2 NL1	460	460

Marcel

Nominal Ledger

Suspense account   Page 1

Date	Details	Folio	$	Date	Details	Folio	$
20–6 Nov 4	Sales	NL2	1 000	20–6 Oct 31 Nov 4	Difference on Trial Balance Purchases Pierre Nicole	 NL3 PL1 PL2	 380 140 20 460
			1 000				1 000

Chapter 13 – Journal entries and correction of errors   151

It is important to remember that only items affecting the balancing of the trial balance are corrected through a suspense account. A suspense account is **not** used to correct items which do not affect the balancing of the trial balance.

Effect on profit of correcting errors

If errors are corrected *after* the final accounts are prepared, the profit may have to be adjusted. If an error affected an item in the Profit and Loss Account, the net profit will be incorrect. Where an error affected an item in the Trading Account, both the gross profit and the net profit will be incorrect. It is usual to draw up a statement showing how the errors affect the profit calculation and the corrected profit.

■ **Example**

Rango Traders prepared a trial balance on 31 December 20–1. The totals of the trial balance agreed and final accounts were prepared for the year ended 31 December 20–1, showing a net profit of $20 000.

The following errors were discovered on 7 January 20–2:
(a) Repairs to fixtures, $125, had been debited to the fixtures account.
(b) Sales on credit to Wiese, $154, had been entered in the account of A. Wise.
(c) Cash drawings of $200 had been completely omitted from the books.
(d) The purchases account had been under-cast by $100 and the wages account had been over-cast by $100.
(e) Purchases on credit, $495, from Kotze, were entered in the books as $594.
(f) A cheque, $300, received from Botha, was debited in his account and credited in the bank account.

Prepare a statement to show the corrected net profit for the year ended 31 December 20–1.

Notes: (a) Repairs to fixtures increase, so the net profit will decrease by $125.
(b) This has no effect on the calculation of the net profit.
(c) This has no effect on the calculation of the net profit.
(d) Purchases increase, so the gross profit, and consequently the net profit, will decrease by $100.
Wages decrease, so the net profit will increase by $100.
(e) Purchases decrease, so the gross profit, and consequently the net profit, will increase by $99.
(f) This has no effect on the calculation of the net profit.

Rango Traders

Statement of Corrected Net Profit for the year ended 31 December 20–1

	$	$
Net Profit from Profit and Loss Account		20 000
Add Wages over-cast (d)	100	
Purchases over-stated (e)	99	199
		20 199
Less Repairs under-stated (a)	125	
Purchases under-cast (d)	100	225
Corrected Net Profit		19 974

Effect on Balance Sheet of correcting errors

If errors are corrected *after* the final accounts are prepared, the Balance Sheet may have to be adjusted. If it was necessary to correct the net profit, this will obviously affect the capital section of the Balance Sheet. Where an error affected an asset, a liability or the capital, the figure shown in the Balance Sheet will not be accurate and must be corrected.

■ Example

Rango Traders prepared a trial balance on 31 December 20–1. The totals of the trial balance agreed and final accounts were prepared for the year ended 31 December 20–1. The following errors were discovered on 7 January 20–2:

(a) Repairs to fixtures, $125, had been debited to the fixtures account.
(b) Sales on credit to Wiese, $154, had been entered in the account of A. Wise.
(c) Cash drawings of $200 had been completely omitted from the books.
(d) The purchases account had been under-cast by $100 and the wages account had been over-cast by $100.
(e) Purchases on credit, $495, from Kotze, were entered in the books as $594.
(f) A cheque, $300, received from Botha, was debited in his account and credited in the bank account.

The corrected net profit for the year ended 31 December 20–1 was $19 974.

Explain how each of the errors will affect the Balance Sheet of Rango Traders as at 31 December 20–1.

(a) To correct this error of principle, where revenue expenditure had been treated as capital expenditure, the fixtures in the fixed assets section are decreased by $125.
(b) This error of commission has no effect on the Balance Sheet, although the sales ledger accounts of Wiese and A. Wise need to be amended.

(c) To correct this error of omission, the cash in the current assets section is decreased by $200, and the capital section is also decreased as the drawings increase by $200.
(d) These compensating errors do not affect the Balance Sheet.
(e) To correct this error of original entry, the creditors in the current liabilities section are decreased by $99.
(f) To correct this error of complete reversal, the bank in the current assets section is increased by $600 and the debtors in the current assets section is decreased by $600.

The capital section will also decrease by $26 because of the decrease in the net profit.
The Balance Sheet will still balance after all the adjustments are made.

Review questions

1. (a) State **one** use of the journal.
[IGCSE 1999]
   (b) In connection with journal entries –
      (i) what is a narrative?
      (ii) why is a narrative required?
   (c) Name the account which may be opened when a trial balance does not agree.
[IGCSE 1998]
   (d) The purchase of stationery for use in a business was debited to the purchases account.
      (i) What type of error is this?
      (ii) Will a correcting entry in a suspense account be required? Give reasons.
      (iii) How will the gross profit and net profit be affected when this error is corrected?
      (iv) How will the Balance Sheet be affected when this error is corrected?
   (e) Joe began trading on 1 April 2000 and paid $10 000 into a business bank account. He borrowed a further $5 000 from his sister, Freda, and also paid this into the bank account. Joe keeps full accounting records. Give the entries required in Joe's journal to record the above transactions. Narratives are **not** required.
[IGCSE 2000]

2. Hugh makes up his annual accounts to 31 March. In his trial balance drawn up on 31 March 1999, the amount shown for trade debtors was $20 500. After this trial balance was prepared:
   1. Hugh was notified by Finn's Furnishings that it was not able to pay the balance of $500 owing to him. Hugh wrote off this amount as a bad debt.
   2. Hugh then created a provision for doubtful debts equal to 5% of trade debtors.

Give the journal entries required to record the adjustments 1. and 2. Include a narrative below each entry.

[IGCSE 1999]

3. (a) State **five** types of error that do not affect a trial balance.
   (b) The following trial balance at 30 April 1997 has some errors.

	Debit $	Credit $
Capital at 1 May 1996		20 000
Drawings	5 000	
Sales		60 525
Purchases	29 900	
Stock at 1 May 1996	8 750	
Stock at 30 April 1997		7 300
Administration expenses	15 017	
Discounts allowed		1 100
Discounts received	930	
Fixed assets	25 000	
Cash in hand	200	
Bank overdraft	1 760	
Trade debtors	3 588	
Provision for doubtful debts	140	
Trade creditors		2 200
Suspense account	840	
	91 125	91 125

Rewrite the trial balance to correct the errors. Enter any difference remaining on the trial balance as a balance on the suspense account.

(c) After the trial balance was re-written, the following errors were discovered:
   (i) $600 received from Bokko Ltd. was entered correctly in the cash book, but was debited in Bokko's account in the sales ledger.
   (ii) $200 paid to Kember Ltd. was debited in Kember Ltd.'s account as $2 000.
   (iii) A sale of goods on credit to Sihan Ltd. for $2 500 was omitted entirely from the books.

Prepare journal entries to correct these errors. Brief narratives are required.

(d) It is not possible to record all aspects of a business in money terms. Name **two** such aspects of a business.

[IGCSE 1997]

4. On 31 October 1999 a trial balance showed a difference which was posted to a suspense account. The following errors were later discovered:
   1. A payment of £520 for electricity had been entered on the debit side of the electricity account as $620.
   2. Machinery repairs costing $1 000 had been debited to the machinery account.
   3. Insurance premiums paid, $1 200, had been posted to the credit side of the insurance account.

   (a) Give the journal entries, without narratives, to correct the above errors.
   (b) Write up the Suspense account, including your figure for the opening balance. Show your calculation.
   [IGCSE 1999]

5. A trial balance failed to agree because the debit side totalled $144 000 and the credit side totalled $140 800. The difference was entered in a suspense account.

   Later, the following errors were discovered:
   1. One page of the sales journal had not been entered in the sales account in the nominal ledger. The total of the page was $1 400.
   2. One page of the purchases journal had been over-cast by $400.
   3. The total of discounts allowed for March, $600, had not been entered in the discounts account.
   4. Cash received from a debtor, $800, had been entered in the cash book but had not been entered in the customer's account in the sales ledger.
   5. A payment of $1 200 to a supplier had been entered twice in that supplier's account in the purchases ledger.

   (a) Prepare journal entries to correct errors 1 to 5. Narratives are **not** required.
   (b) Prepare the Suspense account to show how it will appear after all the errors have corrected.
   (c) State **two** types of error which do not affect the trial balance. State **one** example of each of the two types.
   [IGCSE 1998]

*6. (a) Explain **one** purpose of using the journal to record business transactions.
   (b) Millie Plainfeather is a sole trader who keeps a full set of books including a journal. You have been informed of the following:
      (i) 1 June 1996: a motor vehicle was bought on credit for $10 000 from the Star Garage. No entry has been made in Millie's books regarding this transaction.

(ii) 5 June 1996: Millie paid $300 in cash for electricity. This had been correctly entered in the cash book but had been wrongly entered on the debit side of the rent account. No entries have yet been made in Millie's books to correct this.

Give the entries now required regarding each of the above matters in Millie's journal. Include a narrative below each transaction.

(c) Millie's draft accounts for the year ended 30 June 1996 showed a net profit of $26 800. After these accounts were prepared, it was decided to make adjustments for the following:
   (i) A provision for doubtful debts of $900 was to be created.
   (ii) Depreciation of $400 was to be charged on office equipment.
   (iii) Motor expenses were to include a bill from Star Garage for $500 for work done on 27 June. The bill was not received until 4 July.

Complete a statement to show the effect of each of these adjustments (i) to (iii) on Millie's original net profit. Calculate the corrected net profit figure.

[IGCSE 1996]

7. Fred Zero's draft Trading and Profit and Loss Account for the year to 30 September 1997 showed the following:

	$
Gross Profit	42 880
Net Profit	9 526

It was later discovered that no entries had been made for the following items:
1. Fred Zero had taken goods which had cost $1 300 from the business for his own use.
2. On 30 September 1997, Fred Zero had received goods costing $800. He has included these goods in his closing stock. He had not paid for the goods nor received an invoice for them.
3. $350 had been debited to the carriage outwards account. This should have been debited to the carriage inwards account.

(a) State the effect on the gross profit **and** the net profit of the adjustment of **each** of the **three** discoveries 1–3. If any item has no effect on the gross profit or the net profit, state 'no effect'.
(b) Calculate the amended gross profit and amended net profit after the adjustments have been made.

[IGCSE 1997]

8. The draft Balance Sheet of a business at 31 March 1999 is shown.

	$		$	$
Capital account		Fixed assets		30 000
Balance at 1 April 1998	55 000			
Net Profit for year	27 000			
	82 000	Current assets		
Less Drawings	25 000	Stock	18 000	
Balance at 31 March 1999	57 000	Debtors	12 000	
		Bank	5 000	35 000
Current liabilities				
Creditors	8 000			
	65 000			65 000

After the draft Balance Sheet is prepared, the following matters are discovered:

(a) The stock at 31 March 1999 includes goods which are damaged. They have been included in stock at their cost of $3 000, but can now only be sold for $1 000.

(b) A debtor owing $1 000 paid $950 in full settlement of his account on 31 March 1999. This has not been recorded in the books.

(c) A debtor owing $500 at 31 March 1999 has stated that he is unable to pay.

(d) Goods which cost $800 were returned to the supplier on 30 March 1999. No record of this has been made in the books.

Prepare a revised Balance Sheet.

[IGCSE 1999]

CHAPTER 14

Control accounts

Control accounts are sometimes known as **total accounts**. A control account acts as a summary of the ledger which it 'controls'.

If the totals of a trial balance drawn up at the end of an accounting period fail to agree, it is necessary to check the accounting records. This can be a time-consuming task and errors may be difficult to locate. The task can be made easier if sections of the ledger have control accounts. These accounts act as a check on the individual accounts in that section of the ledger, and so prove that the entries in that ledger are arithmetically correct. As with a trial balance, a control account only checks the arithmetical accuracy: there are some errors, such as errors of commission, which will not be revealed by a control account.

It has already been explained how the ledger is divided into –
- Sales ledger – which contains the accounts of the debtors
- Purchases ledger – which contains the accounts of the creditors
- Nominal ledger – which contains all the other accounts, except cash, bank and petty cash.

It is usual to prepare a control account for the sales ledger and a control account for the purchases ledger.

Sales ledger control accounts

A sales ledger control account is sometimes known as a **total debtors account**. The control account is balanced at the end of the period in the same way as any other ledger account. When the balances on all the individual accounts in the sales ledger are added together they should agree with the balance on the sales ledger control account. If the balance on the control account differs from the total of the individual debtor's balances an error must have occurred, either in the sales ledger or within the control account, so further investigation is required.

A sales ledger control account resembles the account of an individual debtor. It is, however, an account recording, in total, the transactions affecting *all* the debtors. If there is an error in the sales ledger it will not be revealed by a control account prepared from the individual accounts in that ledger. It is therefore essential that the information required to prepare a sales ledger control account is obtained from **books of prime entry**, not the sales ledger itself.

Items appearing in a sales ledger control account, and the source of the information for each item are summarised below.

Debit entries	Source of information
Opening balance b/d	Previous closing balance c/d
Sales on credit	Sales journal
Cheques dishonoured	Cash book
Cash refunded to debtors	Cash book

Credit entries	Source of information
Sales returns	Sales returns journal
Cash and cheques received	Cash book
Discount allowed	Cash book
Bad debts	Journal

■ **Example**

The following figures are taken from the books of Jane:

		$
20–2 June 1	Balances brought down in sales ledger	10 260
30	Totals for the month –	
	Sales journal	71 500
	Sales returns journal	1 380
	Cheques received from debtors	68 800
	Cash received from debtors	1 050
	Discount allowed	1 440
	Bad debts written off	160
	Cheque received (included in figure given above) later dishonoured	870

Prepare Jane's Sales Ledger Control account for the month of June 20–2.

Jane

Sales Ledger Control account

Date	Details	Folio	$	Date	Details	Folio	$
20–2				20–2			
June 1	Balances	b/d	10 260	June 30	Sales returns		1 380
30	Sales		71 500		Bank		68 800
	Bank (dis-				Cash		1 050
	honoured				Discount		
	cheque)		870		allowed		1 440
					Bad debts		160
					Balances	c/d	9 800
			82 630				82 630
20–2							
July 1	Balances	b/d	9 800				

Purchases ledger control accounts

A purchases ledger control account is sometimes known as a **total creditors account**. At the end of the period the balance on the purchases ledger control account should agree with the total of the balances of all the individual accounts in the purchases ledger. If the balance on the control account differs from the total of the individual creditor's balances there must be an error, either in the purchases ledger or in the control account.

A purchases ledger control account resembles the account of an individual creditor. The information required to prepare a purchases ledger control account must be obtained from books of prime entry, not from the purchases ledger itself – otherwise errors within the ledger will not be revealed.

Items appearing in a purchases ledger control account and the source of the information for each item are summarised below.

Debit entries	Source of information
Purchases returns	Purchases returns journal
Cash and cheques paid	Cash book
Discount received	Cash book

Credit entries	Source of information
Opening balance b/d	Previous closing balance c/d
Purchases on credit	Purchases journal
Cash refunded by creditors	Cash book

■ **Example**

The following figures are taken from the books of Jane:

		$
20–2 June 1	Balances brought down in purchases ledger	5 900
30	Totals for the month –	
	Purchases journal	49 700
	Purchases returns journal	1 070
	Cheques paid to creditors	47 080
	Cash paid to creditors	950
	Discount received	860

Prepare Jane's Purchases Ledger Control account for the month of June 20–2.

Jane

Purchases Ledger Control account

Date	Details	Folio	$	Date	Details	Folio	$

20–2
June 30
	Purchases
	    returns
	Bank
	Cash
	Discount
	    received
	Balances
		
		c/d
			
			1 070
			47 080
			950
			
			860
			5 640
			55 600
				20–2
				June 1
				         30
				
				20–2
				July 1
					Balances
					Purchases
					
					Balances
						b/d
						
						b/d
							5 900
							49 700
							
							55 600
							5 640

Balances on both sides of a control account

It may happen that there is a small opening credit balance brought down on a sales ledger control account, in addition to the usual opening debit balance. Where a debtor has overpaid his account, or has returned goods after paying his account, the individual sales ledger account will show a credit balance.

In the sales ledger control account it is usual to show any credit balances as a separate item rather than simply showing the overall net debit balances. When balancing a sales ledger control account, any small closing balance is debited and carried down as a credit balance. The account can then be balanced in the usual way and the balance credited and carried down as a debit balance.

Similarly, it can happen that there is a small opening debit balance on a purchases ledger control account, in addition to the usual opening credit balance. Where the business has overpaid a creditor, or has returned goods after paying the account, the individual purchases ledger account will show a debit balance.

In the purchases ledger control account it is usual to show any debit balances as a separate item instead of showing the overall net credit balances. When balancing a purchases ledger control account, any small closing balance is credited and carried down as a debit balance. The account can then be balanced in the usual way and the balance debited and carried down as a credit balance.

Example

The following figures are taken from the books of Jane:

		$
20–2 Aug 1	Balances brought down in the purchases ledger –	
	Credit balances	6 230
	Debit balances	160
31	Totals for the month –	
	Purchases journal	48 600
	Purchases returns journal	950
	Cheques paid to creditors	47 030
	Discount received	970
31	Purchases ledger debit balances	130

(a) Prepare Jane's Purchases Ledger Control account for the month of August 20–2.

(b) After the preparation of the control account it is found that the total of the credit balances in the purchases ledger on 31 August 20–2 amounts to $5 950. What can be inferred in relation to the purchases ledger?

Jane

(a) **Purchases Ledger Control account**

Date	Details	Folio	$	Date	Details	Folio	$
20–2 Aug 31	Balances	b/d	160	20–2 Aug 1	Balances	b/d	6 230
	Purchases returns		950	31	Purchases		48 600
	Bank		47 030		Balances	c/d	130
	Discount received		970				
	Balances	c/d	5 850				
			54 960				54 960
20–2 Sept 1	Balances	b/d	130	20–2 Sept 1	Balances	b/d	5 850

(b) The purchases ledger control account shows credit balances of $5 850 but the total of the balances on the individual creditor's accounts is $5 950. This would imply that there is an error of $100 either in the purchases ledger or in the purchases ledger control account.

A similar process is applied to a sales ledger control account which has balances on both sides.

Advantages of control accounts

It has already been explained that control accounts can help in locating errors by proving the arithmetical accuracy of the ledgers which they control.

It is not necessary to balance all the individual accounts and add up the total of these balances in order to find the total amount owed by debtors and the total amount owed to creditors on a certain date. The balances on the control accounts can be regarded as being equal to the debtors and creditors on a certain date, so this information can be obtained immediately. Draft final accounts can also be prepared quickly because of the balances provided by the control accounts.

Fraud is made more difficult by the use of control accounts. A responsible person should prepare the control accounts, and this person should not be the same person who made the entries in the sales and purchases ledgers.

Control accounts also provide a summary of the transactions affecting the debtors and creditors for the financial period.

Review questions

1. (a) Name the account which summarises all the sales ledger accounts.
   [IGCSE 1997]
   (b) Name the ledger account which summarises all the accounts of buyers of goods on credit.
   [IGCSE 1996]
   (c) State **one** reason for keeping control accounts.
   [IGCSE 1998]
   (d) The purchases ledger control account is prepared from information provided by books of prime entry. Name **two** of these books.

2. The entries in the sales ledger control account of a business during April 1998 were as follows.

	$
Balances brought forward 1 April 1998	40 180
Credit sales	102 000
Goods returned by customers	1 420
Cash received from debtors	112 000
Discounts allowed to debtors	2 670

   (a) From the information given, prepare the Sales Ledger Control account for the month of April 1998.
   (b) State **two** advantages of using control accounts.
   [IGCSE 1998]

*3. The following figures are taken from the books of David.

		$
20–4 Sept 31	Balances brought down in purchases ledger –	
	Debit	40
	Credit	2 800
30	Totals for the month –	
	Purchases journal	6 300
	Purchases returns journal	1 100
	Cheques paid to creditors	5 750
	Discount received	110
	Cash refunded by creditors	10
30	Purchases ledger debit balances	30

(a) Prepare David's Purchases Ledger Control account for the month of September 20–4.
(b) It is found that the total of the purchase returns journal for the month of September 20–4 should be $1 000, not $1 100. What effect, if any, will this error have on the closing credit balances of the purchases ledger control account?

4. The following information for the month of March 20–6 is taken from the books of Hussein & Company.

		$
March 1	Purchases ledger balances	24 100 credit
	Sales ledger balances	29 500 debit
	Sales ledger balances	210 credit
31	Totals for the month –	
	Sales journal	59 480
	Purchases journal	46 300
	Sales returns journal	620
	Purchases returns journal	440
	Cheques paid to creditors	46 900
	Cheques received from debtors	54 660
	Cash received relating to a bad debt written off in June 20–1	200
	Cheque received from credit customer (included in cheques received listed above) later dishonoured	120
	Cash refunded to credit customer in respect of overpayment	10
	Cash purchases	5 800
	Discount allowed	690
	Discount received	730
	Increase in provision for doubtful debts	90
31	Sales ledger credit balances	160

(a) Select the appropriate figures from those given above and prepare a Sales Ledger Control account and a Purchases Ledger Control account for Hussein & Company for the month of March 20–6.
(b) List the items which have **not** been entered in either control account. Explain why **each** of those items has been omitted from the control accounts.
(c) The total of the balances in the sales ledger and purchases ledger on 31 March 20–6 were –

	$
Purchases ledger balances	23 060 credit
Sales ledger balances	33 090 debit
Sales ledger balances	160 credit

What can be inferred in relation to the accuracy of the sales ledger and the purchases ledger?

CHAPTER 15

Incomplete records

Sometimes businesses, especially small businesses, do not maintain a full set of double entry records. Consequently, no trial balance will be produced and a complete set of final accounts cannot be prepared without further analysis of the records that do exist.

Where the only records available are the assets and liabilities at the beginning of the year and at the end of the year, it is not possible to prepare a Trading and Profit and Loss Account. The assets and liabilities are usually listed in a **Statement of Affairs**. This would have been called a Balance Sheet if it had been drawn up from a set of double entry records. Like a Balance Sheet, a Statement of Affairs can be prepared horizontally or vertically.

The only way the profit for the year can be found is by comparing the capital shown in the opening Statement of Affairs with the capital shown in the closing Statement of Affairs. The basic formula is –

Closing capital – Opening capital = Profit

It may be that the owner has made drawings during the year, which will account for some of the difference in the capital figures. The formula must, therefore, be modified –

Closing capital – Opening capital + Drawings = Profit

If the owner has introduced more capital during the year, this will also account for some of the difference in the capital figures. The formula must again be modified –

Closing capital – Opening capital + Drawings – Capital introduced = Profit

The missing figure for profit could also be calculated in the form of a capital account –

Capital account

Date	Details	Folio	$	Date	Details	Folio	$
Yr 1 Dec 31	Drawings Balance	c/d		Yr 1 Jan 1 Dec 31 Yr 2 Jan 1	Balance Bank Net Profit Balance	b/d b/d	?

Calculating the profit from the change in the capital is far from satisfactory, as it does not provide any information about sales, purchases, expenses and gross profit. It may, however, be the only calculation possible from the limited information available.

■ **Example**

Ruth Moshana is a trader who does not keep a full set of double entry records. She supplies the following information about her assets and liabilities:

	1 January 20–1 $	31 December 20–1 $
Machinery at cost	7 000	?
Equipment at cost	2 500	?
Motor vehicle at cost		1 800
Stock	1 050	1 290
Debtors	630	660
Creditors	970	860
Bank	2 700	–
Bank overdraft		120
Prepayments	120	40
Accruals	30	20
Loan from Easifinance	5 000	2 000

On 31 December 20–1 it was decided that the machinery and the equipment should be depreciated by 10% on cost. During the year Ruth took drawings of $20 per week. On 1 July 20–1 Ruth brought her private motor vehicle into the business at a valuation of $1 800.

168 Accounting: IGCSE

(a) Prepare the Statement of Affairs of Ruth Moshana as at (i) 1 January 20–1 and (ii) 31 December 20–1.
(b) Calculate Ruth Moshana's profit or loss for the year ended 31 December 20–1.

Ruth Moshana

Statement of Affairs as at 1 January 20–1

	$	$	$
Fixed assets			
Machinery at cost			7 000
Equipment at cost			2 500
			9 500
Current assets			
Stock		1 050	
Debtors		630	
Prepayments		120	
Bank		2 700	
		4 500	
Less Current liabilities			
Creditors	970		
Accruals	30	1 000	
Working capital			3 500
			13 000
Less Long-term liabilities			
Loan – Easifinance			5 000
			8 000
Financed by			
Capital			
Balance			8 000
			8 000

The missing figure of capital is inserted to make the Balance Sheet balance.

Ruth Moshana

Statement of Affairs as at 31 December 20–1

	$ Cost	$ Depreciation to date	$ Net book value
Fixed assets			
Machinery	7 000	700	6 300
Equipment	2 500	250	2 250
Motor vehicle	1 800	–	1 800
	11 300	950	10 350
Current assets			
Stock		1 290	
Debtors		660	
Prepayments		40	
		1 990	
Less Current liabilities			
Creditors	860		
Accruals	20		
Bank overdraft	120	1 000	
Working capital			990
			11 340
Less Long-term liabilities			
Loan – Easifinance			2 000
			9 340
Financed by			
Capital			
Balance			9 340
			9 340

The missing figure of capital is inserted to make the Balance Sheet balance.

Note: The Balance Sheets have been shown in vertical format, but horizontal format is equally acceptable. A columnar style of presentation could also have been used showing the Balance Sheets side by side.

Ruth Moshana

Calculation of profit for the year ended 31 December 20–1

	$
Capital at 31 December 20–1	9 340
Less capital at 1 January 20–1	8 000
	1 340
Add drawings during the year (52 × $20)	1 040
	2 380
Less capital introduced	1 800
Profit for the year	580

A business may be able to provide other information, in addition to the assets and liabilities at the beginning and end of the year. Where details of money paid and received are also available, it is possible to calculate the sales, purchases and expenses, and so prepare a Trading and Profit and Loss Account.

The procedure may be summarised as follows –
1. Calculate the opening capital.
2. Calculate the sales for the year.
3. Calculate the purchases for the year.
4. Calculate the closing bank balance (where necessary).
5. Prepare the final accounts.

■ **Example**

Tobias Ambunda is a sole trader who keeps a bank account, but very few other accounting records. He provides the following information:

	1 November 20–7 $	31 October 20–8 $
Premises at cost	15 000	15 000
Fixtures at cost	2 500	?
Stock	2 650	2 950
Debtors	3 330	3 660
Creditors	2 900	3 080
Bank	1 300	?
General expenses accrued	80	120

A summary of his bank account for the year to 31 October 20–8 shows –

Receipts	$	Payments	$
Cash sales	2 570	Payments to creditors	32 320
Receipts from debtors	41 100	Cash purchases	1 100
		Payment of expenses	5 410
		Purchase of fixtures	1 000
		Drawings for personal use	2 000

Fixtures are to be depreciated by 10% per annum on the cost of fixtures held at 31 October 20–8.

Prepare the Trading and Profit and Loss Account of Tobias Ambunda for the year ended 31 October 20–8, and a Balance Sheet as at 31 October 20–8.

Calculation of Opening Capital

Tobias Ambunda

Statement of Affairs as at 31 October 20–8

	$	$	$
Fixed assets			
Premises at cost			15 000
Fixtures at cost			2 500
			17 500
Current assets			
Stock		2 650	
Debtors		3 330	
Bank		1 300	
		7 280	
Less Current liabilities			
Creditors	2 900		
Accruals	80	2 980	
Working capital			4 300
			21 800
Financed by			
Capital			
Balance			21 800
			21 800

172 Accounting: IGCSE

Calculation of Sales

The amount actually received from debtors is not necessarily equal to the credit sales. Some of the money received relates to the amount owing at the start of the year, for sales made in the previous year. In addition, the debtors have not yet paid for some of the goods sold on credit to them during the current financial year. The credit sales for the year may be calculated –

	$
Receipts from debtors	41 100
Less debtors at 1 November 20–7	3 330
	37 770
Plus debtors at 31 October 20–8	3 660
Credit sales for the year	41 430

Alternatively, the calculation may be presented in the form of a total debtors account. The amount of credit sales is inserted as the balancing figure.

Total Debtors account

Date	Details	Folio	$	Date	Details	Folio	$
20–7				20–8			
Nov 1	Balance		3 330	Oct 31	Bank		41 100
20–8					Balance	c/d	3 660
Oct 31	Sales*		41 430				
			44 760				44 760
20–8							
Nov 1	Balance	b/d	3 660				

*Inserted as balancing figure

The total sales for the year are the credit sales plus the cash sales –

	$
Credit sales	41 430
Cash sales	2 570
	44 000

Calculation of Purchases

The amount actually paid to the creditors is not necessarily equal to the credit purchases. Some of the money paid relates to the amount owing at the start of the year for credit purchases made in the previous year. In addition, the creditors have not yet been paid for some of the goods purchased on credit from them during the current financial year.

The credit purchases may be calculated –

		$
Payments to creditors		32 320
Less creditors at 1 November 20–7		2 900
		29 420
Plus creditors at 31 October 20–8		3 080
Credit purchases for the year		32 500

Alternatively, the calculation may be presented in the form of a total creditors account. The amount of credit purchases is inserted as the balancing figure.

Total Creditors account

Date	Details	Folio	$	Date	Details	Folio	$
20–8				20–7			
Oct 31	Bank		32 320	Nov 1	Balance		2 900
	Balance	c/d	3 080	20–8			
				Oct 31	Purchases*		32 500
			35 400				35 400
				20–8			
				Nov 1	Balance	b/d	3 080

*Inserted as balancing figure

The total purchases for the year are the credit purchases plus the cash purchases –

	$
Credit purchases	32 500
Cash purchases	1 100
	33 600

Calculation of Closing Bank Balance

The bank balance at 31 October 20–8 is calculated by preparing a summary of the bank account. The opening balance is shown, together with the total amount received and the total amount paid (it is not necessary to itemise these unless the question requires this) and the account is then balanced.

Bank account

Date	Details	Folio	$	Date	Details	Folio	$
20–7				20–8			
Nov 1	Balance		1 300	Oct 31	Total payments		41 830
20–8					Balance	c/d	3 140
Oct 31	Total receipts		43 670				
			44 970				44 970
20–8							
Nov 1	Balance	b/d	3 140				

Preparation of Trading and Profit and Loss Account

Tobias Ambunda

Trading and Profit and Loss Account for the year ended 31 October 20–8

	$	$
Sales		44 000
Less Cost of goods sold		
Opening stock	2 650	
Purchases	33 600	
	36 250	
Less Closing stock	2 950	33 300
Gross Profit		10 700
Less General expenses (5 410 + 120 – 80)	5 450	
Depreciation of fixtures 10% × (2 500 + 1 000)	350	5 800
Net Profit		4 900

Chapter 15 – Incomplete records

Preparation of Balance Sheet

Tobias Ambunda
Balance Sheet as at 31 October 20–8

	$	$	$
Fixed assets	Cost	Depreciation to date	Net book value
Premises	15 000	–	15 000
Fixtures	3 500	350	3 150
	18 500	350	18 150
Current assets			
Stock		2 950	
Debtors		3 660	
Bank		3 140	
		9 750	
Less Current liabilities			
Creditors	3 080		
Accruals	120	3 200	
Working capital			6 550
			24 700
Financed by			
Capital			
Opening balance			21 800
Plus Net Profit			4 900
			26 700
Less Drawings			2 000
			24 700

Note: The final accounts could have been presented in horizontal format.

Discount Allowed and Discount Received

A business may allow its customers a cash discount if they pay promptly. In the same way, a business may receive a cash discount from its suppliers if their accounts are settled within the set time. These discounts affect the calculation of credit sales and credit purchases and must be included in the calculation.

Example

Tobias Ambunda supplied the following information:

	1 November 20–7 $	31 October 20–8 $
Debtors	3 330	3 660
Creditors	2 900	3 080

During the year ended 31 October 20–8, Tobias received $41 100 from his debtors, after deduction of $1 010 cash discount, and he paid $32 320 to his creditors, after $2 160 cash discount was deducted.

Calculate the credit sales and credit purchases for the year ended 31 October 20–8.

Tobias Ambunda

Total Debtors account

Date	Details	Folio	$	Date	Details	Folio	$
20–7				20–8			
Nov 1	Balance		3 330	Oct 31	Bank		41 100
20–8					Discount		1 010
Oct 31	Sales*		42 440		Balance	c/d	3 660
			45 770				45 770
20–8							
Nov 1	Balance	b/d	3 660				

*Inserted as balancing figure

Total Creditors account

Date	Details	Folio	$	Date	Details	Folio	$
20–8				20–7			
Oct 31	Bank		32 320	Nov 1	Balance		2 900
	Discount		2 160	20–8			
	Balance	c/d	3 080	Oct 31	Purchases*		34 660
			37 560				37 560
				20–8			
				Nov 1	Balance	b/d	3 080

*Inserted as balancing figure

The discounts would also be shown in the Profit and Loss Account in the usual way.

Mark-up, margin, and stock turnover

It is sometimes necessary to use percentages to calculate missing information in incomplete records.

Mark-up and Margin

The **margin** is the gross profit measured as a percentage of the selling price. The **mark-up** is the gross profit measured as a percentage of the cost price; this is the amount added to the cost price to determine the selling price.

■ **Example**

The sales of a business for July were $50 000. The cost of goods sold was $40 000. Calculate (i) the mark-up (ii) the margin.

(i) Mark-up = $\dfrac{\text{Gross Profit}}{\text{Cost of sales}} \times \dfrac{100}{1} = \dfrac{\$10\,000}{\$40\,000} \times \dfrac{100}{1} = 25\%$

(ii) Margin = $\dfrac{\text{Gross Profit}}{\text{Sales}} \times \dfrac{100}{1} = \dfrac{\$10\,000}{\$50\,000} \times \dfrac{100}{1} = 20\%$

These calculations can be used to calculate a missing figure in a Trading Account.

■ **Example**

A business provides the following information for the year ended 30 April 20–3:

	$
Sales	30 000
Stock 1 May 20–2	2 500
Stock 30 April 20–3	3 200
Average Mark-up 50%	

Prepare a Trading Account to show the calculation of the purchases for the year.

Trading Account for the year ended 30 April 20–3

	$	$
Sales		30 000
Less Cost of goods sold		
Opening stock	2 500	
Purchases	20 700(c)	
	23 200(b)	
Less Closing stock	3 200	20 000(a)
Gross Profit		10 000

178 Accounting: IGCSE

Notes:
1. The Trading account was drawn up and the figures for sales, opening stock, and closing stock were inserted, leaving gaps for purchases, cost of sales and gross profit.
2. The gross profit was calculated and inserted in the account.

   Cost price + Profit = Selling price   Therefore 100 + 50 = 150
   Selling price = $30 000 = 150%

   $$\text{Gross Profit} = \frac{50}{150} \times \frac{\$30\,000}{1} = \$10\,000$$

3. The purchases figure was calculated by working "backwards" from the gross profit – steps (a) to (c).

Calculations on mark-up and margin can be used to find any one unknown figure in a Trading Account.

Rate of Stock Turnover

This is the number of times a business replaces its stock in a given period. The formula is –

$$\frac{\text{Cost of goods sold}}{\text{Average stock}}$$

The importance of stock turnover will be explained in Chapter 20.

It is sometimes necessary to use this formula to calculate a missing figure in a Trading Account.

■ **Example**

A business provided the following information for the year ended 30 September 20–5:

	$
Stock 1 October 20–4	6 800
Stock 30 September 20–5	6 000
Mark-up 25%	
Rate of turnover 5 times a year	

Prepare a Trading Account for the year ended 30 September 20–5. Show all workings.

Calculations:

1. Average stock = $\frac{\$6\,800 + \$6\,000}{2} = \$6\,400$

2. Rate of turnover = $5 = \frac{\text{Cost of goods sold}}{\text{Average stock}} = \frac{\text{Cost of goods sold}}{\$6\,400}$

   Therefore Cost of goods sold = 5 × $6 400 = $32 000

Chapter 15 – Incomplete records

3. Mark-up = 25%
   Therefore gross profit = 25% × $32 000 = $8 000

4. Sales and purchases are found by working "backwards" from the gross profit and cost of goods sold in the Trading Account.

Trading Account for the year ended 30 September 20–5

	$	$
Sales		40 000
Less Cost of goods sold		
Opening stock	6 800	
Purchases	31 200	
	38 000	
Less Closing stock	6 000	32 000
Gross Profit		8 000

Review questions

1. (a) (i) What is a Statement of Affairs?
       (ii) In what circumstances is a Statement of Affairs prepared?
   (b) (i) Explain the difference between mark-up and margin.
       (ii) A trader bought goods for $200 and sold them for $250. What is
            1. the mark-up, expressed as a percentage, and
            2. the margin, expressed as a percentage.
   (c) A business provided the following information for the year ended 31 May 20–4:

	$
Sales	82 000
Cost of sales	45 000
Stock 1 June 20–3	8 000
Stock 31 May 20–4	12 000

   What was the rate of turnover for the year ended 31 May 20–4?

2. Mike Kimathi has a food store. On the evening of 31 March 20–6 his shop was flooded and all the stock destroyed. On 1 January 20–6 Mike's stock was valued at $14 000. From 1 January to 31 March 20–6 his sales were $70 000 and his purchases were $48 000. His profit margin is 25%.
   Calculate the cost of the stock destroyed. Show your answer in the form of a Trading Account.

3. Johnny Neumbo runs a small electrical business, buying and selling entirely on credit terms. His financial year-end is 31 March. He does not keep complete accounting records, but is able to provide the following information about his financial position.

	At 1 April 1996	At 31 March 1997
	$	$
Trade debtors	2 000	3 000
Trade creditors	1 200	1 500
Stock of goods	4 800	5 200

During the year ended 31 March 1997 –
Cheques received from trade debtors amounted to $10 000
Cheques paid to trade creditors totalled $6 700.

(a) Calculate Johnny's sales and purchases for the year ended 31 March 1997. Show your workings.

(b) Calculate Johnny's gross profit for the year ended 31 March 1997. Show your workings.

[IGCSE 1997]

4. Estelle owns a general store, buying all her goods on credit. Sales are on both cash and credit terms. Full accounting records are not kept, but Estelle supplies the following information about her business for the year ended 30 September 2000:

	At 1 October 1999	At 30 September 2000
	$	$
Stock	26 000	16 000
Debtors	15 000	12 000
Creditors	11 500	14 000

Other information for the year is as follows:

	$
Receipts from debtors	125 000
Payments to creditors	85 000
Discounts allowed	3 000
Discounts received	2 500
Cash sales	25 000

(a) Extract the necessary information from the above figures and calculate Estelle's sales and purchases for the year ended 30 September 2000. Show your workings.

(b) Use your answer to (a), together with other information you have been given, to prepare Estelle's Trading Account for the year ended 30 September 2000.

[IGCSE 2000]

5. Ashraf Latiff is a sole trader who does not keep full accounting records. He is able to provide the following information:

	At 1 May 20–4 $	At 30 April 20–5 $
Fixed assets at cost	40 000	53 000
Current assets	20 000	33 000
Current liabilities	16 000	24 000

It is decided that the fixed assets held at 30 April 20–5 should be depreciated by 15% on cost. Ashraf estimates that he has withdrawn $9 000 from the business for his own use during the year ended 30 April 20–5.
(a) Draw up Ashraf's Statement of Affairs at 1 May 20–4.
(b) Draw up Ashraf's Statement of Affairs at 30 April 20–5.
(c) Calculate Ashraf's profit or loss for the year ended 30 April 20–5.

*6. Maria carries on business as a trader. She has not kept proper records of her transactions for the year to 30 April 1998. However, the following information is available:

	At 1 May 1997 $	At 30 April 1998 $
Fixtures and fittings	12 000	10 000
Stock	4 000	5 000
Debtors	600	720
Creditors	120	300
Rent owing	400	–
Rates paid in advance	140	180
Balance at bank	6 025	to be found

Maria's receipts and payments for the year to 30 April 1998 were –

		$
Receipts (all banked)	Cash sales	19 000
	Receipts from debtors	5 640
Payments (by cheque)	Payments to creditors	3 660
	Wages	2 200
	Rent	6 000
	Rates	5 100
	Electricity	615
	Personal drawings	14 000

There were no purchases or sales of fixed assets during the year.
(a) Prepare Maria's cash book (bank columns) for the year to 30 April 1998.
(b) Prepare Maria's Trading and Profit and Loss Account for the year to 30 April 1998.
(c) State and explain the advice you would give Maria about her drawings from the business during the year to 30 April 1998. Use your answers to (a) and (b).

[IGCSE 1998]

7. Glenn Charles is a retailer. He does not keep a complete accounting system, but the following information is available from his records:

	At 31 March 1995 $	At 31 March 1996 $
Stock	4 000	6 000
Trade debtors	2 500	3 600
Trade creditors	2 000	2 500
Shop fittings	5 000	4 500
Balance at bank	1 100	1 800

His bank account for the year ended 31 March 1996 showed –
(i) cheques received from trade debtors $20 500
(ii) cash sales banked $2 500
(iii) cheques paid to trade creditors $17 200
Glenn's drawings for the year were $7 200.

From the above information, calculate Glenn's
(a) Purchases and sales for the year ended 31 March 1996;
(b) Capital at 31 March 1995 **and** 31 March 1996;
(c) Net profit for the year ended 31 March 1996.

[IGCSE 1996]

CHAPTER 16

Accounts of clubs and societies

The previous chapters have been concerned with the accounts of businesses. Accounts are also maintained by non-trading organisations such as sports clubs, drama groups, youth clubs and so on.

The main aim of a business is to earn a profit, whereas the main aim of a non-trading organisation is to provide facilities and services for its members. Most businesses maintain double entry accounting records, but many non-trading organisations only maintain a cash book. At the end of the financial year, the treasurer often prepares a summary of the cash book, known as a **Receipts and Payments Account**. If there is some form of regular trading, such as a snack bar, sports shop, etc., a **Trading Account** may be prepared. This is very similar to a Trading Account prepared by a business. A trading organisation prepares a Profit and Loss Account at the end of the financial year. A non-trading organisation prepares an **Income and Expenditure Account** instead of a Profit and Loss Account. A non-trading organisation prepares a Balance Sheet in the same way as a trading business, but capital is replaced by **Accumulated Fund**.

Receipts and payments account

This is a summary of the cash book for the financial period. Any money received during the period is debited and any money paid during the period is credited. The account is then balanced in the usual way. The balance is carried down and becomes the opening balance for the next financial period. This balance may be money in the bank, actual cash, or a combination of the two. A debit balance represents money owned, and is an asset, a credit balance represents a bank overdraft, and is a liability.

This account records all money paid and received during the period. Non-monetary items such as depreciation are not entered in this account, and no adjustments are made for accruals and prepayments. No distinction is made between capital expenditure and revenue expenditure, or between capital receipts and revenue receipts.

■ **Example**

The Hamlet Drama Club was formed some years ago. On 1 July 20–5 it had $3 700 in the bank. All receipts are paid into the bank and all payments are made by cheque.

The treasurer provided the following information of money received and paid during the year ended 30 June 20–6:

	$
Subscriptions received	3 900
Receipts from café sales	3 500
Purchases of café supplies	1 620
Purchase of new equipment	1 750
Wages of part-time café assistant	1 000
Wages of part-time caretaker	1 600
Rates and insurance	480
Receipts from tickets for annual play	2 220
Expenses of annual play	1 650
Administration expenses	740

Prepare the Receipts and Payments Account of the Hamlet Drama Club for the year ended 30 June 20–6.

Hamlet Drama Club

Recepts and Payments Account for the year ended 30 June 20–6

Receipts	$	Payments	$
Balance 1 July 20–5	3 700	Purchases of café supplies	1 620
Subscriptions	3 900	Equipment	1 750
Receipts from café	3 500	Wages – café assistant	1 000
Ticket sales for play	2 220	caretaker	1 600
		Rates and insurance	480
		Expenses of play	1 650
		Administration expenses	740
		Balance 30 June 20–6	4 480
	13 320		13 320

Trading account

Some non-trading organisations do carry out a regular trading activity, but this is not the main purpose of the organisation. Many clubs and societies have a café, a shop, a bar, and so on, where goods are bought and sold. A Trading Account should be prepared for each trading activity in order to calculate the gross profit or loss earned. The gross profit of a business is calculated in the Trading Account and then transferred to the Profit and Loss Account. In a similar way, the gross profit of a trading activity of a non-trading organisation is calculated in the Trading Account and then transferred to the Income and Expenditure Account.

■ **Example** The Hamlet Drama Club was formed some years ago. The club has a café where soft drinks, beverages, sandwiches and confectionery are on sale to members and visitors. The following information is available for the year ended 30 June 20–6:

	$
Stock 1 July 20–5	350
Stock 30 June 20–6	440
Sales	3 500
Purchases	1 620
Wages of part-time café assistant	1 000

Prepare the Trading Account for the Café for the year ended 30 June 20–6

Hamlet Drama Club

Trading Account for the Café for the year ended 30 June 20–6

	$	$
Sales		3 500
Less Cost of sales		
Opening stock	350	
Purchases	1 620	
	1 970	
Less Closing stock	440	
Cost of goods sold	1 530	
Wages of assistant	1 000	2 530
Profit on café (transferred to Income and Expenditure Account)		970

Note: Any direct expenses of the trading activity, the wages of the café assistant in this example, should be added to the cost of the goods in order to calculate accurate figures for cost of sales and profit earned.

The above Trading Account was presented using the vertical format. The horizontal format would be equally acceptable.

It is sometimes necessary to calculate the sales and purchases for the financial period. This is done using a similar calculation to that used for calculating these figures where only incomplete accounting records are available for a business (see Chapter 15).

■ **Example**   The Hamlet Drama Club has a café. All the sales are for cash and all purchases are made on credit terms. The following information is available –

	$
Creditors 1 July 20–5	60
Creditors 30 June 20–6	80

The Receipts and Payments Account for the year ended 30 June 20–6 showed $1 620 was paid to creditors during the year.

Calculate the purchases for the year.

Total Creditors account

Date	Details	Folio	$	Date	Details	Folio	$
20–6				20–5			
June 30	Bank		1 620	July 1	Balance		60
	Balance	c/d	80	20–6			
				June 30	Purchases		1 640
			1 700				1 700
				20–6			
				July 1	Balance	b/d	80

The purchases for the year of $1 640 would appear in the Trading Account (instead of the $1 620 shown in the previous example). The profit on the café transferred to the Income and Expenditure Account would therefore be $950.

Income and expenditure account

This is similar to the Profit and Loss Account prepared for a business. It lists all the expenses of the organisation and all the gains. Where the expenses are lower than the gains, the difference is referred to as a **Surplus** or **Excess of Income over Expenditure**. A business refers to this difference as a net profit. Where the expenses are more than the gains, the difference is referred to as a **Deficit** or **Excess of Expenditure over Income**. A business refers to this difference as a net loss.

In preparing a Profit and Loss Account for a trading business, the **matching** concept is applied and expenses are adjusted for accruals and prepayments. This is also applied when an Income and Expenditure Account is prepared. Any non-monetary expenses, such as depreciation, are also taken into account in the Income and Expenditure Account, in the same way as in a Profit and Loss Account. Capital receipts and capital expenditure do not appear in a Profit and Loss Account, nor do they appear in an Income and Expenditure Account.

The Income and Expenditure Account of a non-trading organisation is prepared from the Receipts and Payments Account, together with any information supplied about accruals, prepayments, depreciation, profits or losses on sales of fixed assets, and any profits or losses from any trading activities.

■ Example

The Hamlet Drama Club was formed some years ago. The following is the Receipts and Payments Account for the year ended 30 June 20–6.

Hamlet Drama Club

Receipts and Payments Account for the year ended 30 June 20–6

Receipts	$	Payments	$
Balance 1 July 20–5	3 700	Purchases of café supplies	1 620
Subscriptions	3 900	Equipment	1 750
Receipts from café	3 500	Wages – café assistant	1 000
Ticket sales for play	2 220	caretaker	1 600
		Rates and insurance	480
		Expenses of play	1 650
		Administration expenses	740
		Balance 30 June 20–6	4 480
	13 320		13 320

1. At 30 June 20–6 –
   Subscriptions owed by members for the current financial year amounted to $180.
   Subscriptions received from members for the next financial year amounted to $90.
   Insurance prepaid amounted to $75.
   Caretaker's wages outstanding amounted to $35.
   Equipment is to be depreciated by $750.
2. The profit on the café for the year ended 30 June 20–6 was $950.

Prepare the Income and Expenditure Account of the Hamlet Drama Club for the year ended 30 June 20–6.

Hamlet Drama Club

Income and Expenditure Account for the year ended 30 June 20–6

	$	$
Income		
Subscriptions (3900 + 180 – 90)		3 990
Profit on café		950
Annual play – Ticket sales	2 220	
Less expenses	1 650	570
		5 510
Expenditure		
Wages of caretaker (1600 + 35)	1 635	
Rates and insurance (480 – 75)	405	
Administration expenses	740	
Depreciation of equipment	750	3 530
Surplus for the year		1 980

The above Income and Expenditure Account was presented using the vertical format.

If the horizontal format were used it would be shown as follows:

Hamlet Drama Club

Income and Expenditure Account for the year ended 30 June 20–6

Expenditure	$	Income	$	$
Wages of caretaker (1600 + 35)	1 635	Subscriptions		
Rates & insurance (480 – 75)	405	(3900 + 180 – 90)		3 990
Administration expenses	740	Profit on café		950
Depreciation of equipment	750	Annual play –		
Surplus for the year	1 980	Ticket sales	2 220	
		Less expenses	1 650	570
	5 510			5 510

Chapter 16 – Accounts of clubs and societies

Notes:
1. The subscriptions, insurance and wages have all been adjusted for accruals and/or prepayments, so that each item shows the total relating to the current financial year.
2. The purchase of equipment does not appear under expenditure as this is capital expenditure. The loss in value of equipment, the non-monetary expense of depreciation, is shown under expenditure.
3. The opening and closing bank balances are not included as these are neither items of income nor items of expenditure.
4. The income and expenses of the annual play have been set against each other so the profit on the activity can be clearly seen. This should be done for any fund-raising activity held by a non-trading organisation.

Balance sheet

The Balance Sheet of a non-trading organisation is very similar to a Balance Sheet of a trading business. The main difference is that a non-trading organisation has no capital. When a business is set up, the owner usually invests capital in the business, which may be added to at a later date. The capital will increase if the business makes a profit and will decrease if the business makes a loss or when the owner makes drawings.

The members of a non-trading organisation do not invest in the organisation with a view to earning a profit, and therefore cannot make withdrawals of profit if the organisation makes a surplus. The surpluses accumulate within the organisation and form a capital fund, known as the **Accumulated Fund**. If the organisation makes a deficit, this will reduce the accumulated fund.

The accumulated fund is shown in the Balance Sheet of a non-trading organisation in a similar way to the capital in the Balance Sheet of a trading business.

■ **Example**

The Hamlet Drama Club was formed some years ago. On 1 July 20–5 the assets and liabilities were as follows –

	$
Premises at cost	24 000
Equipment at cost	5 750
Bank	3 700
Café stock	350
Creditors for café supplies	60
Accumulated Fund	33 740

The Income and Expenditure for the year ended 30 June 20–6 showed a surplus of $1 980, after charging depreciation on equipment of $750.

During the year ended 30 June 20–6 purchases of equipment amounted to $1 750.

At 30 June 20–6 –

	$
Bank	4 480
Café stock	440
Creditors for café supplies	80
Subscriptions owing by members	180
Subscriptions paid in advance by members	90
Wages outstanding	35
Insurance prepaid	75

Prepare the Balance Sheet of the Hamlet Drama Club as at 30 June 20–6.

Hamlet Drama Club

Balance Sheet as at 30 June 20–6

	$	$	$
Fixed assets	Cost	Depreciation to date	Net book value
Premises	24 000	–	24 000
Equipment (5750 + 1750)	7 500	750	6 750
	31 500	750	30 750
Current assets			
Stock in café		440	
Subscriptions owing by members		180	
Prepayment		75	
Bank		4 480	
		5 175	
Less Current liabilities			
Creditors	80		
Subscriptions prepaid by members	90		
Accrual	35	205	4 970
			35 720
Financed by			
Accumulated Fund			
Opening balance			33 740
Plus Surplus for year			1 980
			35 720

The above Balance Sheet was presented using the vertical format. The horizontal format would be equally acceptable.

It is sometimes necessary to calculate the accumulated fund, as this information is not always supplied. This can be calculated in the same way as the capital of a business is calculated. The assets on a certain date less the liabilities on that date will equal the accumulated fund.

■ Example

On 1 July 20–5 the assets and liabilities of the Hamlet Drama Club were as follows –

	$
Premises at cost	24 000
Equipment at cost	5 750
Bank	3 700
Café stock	350
Creditors for café supplies	60

Calculate the Accumulated Fund as at 1 July 20–5.

Hamlet Drama Club

Calculation of Accumulated Fund as at 1 July 20–5

		$	$
Assets	Premises	24 000	
	Equipment	5 750	
	Bank	3 700	
	Café stock	350	33 800
Liabilities	Creditors for café supplies		60
			33 740

Subscriptions

The subscriptions shown in an Income and Expenditure Account must be the subscriptions relating to the period of time covered by that account. The amount received is adjusted for accruals and prepayments. This calculation may be shown in a ledger account.

A subscriptions account shows the subscriptions relating to all the members of the organisation. It is important to remember that subscriptions are an item of income from the organisation's viewpoint. Any subscriptions owing by the members are an asset and will appear as a debit balance on the subscriptions account. Any subscriptions paid in advance by members are a liability (the organisation has an obligation to provide a period of membership for which the members have already paid), and will appear as a credit balance on the subscriptions account. Because the subscriptions account shows subscriptions relating to all the members, it is possible to have two balances on the account as some members may be in arrears and others may have paid in advance.

■ **Example** During the year ended 30 June 20–6 the Hamlet Drama Club received subscriptions totalling $3 900, which included $90 relating to the next financial year. On 30 June 20–6 members owed $180 subscriptions for the current financial year.

During the year ended 30 June 20–7 the Hamlet Drama Club received subscriptions totalling $4 200, which included $70 relating to the next financial year. There were no subscriptions outstanding for the year ended 30 June 20–7.

Prepare the Subscriptions account for **each** of the years ended 30 June 20–6 and 30 June 20–7.

Hamlet Drama Club

Subscription account

Date	Details	Folio	$	Date	Details	Folio	$
20–6 June 30	Income & Expenditure Balance	c/d	3 990 90	20–6 June 30	Bank Balance	c/d	3 900 180
			4 080				4 080
20–6 July 1	Balance	b/d	180	20–6 July 1	Balance	b/d	90
20–7 June 30	Income & Expenditure Balance	c/d	4 040 70	20–7 June 30	Bank		4 200
			4 290				4 290
				20–7 July 1	Balance	b/d	70

Review questions

1. (a) A school sports club makes a profit by selling sports equipment to the pupils. At the end of the financial year, to which account is this profit transferred?

    [IGCSE 1997]

    (b) State the term used in the Income and Expenditure Account of a non-trading organisation when income for a period exceeds the expenditure.

    [IGCSE 1998]

    (c) State the term used to describe the capital of a non-trading organisation.

    [IGCSE 1998]

(d) In connection with non-trading organisations, what are subscriptions?
(e) Explain why subscriptions paid in advance by members of a club are a liability to the club.

2. On 1 January 1997, the Blennerhasset Sports and Social Club had the following assets and liabilities:

	$
Club premises	20 000
Bar stocks	2 000
Bar creditors	1 800
Subscriptions received in advance	200
Balance at bank	1 300
Cash in hand	200
Electricity charges owing	500

(a) Calculate the balance of the club's Accumulated Fund on 1 January 1997. Show your workings.
(b) State and explain the difference between a Receipts and Payments Account and an Income and Expenditure Account.

[IGCSE 1998]

3. (a) Explain what is meant by the matching principle.
(b) Explain the importance of including in an organisation's final accounts all expenditure paid in advance and all income received in advance.
(c) On 1 April 1995, balances in the ledger of the Nomads Cricket Club included the following:

	$
Insurance (debit)	200
Subscriptions (credit)	500

During the year ended 31 March 1996, the club paid $1 800 for insurance by cheque, and received cheques totalling $2 600 for subscriptions.

On 31 March 1996: insurance paid in advance was $250
subscriptions received in advance were $300.

Write up the club's ledger accounts for Insurance and Subscriptions for the year ended 31 March 1996, showing the balances carried down at that date.

[IGCSE 1996]

4. The following information is extracted from the books of a sports club for the year to 30 April 1999:

	$
Subscriptions owing at 1 May 1998	160
Subscriptions received in the year	2 310
Subscriptions owing at 30 April 1999	200
Stock of refreshments at 1 May 1998	600
Refreshments purchased during the year	4 000
Stock of refreshments at 30 April 1999	370
Sales of refreshments	3 980

(a) Prepare the following accounts for the year to 30 April 1999:
  (i) Subscriptions account
  (ii) Refreshments account.
(b) During each of the past three years, the club's expenditure has exceeded its income.
  (i) State the reason why this should not be allowed to continue.
  (ii) Suggest **two** actions that the club can take to improve the situation.
(c) The club's treasurer says that a club that does not make a good profit every year should be closed. Discuss the treasurer's statement.

[IGCSE 1999]

*5. The following Trial Balance was extracted from the books of the Newport Social Club on 31 August 1996.

	Debit $	Credit $
Accumulated Fund 1 September 1995		48 650
Bar Stocks 1 September 1995	5 200	
Bar purchases	37 200	
Land and buildings	50 000	
Cash at bank	4 550	
Cash in hand	1 750	
Bar takings		83 400
Wages	29 250	
Sports equipment	10 000	
Treasurer's salary	5 000	
Secretarial expenses	3 100	
General expenses	2 500	
Rates and insurance	4 250	
Subscriptions received		17 000
Profit on social events		3 750
	152 800	152 800

The treasurer gave you the following information:
1. All bar purchases and takings were for cash.
2. At 31 August 1996: subscriptions due but unpaid were $700 and bar stocks were $6 000.
3. Of the wages total of $29 250, wages of bar staff were $12 500.
4. Depreciation is to be written off sports equipment at 10% per annum, calculated on the book value at 31 August 1996.

(a) Prepare for the year ended 31 August 1996, the club's
   (i) Bar Trading Account
   (ii) Income and Expenditure Account.
(b) Prepare the club's Balance Sheet as at 31 August 1996.

[IGCSE 1996]

6. (a) State **three** differences between the accounting terms used in trading businesses and those used in non-trading organisations.
   Example:
   Trading business   **Non-trading organisation**
   Cash book   Receipts and Payments Account

On 1 March 1999 Lomas United Football Club had $11 050 in the bank and equipment which had originally cost $1 770. At that date, $10 was outstanding for travelling expenses and insurance was prepaid by $15.

The treasurer produced the following information relating to the year ended 29 February 2000:

	$
Subscriptions received	2 280
Payment of football league fees	50
Ground rent	300
Travelling expenses to away matches	385
General expenses	1 195
Insurance	225
Purchase of new equipment	1 430
Receipts from spectators at home matches	1 500
Net proceeds from New Year party	320

Additional notes

1. All receipts were paid into the bank and all payments were made by cheque.

2. At 29 February 2000 insurance prepaid amounted to $20 and subscriptions owing by members amounted to $120.

3. Equipment is depreciated at 25% p.a. on the total cost of equipment held at the end of the year.

(b) Prepare the Receipts and Payments Account for the year ended 29 February 2000.
(c) Prepare the Income and Expenditure Account for the year ended 29 February 2000.
(d) The Lomas United Football Club hopes to purchase its own football pitch in two year's time. Suggest **four** ways in which the club could raise the extra funds that will be required.

[IGCSE 2000]

CHAPTER 17 Partnership accounts

A partnership is a business in which two or more people work together as owners with a view to making profits. Normally there cannot be more than twenty partners.

A partnership may be formed when a sole trader wishes to expand his (or her) business, or a new business may be established in the form of a partnership. A sole trader may be limited in the capital he is able to invest in the business, but he is entitled to all the profits earned. More capital may be available if a partnership is formed, but the profits have to be shared amongst the partners.

A sole trader must rely on his own judgement and skill and is solely responsible for the day-to-day running of the business. A partnership can take advantage of each partner's knowledge and experience, and the responsibility of managing the business can be shared. All partners can take part in the decisions affecting the business, but this can result in decisions taking longer to put into effect. All the partners must abide by any joint decisions, even if they were not personally in favour of them. In a partnership, as in any group of people working as a team, disagreements may occur. A sole trader is solely responsible for the debts of the business whereas in a partnership all the partners are personally responsible for the debts of the business.

Partnership agreement

It is usual for an agreement to be drawn up when a partnership is formed. This is not legally necessary, but eliminates any confusion and misunderstandings which may arise if no written agreement is prepared. The contents of a partnership agreement in relation to accounting matters should include –

(a) **The amount of capital to be invested by each partner**
It is not necessary for the partners to invest equal amounts. They should agree how much each of them will invest.

(b) **How the profits and losses are to be shared between the partners**
The partners must decide how they will share the profits and losses. They may be shared –
(i) equally
(ii) in proportion to the capital invested by each partner
(iii) in some other ratio.

(c) **If interest on partners' capital is to be paid, and, if so, at what rate**
The partners should decide whether interest will be paid on the capital invested by each partner. If all partners invest the same amount of capital, they may decide that interest will not be paid. Interest is a form of compensation for the interest the partners will lose by investing capital in the business rather than making an investment elsewhere. It is also a form of compensation to a partner who has invested more capital than the other partners.

(d) **If salaries are to be paid to the partners, and, if so, what amount**
The partners must decide whether a salary will be paid to one or more of the partners. They may decide not to pay partners' salaries if they share the work and responsibilities equally. Where one partner has a greater workload or greater responsibilities, it may be decided that a salary will be paid as a form of compensation.

(e) **If interest is to be charged on partners' drawings, and, if so, at what rate**
The partners may decide that they will impose a 'penalty' on those partners who make drawings from the business, in an attempt to deter excessive drawings. Interest is charged on the amount withdrawn, from the date of withdrawal to the end of the financial year.

(f) **If an upper limit is placed on partners' drawings, and, if so, what amount**
The partners must consider whether an upper limit should be placed on partners' drawings, which they will not be allowed to exceed. It is much better for the business if drawings are kept to a minimum.

(g) **If interest on partners' loans is to be paid, and, if so, at what rate**
The partnership business may borrow from one of the partners when extra funds are required. The partners must decide on the rate of interest to be paid if such a loan is obtained. A loan from a partner is *not* regarded as part of that partner's capital, and a separate loan account is opened. The loan interest appears with any other loan interest in the Profit and Loss Account, and the loan appears with any other loans in the long-term liabilities section of the Balance Sheet.

Profit and Loss Appropriation Account

After the preparation of the Profit and Loss Account for the financial year, a partnership business draws up an Appropriation Account to show how the net profit is shared out between the partners. The first step is to add to the net profit any interest charged on drawings. Then the appropriations, or profit shares, set out in the partnership agreement, such as interest on capital and partners' salaries, are deducted. The difference is known as the **residual profit**. This is divided between the partners in the agreed profit-sharing ratio.

■ **Example**

Ann and Joe are in partnership. Their financial year ends on 31 July. Their partnership agreement states –
1. Interest on capital is allowed at 10% per annum.
2. Interest on drawings is charged at 4% on the total drawings for the year.
3. Ann is to receive a salary of $5 000 per annum.
4. The balance of the profit is shared in proportion to the capital invested by each partner.

On 1 August 20–5 the partners' capitals were –
Ann $8 000   Joe $12 000

During the year ended 31 July 20–6 the partners made the following drawings –
Ann $4 000   Joe $3 000

The net profit for the year ended 31 July 20–6 was $9 220.

Prepare the Profit and Loss Appropriation Account of Ann and Joe for the year ended 31 July 20–6.

Ann and Joe
Profit and Loss Appropriation Account for the year ended 31 July 20–6

			$	$	$
Net Profit					9 220
Add Interest on drawings –	Ann			160	
	Joe			120	280
					9 500
Less Interest on capital –	Ann		800		
	Joe		1 200	2 000	
Partner's salary –	Ann			5 000	7 000
					2 500
Profit shares –	Ann (8/20 × $2 500)			1 000	
	Joe (12/20 × $2 500)			1 500	2 500

The above Profit and Loss Appropriation Account was presented using the vertical format. If the horizontal format were used it would be shown as follows –

Ann and Joe
Profit and Loss Appropriation Account for the year ended 31 July 20–6

	$	$		$	$
Interest on capital –			Net Profit		9 220
Ann	800		Interest on drawings –		
Joe	1 200	2 000	Ann	160	
Partner's salary –			Joe	120	280
Ann		5 000			
Profit shares –					
Ann	1 000				
Joe	1 500	2 500			
		9 500			9 500

Partners' ledger accounts

Each partner has a **capital account** in the nominal ledger of the business. Most partnerships restrict the entries in the partners' capital accounts to the actual capital introduced into the business, plus any further capital invested or any permanent decrease in the capital. The capital accounts maintained on this method are referred to as 'fixed' capital accounts.

Another account is required for each partner, in which amounts to which he becomes entitled and amounts with which he is charged are entered. These accounts are known as **current accounts**. Interest on capital, partner's salary, and profit share are credited to the partner's current account, as these are amounts owed to the partner. Interest on drawings and drawings are debited to the partner's current account, as these reduce the amount owed to the partner.

The capital accounts have credit balances as these represent the amount the business owes the partners. The current accounts may have either a credit balance or a debit balance. Where the partner's drawings exceed the total amount of profit to which he is entitled, the account will have a debit balance, representing the amount owed by the partner to the business. Where the partner's drawings are less than the total amount of profit to which he is entitled, the account will have a credit balance representing the amount owed by the business to the partner.

A **drawings account** may also be maintained for each partner. Where this is done, the total will be transferred to the partner's current account at the end of the financial year.

Example

Ann and Joe are in partnership. Their financial year ends on 31 July. The following information is provided for the year ended 31 July 20–6:

	Ann $	Joe $
Capital account 1 August 20–5	8 000	12 000
Current account 1 August 20–5	500 (Cr.)	200 (Cr.)
Drawings for the year	4 000	3 000
Interest on drawings	160	120
Interest on capital	800	1 200
Partner's salary	5 000	–
Profit shares	1 000	1 500

Prepare the Capital account and the Current account of Ann for the year ended 31 July 20–6.

Ann and Joe

Ann Capital account

Date	Details	Folio	$	Date	Details	Folio	$
				20–2 Aug 1	Balance	b/d	8 000

Ann Capital account

Date	Details	Folio	$	Date	Details	Folio	$
20–6 July 31	Drawings		4 000	20–5 Aug 1	Balance	b/d	500
	Interest on drawings		160	20–6 July 31	Interest on capital		800
	Balance	c/d	3 140		Salary		5 000
					Profit share		1 000
			7 300				7 300
				20–6 Aug 1	Balance	b/d	3 140

202 Accounting: IGCSE

Where an examination question involves the preparation of capital and current accounts for more than one partner, it is quicker to set the accounts out in columnar format, showing the accounts side by side.

■ **Example**

Using the information provided in the previous example, prepare the Capital accounts and Current accounts of Ann and Joe for the year ended 31 July 20–6. Present the accounts in columnar format.

Ann and Joe

Capital accounts

Date	Details	Folio	Ann $	Joe $	Date	Details	Folio	Ann $	Joe $
					20–5 Aug 1	Balance	b/d	8 000	12 000

Current accounts

Date	Details	Folio	Ann $	Joe $	Date	Details	Folio	Ann $	Joe $
20–6 July 31	Drawings		4 000	3 000	20–5 Aug 1	Balance	b/d	500	200
	Interest on drawings		160	120	20–6 July 31	Interest on capital		800	1 200
	Balance	c/d	3 140			Salary		5 000	
						Profit share		1 000	1 500
						Balance	c/d		200
			7 300	3 120				7 300	3 120
20–6 Aug 1	Balance	b/d		220	20–6 Aug 1	Balance	b/d	3 140	

Chapter 17 – Partnership accounts 203

Balance sheet

The only difference between the Balance Sheet of a partnership and that of a sole trader is the capital section. This must show the balances on each partner's capital account and current account separately.

An examination question may require current accounts of the partners, and also an extract from the Balance Sheet to show how these accounts appear. In this case, the details of the current accounts need not be written out in full in the Balance Sheet; it is sufficient to put the closing balances. Where an examination question requires only a Balance Sheet extract, it is advisable to show all calculations, which may be within the Balance Sheet or be in the form of a separate working note.

■ **Example**

Ann and Joe are in partnership. Their capital and current accounts for the year ended 31 July 20–6 were shown in the last example.

Prepare a relevant extract from the Balance Sheet of Ann and Joe as at 31 July 20–6 showing the capital and current accounts.

Where the current accounts are shown in full, the Balance Sheet extract would be as follows –

Ann and Joe

Extract from Balance Sheet as at 31 July 20–6

	$ Ann	$ Joe	$ Total
Capital accounts	8 000	12 000	20 000
Current accounts			
Opening balance	500	200	
Interest on capital	800	1 200	
Partner's salary	5 000	–	
Profit share	1 000	1 500	
	7 300	2 900	
Less Drawings	4 000	3 000	
Interest on drawings	160	120	
	4 160	3 120	
	3 140	(220)	2 920
			22 920

Note: The debit balance on Joe's Current account is shown as a minus, reducing the amount owed by the business to the partners.

Where it is only necessary to show the balances of the current accounts, the Balance Sheet extract would be as follows –

Ann and Joe

Extract from Balance Sheet as at 31 July 20–6

	$ Ann	$ Joe	$ Total
Capital accounts	8 000	12 000	20 000
Current accounts	3 140	(220)	2 920
			22 920

Admission of a new partner

When there is any change to the membership of the partnership, this is technically the end of the partnership. One partner may leave the business, or, if more capital and/or skill are required, a new partner may join the partnership. In each case, this is the start of a new partnership.

When a new partner is admitted to the partnership, it is necessary to make adjustments for **Goodwill**. This is an **intangible fixed asset** – it has a monetary value, but no separate physical existence. Intangible fixed assets belong to the business and have a value, but cannot be seen and touched. In addition to Goodwill, other intangible assets are trademarks and brand names.

Applying the concept of **prudence**, Goodwill does not usually appear in the books of a business. Goodwill is the value of a business over and above the value of its recorded assets. This is affected by such factors as the location of the business premises; the reputation of the business; the quality of goods or services provided by the business; the possession of trademarks and brand names; the efficiency of the workforce; the number of regular customers; the contacts with reliable suppliers, and so on.

When an existing business is taken over, the new owner benefits from the Goodwill built up by the previous owner. The difference between the value of the identifiable net assets and the purchase price, is the amount paid for this Goodwill.

In a similar way, a new partner joining an existing partnership will benefit from the Goodwill built up by the existing partners, who must be compensated for this. Even if Goodwill does not appear on the books, a value must be placed on it. A Goodwill account is opened, and the necessary adjustments recorded.

If it is decided that an account for Goodwill will be kept on the books the entries may be summarised as –

Debit Goodwill account
Credit Capital accounts of the partners in the old firm
} with the Goodwill split in the old profit-sharing ratio.

In this case the Goodwill account remains open and would appear in any future Balance Sheet as an intangible fixed asset.

If it is decided that an account for Goodwill will *not* be kept on the books, the entries may be summarised as –

Debit Goodwill account
Credit Capital accounts of the partners in the old firm
} with the Goodwill split in the old profit-sharing ratio.

Debit Capital accounts of the partners in the new firm
Credit Goodwill account
} with the Goodwill split in the new profit-sharing ratio.

In this case, the Goodwill account is opened and then immediately closed.

■ **Example**

Ann and Joe are in partnership. Their financial year ends on 31 July. They share profits and losses in proportion to the capital invested by each partner.

On 1 August 20–7 their capitals were –
Ann $8 000   Joe $12 000

Goodwill did not appear on the books but was valued at $6 000 on 1 August 20–7.

On that date they decided to admit Ken to the partnership. He agreed to pay $10 000 into the business bank account.

Profits and losses in the new partnership are to be shared in the ratio –
Ann – 2/6   Joe – 3/6   Ken – 1/6

(a) Assume that Goodwill is to be kept on the books.
Show the Goodwill account and the Capital accounts of Ann, Joe and Ken immediately after the admission of Ken.

(b) Assume that Goodwill is **not** to be kept on the books.
Show the Goodwill account and the Capital accounts of Ann, Joe and Ken immediately after the admission of Ken.

Ann, Joe and Ken

(a) Assuming Goodwill is kept on the books

Goodwill account

Date	Details	Folio	$	Date	Details	Folio	$
20–7 Aug 1	Capital Ann Joe		2 400 3 600 6 000	20–7 Aug 1	Balance	c/d	6 000 6 000
20–7 Aug 2	Balance	b/d	6 000				

Capital accounts

			Ann	Joe	Ken				Ann	Joe	Ken
Date	Details	Folio	$	$	$	Date	Details	Folio	$	$	$
20–7 Aug 1	Balance	c/d	10 400 10 400	15 600 15 600	10 000 10 000	20–7 Aug 1	Balance Bank Goodwill	b/d	8 000 2 400 10 400	12 000 3 600 15 600	 10 000 10 000
						20–7 Aug 2	Balance	b/d	10 400	15 600	10 000

(b) Assuming Goodwill is not kept on the books

Goodwill account

Date	Details	Folio	$	Date	Details	Folio	$
20–7 Aug 1	Capital Ann Joe		2 400 3 600 6 000	20–7 Aug 1	Capital Ann Joe Ken		2 000 3 000 1 000 6 000

Capital accounts

Date	Details	Folio	Ann $	Joe $	Ken $	Date	Details	Folio	Ann $	Joe $	Ken $
20–7 Aug 1	Goodwill Balance	c/d	2 000 8 400	3 000 12 600	1 000 9 000	20–7 Aug 1	Balance Bank Goodwill	b/d	8 000 2 400	12 000 3 600	– 10 000
			10 400	15 600	10 000				10 400	15 600	10 000
						20–7 Aug 2	Balance	b/d	8 400	12 600	9 000

Review questions

1. (a) You are preparing the final accounts of a partnership. In which of these final accounts are the following items shown?
    1. Interest on partners' capital accounts
    2. Interest on a partner's loan account
    3. Rent of partnership offices

    [IGCSE 1997]

   (b) Explain what is meant by a Profit and Loss Appropriation Account in a partnership.

   [IGCSE 1996]

   (c) Name **two** items that would appear in a partner's current account.

   [IGCSE 1995]

   (d) Name **one** item which would appear in a partnership's Profit and Loss Appropriation Account.

   [IGCSE 2000]

   (e) (i) Name the final account of a partnership which shows the division of profits.

   (ii) Bill and Ben are partners, sharing profits and losses in the ratio of 3:2. Ben receives an annual salary of $10 000. For the year ending 31 March 2000, the partnership's net profit is $40 000. Calculate the amount credited to Ben's Current account on 31 March 2000. Show your workings.

   [IGCSE 2000]

   (f) A business is purchased for $100 000. The value of the net assets is only $92 000.
   (i) What is the name given to the difference between these two figures?
   (ii) Where will this appear in the Balance Sheet of the new business?

2. Abee and Seedy are in partnership. The following details are available: The partners are charged interest on drawings at 10% per annum and are allowed interest on capital at 10% per annum.

The partners' capital account balances at 1 October 1997 were as follows –
Abee $10 000   Seedy $5 000

During the year to 30 September 1998, the partners made drawings as follows –
Abee $8 000   Seedy $6 000

Seedy receives a salary of $4 000 per annum.

The balance of profits and losses is shared as follows –
Abee 2/3   Seedy 1/3

The profit for the year ended 30 September 1998 was $40 100.
 (a) Prepare the partners' Profit and Loss Appropriation Account for the year ended 30 September 1998.
 (b) The balances on the partners' Current accounts at 1 October 1997 were:
    Abee $5 000 (Credit)   Seedy $2 000 (Credit)

Prepare the partners' current accounts for the year ended 30 September 1998.

[IGCSE 1998]

3. A and B are partners in a business. State **two** advantages, and **two** disadvantages, of admitting an additional partner, C.

[IGCSE 1999]

4. Kafri and Ogus are partners. They have agreed the following:
 (i) Interest is to be allowed on capital at 7% per annum.
 (ii) Interest is to be charged on drawings at 5% per annum.
 (iii) Ogus is to receive an annual salary of $12 000.
 (iv) Profits and losses are to be shared in proportion to their capital.

 (a) Explain **why** the partnership agreement of Kafri and Ogus included arrangements for each of the following:
    (i) Interest on capital
    (ii) Interest on drawings
    (iii) Partner's salary for Ogus

For the year ended 31 August 2000 the partnership earned a net profit of $24 600.

Chapter 17 – Partnership accounts 209

On 31 August 2000 the following balances appeared in the partnership books:

			$
Capital account (at 1 September 1999)	Kafri		30 000
	Ogus		20 000
Current account (at 1 September 1999)	Kafri		3 600 (Credit)
	Ogus		1 200 (Debit)
Drawings during the year ended	Kafri		9 000
31 August 2000	Ogus		17 000

(b) Prepare the Profit and Loss Appropriation Account of Kafri and Ogus for the year ended 31 August 2000.
(c) Prepare the partners' Current accounts as they would appear in the ledger for the year ended 31 August 2000.
(d) Show, by means of a Balance Sheet extract, how the partners' capital and current accounts would appear in the Balance Sheet of the partnership at 31 August 2000.

[IGCSE 2000]

5. Abe and Sue Jemiyo are partners. The following Trial Balance was drawn up after the preparation of the Trading Account for the year ended 30 June 20–7:

		Debit $	Credit $
Gross Profit			15 316
Capital account 1 July 20–6 – Abe			24 000
	Sue		12 000
Current account 1 July 20–6 – Abe			800
	Sue		200
Drawings	Abe	2 500	
	Sue	1 500	
Loan account	Abe		6 000
Premises at cost		35 000	
Fixtures and Fittings at cost		6 000	
Motor vehicles at cost		10 000	
Stock at 30 June 20–7		4 700	
Debtors		4 000	
Creditors			5 500
Cash		200	
Bank overdraft			1 324
Provision for doubtful debts			220
Provision for depreciation 1 July 20–6 –			
Fixtures and fittings			1 140
Motor vehicles			2 500
Administration expenses		3 100	
Selling expenses		2 000	
		69 000	69 000

(a) At 30 June 20–7 administration expenses prepaid amounted to $200 and selling expenses accrued amounted to $150.
(b) The provision for doubtful debts is to be maintained at 5% of the debtors.
(c) Fixtures and fittings are being depreciated at 10% per annum using the reducing balance method. Motor vehicles are being depreciated at 25% per annum using the straight line method.
(d) The partnership agreement provides for –
Interest on partner's loan at 5% per annum
Interest on capital at 4% per annum
Profits and losses to be shared equally

Prepare the Profit and Loss Account and the Profit and Loss Appropriation Account of Abe and Sue Jemiyo for the year ended 30 June 20–7, and a Balance Sheet as at 30 June 20–7.

*6. (a) A and B were partners in a business. At 1 April 1997, the balances on their capital accounts were:
A $15 000   B $10 000
A and B have shared profits and losses equally.
   On 1 April 1997, A and B decided to admit C as a partner. C agreed to pay $8 000 into the firm's bank account as capital as soon as he was made a partner.
   It was agreed that Goodwill should be valued at $12 000 and that the capital accounts of A and B should be adjusted for Goodwill on the admission of C.

Show how the Capital accounts of A, B and C appeared in the firm's books immediately after C had been made a partner.

(b) When C was admitted as a partner, it was agreed that the partners should be allowed interest on their capital accounts at the rate of 10% per annum. B was allowed a salary of $12 000 per annum. The balance of profits and losses were to be shared equally between A, B and C.
   Current accounts were opened for the partners. Drawings made by the partners in the year to 31 March 1998 were as follows –
$
A   16 000
B   17 000
C   15 000

In the year to 31 March 1998 the partnership made a profit of $81 000.

(i) Prepare the Profit and Loss Appropriation Account of the partnership for the year to 31 March 1998.
(ii) Show how the partners' Current accounts will appear in the books of the partnership at 31 March 1998.

[IGCSE 1998]

7. Miriam and Salem are in partnership. They share profits and losses equally. On 1 February 20–2 they decided to invite their younger brother, Mohsen, to join the partnership.

At that date Miriam's capital was $30 000, and Salem's was $20 000. Goodwill was valued at $10 000, but did not appear on the books. It was agreed that adjustments should be made for Goodwill, but that a Goodwill account would not be maintained on the books.

Mohsen introduced $15 000 into the business bank account. It was agreed that the partners would share profits and losses 2:2:1.

(a) Prepare journal entries, with narratives, to show –
   (i) the admission of Mohsen
   (ii) the adjustments to the Goodwill.
(b) Explain to Mohsen what is meant by 'Goodwill' and how it can arise.
(c) Explain why it is necessary to value Goodwill before Mohsen joins the partnership.

CHAPTER 18

Accounts of manufacturing businesses

All the previous chapters (apart from Chapter 16) have been concerned with the accounts of businesses involved in trading, that is the buying and selling of goods without changing them in any way. Many businesses, however, buy raw material and manufacture products, which are then sold as finished goods.

A manufacturing business maintains all the usual basic double entry records kept by all businesses. At the end of the financial year, in addition to the Trading and Profit and Loss Account (Appropriation Account where needed) and Balance Sheet, a manufacturing business also prepares a **Manufacturing Account**. This account shows how much it cost the business to make (manufacture) the goods produced in the financial year.

Preparation of Manufacturing Accounts

There are four main elements of cost which make up the cost of manufacture (sometimes known as the **cost of production**). These are –

1. **Direct Material**
   This is the raw material that is required to make the finished goods. It is the first essential cost and is the first item shown in a Manufacturing Account. The cost of raw material actually used (or consumed) during the financial year must be calculated. This is similar to the calculation of cost of goods sold. Raw material used is calculated as follows –
   Opening stock of raw material
   Plus purchases of raw material
   Plus carriage inwards on raw material
   Less closing stock of raw material

2. **Direct Labour**
   This is the cost of the wages and salaries of the people who are employed in the actual manufacture of the finished products. The cost of the direct labour, sometimes known as **direct wages**, is the next essential cost of manufacture. In the Manufacturing Account, direct labour is added to the cost of the raw material used.

   Only the wages of the actual factory operatives are included in this figure. Wages and salaries of supervisors, cleaners, etc. are **not** regarded as direct wages.

3. **Direct Expenses**
   These consist of any expense which can be directly identified with each item produced. The hire charge for a special machine to carry out a particular part of the manufacturing process, or a royalty payable to the person who invented the product originally, are examples of direct

expenses. These expenses are added to the direct material and the direct labour in the Manufacturing Account.

4. **Factory Overheads**

   All the other costs of manufacturing are regarded as factory overheads or **indirect factory expenses**. These expenses are the costs of operating the factory, but which cannot be directly linked to the goods being produced. Any expenses of running the factory such as rent and rates, machinery repairs, factory indirect wages, depreciation of factory machinery, and so on, are all regarded as factory overheads. These overheads are added to the direct costs in the Manufacturing Account.

   In a Manufacturing Account the term **Prime Cost** is used to describe the cost of the direct material, plus the cost of the direct labour, plus the cost of the direct expense. The term **Cost of Production** or **Production Cost of Completed Goods** is used to describe the prime cost plus the factory overheads.

■ **Example**

The following balances were taken from the books of Lebengo Manufacturing Company on 31 March 20–8:

		$
Raw material –	Stock 1 April 20–7	4 500
	Purchases	52 000
	Stock 31 March 20–8	4 950
Carriage on raw material		1 050
Factory wages – direct		49 800
	indirect	32 600
Factory light and power		2 750
Factory general expenses		4 100
Factory machinery repairs		1 950
Depreciation of factory machinery		5 000

Prepare the Manufacturing Account of Lebengo Manufacturing Company for the year ended 31 March 20–8.

Lebengo Manufacturing Company

Manufacturing Account for the year ended 31 March 20–8

	$	$
Cost of material consumed		
Opening stock of raw material	4 500	
Purchases of raw material	52 000	
Carriage on purchases	1 050	
	57 550	
Less Closing stock of raw material	4 950	52 600
Direct wages		49 800
Prime Cost		102 400
Factory overheads		
Indirect wages	32 600	
Light and power	2 750	
General expenses	4 100	
Machinery repairs	1 950	
Depreciation of machinery	5 000	46 400
Production cost of goods completed		148 800

The above Manufacturing Account was presented using the vertical format. If the horizontal format were used it would be shown as follows –

Lebengo Manufacturing Company

Manufacturing Account for the year ended 31 March 20–8

	$	$		$
Cost of material consumed			Production cost of	
Opening stock of raw material		4 500	goods completed c/d	148 800
Purchases of raw material		52 000		
Carriage on purchases		1 050		
		57 550		
Less closing stock of raw material		4 950		
		52 600		
Direct wages		49 800		
Prime cost		102 400		
Factory overheads				
Indirect wages	32 600			
Light and power	2 750			
General expenses	4 100			
Machinery repairs	1 950			
Depreciation of machinery	5 000	46 400		
		148 800		148 800

Work in Progress

In practice it is very probable that some of the goods will only be partly made at the end of the financial year. These items which are partly made, but which are not yet completed, are known as **Work in Progress**. It is necessary to exclude work in progress from the cost of production, as these goods are not yet in a state in which they can be sold. Costs have been incurred in bringing the goods to that point of manufacture, so the work in progress does have some value. Examination questions will state what value is placed on work in progress.

It is important to remember that the closing work in progress at the end of one financial year will become the opening work in progress at the start of the next financial year.

The cost of production must be adjusted for both these stocks of work in progress so that the figure relates only to the cost of goods actually completed in the period. The adjustment is carried out in the same way as for other types of stock – the opening stock is added and the closing stock is deducted.

■ **Example**

The following balances were taken from the books of Lebengo Manufacturing Company on 31 March 20–8:

	$
Prime cost*	102 400
Factory overheads*	46 400
Work in progress – 1 April 20–7	2 100
31 March 20–8	1 900

Prepare the Manufacturing Account of Lebengo Manufacturing Company for the year ended 31 March 20–8.

*Full details would be shown as in the previous example.

Lebengo Manufacturing Company

Manufacturing Account for the year ended 31 March 20–8

	$
Prime Cost	102 400
Factory overheads	46 400
	148 800
Add Opening stock of work in progress	2 100
	150 900
Less Closing stock of work in progress	1 900
Production cost of goods completed	149 000

The above Manufacturing Account was presented using the vertical format. If the horizontal format were used it would be shown as follows –

Lebengo Manufacturing Company

Manufacturing Account for the year ended 31 March 20–8

	$			$
Prime Cost	102 400	Production cost of		
Factory overheads	46 400	goods completed	c/d	149 000
	148 800			
Add Opening stock of work in progress	2 100			
	150 900			
Less Closing stock of work in progress	1 900			
	149 000			149 000

Trading Accounts of manufacturing businesses

The Trading Account of a manufacturing business is very similar to that prepared by any other type of business. It shows the sales less the cost of sales, and the resulting gross profit for the period. As the business actually made the goods, rather than buying them ready-made, the item for purchases is replaced by cost of production. The stocks appearing in a Trading Account are usually referred to as stocks of finished goods, to avoid confusion with stocks of raw material and stocks of work in progress.

It may be that a manufacturing business does purchase *some* finished goods. This occurs where it can purchase them cheaper than it could make them, where it cannot actually make those items, and when it cannot produce enough to meet demand. Purchases of finished goods are added to the cost of production in the Trading Account.

■ **Example**

The following balances were taken from the books of Lebengo Manufacturing Company on 31 March 20–8:

	$
Sales	181 000
Production cost of goods completed*	149 000
Finished goods – Stock 1 April 20–7	5 700
Stock 31 March 20–8	6 200
Purchases of finished goods	2 500

Prepare the Trading Account of Lebengo Manufacturing Company for the year ended 31 March 20–8.

*Calculated in the Manufacturing Account.

Lebengo Manufacturing Company

Trading Account for the year ended 31 March 20–8

	$	$
Sales		181 000
Less Cost of goods sold		
Opening stock of finished goods	5 700	
Production cost of goods completed	149 000	
Purchases of finished goods	2 500	
	157 200	
Less Closing stock of finished goods	6 200	151 000
Gross Profit		30 000

The above Trading Account was presented using the vertical format. If the horizontal format were used it would be shown as follows –

Lebengo Manufacturing Company

Manufacturing Account for the year ended 31 March 20–8

		$		$
Opening stock of finished goods		5 700	Sales	181 000
Production cost of goods completed		149 000		
Purchases of finished goods		2 500		
		157 200		
Less Closing stock of finished goods		6 200		
Cost of goods sold		151 000		
Gross Profit	c/d	30 000		
		181 000		181 000

Profit and Loss Accounts of manufacturing businesses

The Profit and Loss Account of a manufacturing business is exactly the same as that prepared by any other type of business. It shows the gross profit, plus other income, less expenses, and the resulting net profit for the period. It is important to remember that all the expenses relating to the factory have already been entered in the Manufacturing Account, so only administration expenses, selling and distribution expenses, and financial expenses appear in the Profit and Loss Account.

Sometimes expenses relate to the whole of the business, e.g. insurance of buildings, heating and lighting of the buildings. Where this occurs, it is necessary to share the expense between the factory and the offices. Examination questions will state how this apportionment is to be made.

Balance Sheets of manufacturing businesses

The Balance Sheet of a manufacturing business is very similar to that prepared by any other type of business. The only difference is that the manufacturer may have three different types of stock at the date of the Balance Sheet. All three stocks should appear under the current assets in the Balance Sheet.

■ **Example**

The following balances were taken from the books of Lebengo Manufacturing Company on 31 March 20–8:

		$
Stock of raw material –	31 March 20–8	4 950
Stock of work in progress –	31 March 20–8	1 900
Stock of finished goods –	31 March 20–8	6 200

Prepare a relevant extract from Lebengo Manufacturing Company's Balance Sheet as at 31 March 20–8.

Lebengo Manufacturing Company

Extract from Balance Sheet as at 31 March 20–8

	$	$
Current assets		
Stock – Raw material	4 950	
Work in progress	1 900	
Finished goods	6 200	13 050

In order to keep the examples in this chapter as short as possible, year-end adjustments such as accruals and prepayments have not been included. It is important to remember that where such adjustments do occur they should be treated as described in previous chapters.

Review questions

1. (a) State **one** example of factory overhead expenses which might appear in a Manufacturing Account.

    [IGCSE 1998]

   (b) In preparing a Manufacturing Account –
   - (i) name **one** item included in prime cost
   - (ii) name the account to which you would transfer the production cost of finished goods.

    [IGCSE 1997]

   (c) In preparing a Manufacturing Account, state how work in progress at the **end** of the accounting period is shown.

    [IGCSE 1999]

   (d) State the type of expenses in a Manufacturing Account which are added to prime cost to give production cost.

    [IGCSE 1998]

2. Annie Kember owns a business making children's toys. Her accounts are prepared annually to 30 September.

    Balances in Annie's books at 30 September 1996 included the following:

	$
Raw material: Stocks at 1 October 1995	12 000
Purchases	46 000
Carriage inwards	2 000
Factory wages and salaries: Direct	21 000
Indirect	12 000
Factory overheads: Fuel and power	15 000
Rent and rates	8 000

   You are given the following additional information:
   - (a) At 30 September 1996, stocks of raw material were valued at $15 000.
   - (b) There was no work in progress at the beginning or the end of the year.
   - (c) Depreciation of plant and machinery for the year ended 30 September 1996 is to be charged as $10 000.

   Prepare Annie's Manufacturing Account for the year ended 30 September 1996. Show Prime Cost and Factory Cost of Production.

    [IGCSE 1996]

*3. The balances in The X Company's books at 31 March 1999 included the following:

		$
Sales		240 000
Raw material –	Stock at 1 April 1998	13 000
	Purchases	94 000
Carriage inwards		4 400
Finished goods –	Stock at 1 April 1998	11 000
Factory wages –	Direct	36 000
	Indirect	15 000
Factory overheads –	Fuel and power	20 000
	Rent	9 000
Office overheads –	Salaries	16 000
	General expenses	7 600

You are given the following information:
1. Stocks at 31 March 1999

	$
Raw material	15 000
Finished goods	16 000

2. There was no work in progress at the beginning or end of the year.
3. Depreciation for the year ended 31 March 1999 is to be charged as follows –

	$
On factory machinery	18 000
On office equipment	2 000

(a) Prepare The X Company's Manufacturing Account for the year ended 31 March 1999. Show Prime Cost and Factory Cost of Production.
(b) Prepare The X Company's Trading and Profit and Loss Account for the year ended 31 March 1999.

[IGCSE 1999]

4. The following balances were extracted from the books of Bassra Manufacturing Company on 31 May 20–1:

	$
Stocks 1 June 20–0 – Raw material	1 200
Work in progress	2 100
Finished goods	3 200
Purchases of raw material	11 500
Sales	49 500
Wages and salaries – Factory (direct)	14 600
Office	4 200
Rates and insurance	2 650
Manufacturing expenses	850
Provision for depreciation 1 June 20–0 –	
Plant and machinery	4 000
Office equipment	1 400
Plant and machinery at cost	10 000
Office equipment at cost	3 500
Carriage outwards	320
Discount allowed	370
Discount received	490
Factory fuel and power	2 700

Additional information

1. Stocks at 31 May 20–1 were –

	$
Raw material	1 000
Work in progress	2 050
Finished goods	3 400

2. At 31 May 20–0 –

	$
Rates and insurance prepaid amounted to	150
Factory wages accrued amounted to	200

3. Rates and insurance are apportioned – 4/5 factory
   1/5 office

4. Depreciation is written off as follows –
   Plant and machinery – 10% per annum on cost
   Office equipment – 20% per annum on cost

Select the relevant figures from those given above and prepare –
(a) The Bassra Manufacturing Company's Manufacturing Account for the year ended 31 May 20–1
(b) The Bassra Manufacturing Company's Trading and Profit and Loss Account for the year ended 31 May 20–1.

CHAPTER 19

Departmental accounts

If a business has two or more departments, it is important to calculate the contribution made by each department to the business as a whole. The overall profit figure will not reveal which department is earning a profit and which department is operating at a loss. This information is required so that the overall profitability of the business can be improved.

Departmental final accounts show the performance of each department separately. Where the accounts show that a department is not making a profit, changes can be made to try to improve the results, or it may even be decided to close down the department.

Departmental Trading Accounts

A columnar Trading Account is prepared where a business has more than one department. This is prepared in exactly the same way as any other Trading Account. The only difference is that two or more Trading Accounts, one for each department of the business, are prepared side-by-side.

The sales, sales returns, purchases, and purchases returns journals require analysis columns so that separate figures for each department are available. At the end of the financial period, the stock of each department must also be valued separately.

■ **Example**

Nangolo Stores has two departments. Department A sells meat, and Department B sells fruit and vegetables. The following balances were taken from the books of Nangolo Stores on 31 October 20–7.

	Department A $	Department B $
Sales	60 000	20 000
Purchases	40 500	14 000
Stock – 1 November 20–6	8 900	1 500
31 October 20–7	11 100	1 400

Prepare the Departmental Trading Account of Nangolo Stores for the year ended 31 October 20–7.

Nangolo Stores

Departmental Trading Account for the year ended 31 October 20–7

	Department A		Department B		Total	
	$	$	$	$	$	$
Sales		60 000		20 000		80 000
Less Cost of goods sold						
Opening stock	8 900		1 500		10 400	
Purchases	40 500		14 000		54 500	
	49 400		15 500		64 900	
Less Closing stock	11 100	38 300	1 400	14 100	12 500	52 400
Gross Profit		21 700		5 900		27 600

The above Trading Account was presented using the vertical format. If the horizontal format were used it would be shown as follows –

Nangolo Stores

Departmental Trading Account for the year ended 31 October 20–7

		Dept A	Dept B	Total		Dept A	Dept B	Total
		$	$	$		$	$	$
Opening stock		8 900	1 500	10 400	Sales	60 000	20 000	80 000
Purchases		40 500	14 000	54 500				
		49 400	15 500	64 900				
Less Closing stock		11 100	1 400	12 500				
Cost of goods sold		38 300	14 100	52 400				
Gross Profit	c/d	21 700	5 900	27 600				
		60 000	20 000	80 000		60 000	20 000	80 000

Departmental Profit and Loss Accounts

In addition to a columnar Trading Account, it is useful to prepare a columnar Profit and Loss Account. This is prepared in exactly the same way as any other Profit and Loss Account, except that two or more accounts are prepared side-by-side.

It is necessary to share the expenses of the business between the different departments. This must be done in the fairest possible way. Some of the methods of apportioning the expenses between departments are –
(a) The actual cost for each department, where this information is available, e.g. wages of employees in each department.
(b) In proportion to the floor space occupied by each department. This is used for sharing out expenses that are related to area, e.g. insurance, rent, lighting.
(c) In proportion to the sales of each department. This is used for sharing out expenses that are related to the amount of sales, e.g. carriage outwards, advertising.

■ **Example**

Nangolo Stores has two departments. Department A sells meat, and Department B sells fruit and vegetables. The following balances were taken from the books of Nangolo Stores on 31 October 20–7:

	$
Gross Profit for the year ended 31 October 20–7	
Department A	21 700
Department B	5 900
Expenses for the year ended 31 October 20–7	
Wages of sales assistants – Department A	7 000
Department B	4 700
Rent	3 600
Advertising	1 200
Insurance	900
Carriage outwards	1 600

Additional information
$
(a) The sales for the year ended 31 October 20–7 were –
Department A   60 000
Department B   20 000
(b) Department A occupies 2/3 of the total store and Department B occupies 1/3.
(c) The expenses are to be apportioned as follows –
Rent and insurance – on the basis of floor area
Advertising and carriage outwards – on the basis of sales

Prepare the Departmental Profit and Loss Account of Nangolo Stores for the year ended 31 October 20–7.

Nangolo Stores

Departmental Profit and Loss Account for the year ended 31 October 20–7

	Department A		Department B		Total	
	$	$	$	$	$	$
Gross Profit		21 700		5 900		27 600
Less Wages	7 000		4 700		11 700	
Rent	2 400		1 200		3 600	
Advertising	900		300		1 200	
Insurance	600		300		900	
Carriage outwards	1 200	12 100	400	6 900	1 600	19 000
Net Profit (Net Loss)		9 600		(1 000)		8 600

Expenses are apportioned –

		Department A	Department B
Rent		$\frac{2}{3} \times \$3\,600$	$\frac{1}{3} \times \$3\,600$
Insurance		$\frac{2}{3} \times \$900$	$\frac{1}{3} \times \$900$
Advertising		$\frac{\$60\,000}{\$80\,000} \times \$1\,200$	$\frac{\$20\,000}{\$80\,000} \times \$1\,200$
Carriage outwards		$\frac{\$60\,000}{\$80\,000} \times \$1\,600$	$\frac{\$20\,000}{\$80\,000} \times \$1\,600$

The above Profit and Loss Account was presented using the vertical format. If the horizontal format were used it would be shown as follows –

Nangolo Stores

Departmental Profit and Loss Account for the year ended 31 October 20–7

	Dept A	Dept B	Total		Dept A	Dept B	Total
	$	$	$		$	$	$
Wages	7 000	4 700	11 700	Gross Profit b/d	21 700	5 900	27 600
Rent	2 400	1 200	3 600				
Advertising	900	300	1 200				
Insurance	600	300	900				
Carriage outwards	1 200	400	1 600				
Net Profit (Loss)*	9 600	(1 000)	8 600				
	12 700	5 900	27 600		21 700	5 900	27 600

*A net loss is usually shown on the credit side of the Profit and Loss Account. It has been inserted as a minus figure on the debit side so that a total net profit may be shown.

Closure of a department

Departmental final accounts may show that a department is making a loss, or earning only a very low profit. Very careful consideration is needed before a decision is taken to close the department. It may be possible to improve the results, and all possible means should be considered. The methods used to apportion the expenses should be studied to see if they are, in fact, the fairest methods.

The effect of the closure of one department on the rest of the business should be investigated. It must be remembered that not all the expenses apportioned to the department will disappear when the department is closed. Some expenses such as rent and insurance of the building will remain and these will have to be shared among the remaining departments. It may be that one department attracts customers to other departments. Non-monetary factors such as staff morale and the effect on suppliers' and customers' faith in the business are also important.

Finally, the alternative uses of the space becoming available need to be considered. An existing department may be expanded, or a completely new department may be opened, or the space may be rented out to another business.

Review questions

1. (a) State **one** reason why departmental final accounts are prepared.
   (b) Name **two** methods which can be used to apportion expenses between the departments of a business.

2. Pieter's business has two departments – Department A and Department B. The following balances were taken from the books of Pieter on 31 January 20–1:

	Department A $	Department B $
Stock – 1 February 20–0	1 400	2 800
31 January 20–1	1 960	2 170
Sales	14 000	19 000
Purchases	9 900	12 100
Sales returns	150	270
Carriage inwards	210	300

Prepare the Departmental Trading Account of Pieter for the year ended 31 January 20–1.

*3. Sharon Scarlett's shop has two departments. Department A on the ground floor sells ladies' clothing, and Department B on the first floor sells children's clothing.

The following figures were taken from her books at 30 April 2000:

	Department A $	Department B $	Total $
Sales	80 000	40 000	
Stock 1 May 1999	5 500	4 900	
Stock 30 April 2000	5 700	6 300	
Purchases	48 200	31 400	
Expenses –			
Salaries	12 000	8 000	
Rates and insurance			2 000
Administration			4 000
Advertising			1 500
Carriage outwards			600
Depreciation of fixtures			1 000

The expenses are to be apportioned equally between the departments, except for salaries (which are to be charged as shown above), and advertising and carriage outwards, which are to be shared in proportion to the sales of each department.

(a) Prepare Departmental Trading and Profit and Loss Accounts for Sharon Scarlett for the year ended 30 April 2000 to show the gross profit and net profit earned by each department. Total columns are **not** required.

(b) State **two** reasons why it is useful for Sharon to know the results of each department of the business.

(c) Sharon said she was disappointed with the low sales in Department B. She is considering closing that department and operating on the ground floor only.

State **three** items you would advise Sharon to consider before making a decision. You may use your answer to (a).

[IGCSE 2000]

CHAPTER 20
Analysis and interpretation

In order to assess the performance of a business, it is necessary to analyse and interpret the business's final accounts. Analysis involves a detailed review of the information provided in the final accounts. The results of this analysis are interpreted to assess the performance of the business. This may include a comparison with previous years, a comparison with targets or budgets, or even a comparison with other similar businesses.

For a comparison to be meaningful, it is usual to express results in terms of **accounting ratios**. The wording 'accounting ratios' is used to describe all the calculations involved in interpreting accounts, even though some of the calculations are expressed in terms of percentages and time periods. Unless an examination question states otherwise, it is usual to show ratios correct to two decimal places. The ratios may be divided into two groups – those used to measure **profitability** and those used to measure **liquidity**. The information provided in the final accounts of Daniel Duval, shown on the next page, will be used to calculate the main ratios in each group.

The different types of assets and liabilities were explained in Chapter 7. Two uses of the term 'capital' have also been explained. **Capital owned** (or **capital invested**) is the amount owed by a business to the owner of that business on a certain date. **Working capital** is the difference between the current assets and the current liabilities, and is the amount available for the day-to-day running of a business. This is sometimes referred to as **net current assets**.

There is another type of capital which is called **capital employed**. This may be regarded as the total amount of money that is being used in a business, and consists of the owner's capital plus any long-term liabilities. It can also be calculated as fixed assets plus working capital, and is sometimes referred to as **net assets**.

Example

Daniel Duval

Trading and Profit and Loss Account for the year ended 31 March 20–2

	$	$
Sales (all on credit)		100 000
Less Cost of goods sold –		
Opening stock	7 000	
Purchases (all on credit)	72 000	
	79 000	
Less Closing stock	9 000	70 000
Gross Profit		30 000
Less Expenses		20 000
Net Profit		10 000

Balance Sheet as at 31 March 20–2

	$	$
Fixed assets		62 000
Current assets		
Stock	9 000	
Debtors	8 000	
Bank	13 000	
	30 000	
Less Current liabilities		
Creditors	12 000	
Working capital		18 000
		80 000
Less Long-term liabilities		
Loan		12 000
		68 000
Financed by		
Capital		
Opening balance		66 000
Plus Net Profit		10 000
		76 000
Less Drawings		8 000
		68 000

It is possible to define capital employed in several ways – the figure at the start of the period, the figure at the end of the period, or the average of these two figures. Examination questions indicate which definition is to be applied.

Profitability ratios

These are concerned with relating profit figures to other figures within the same final accounts.

Return on capital employed (ROCE)

This is a very important ratio. It shows the profit earned for every $100 of capital employed. This is a measure of the profit as a percentage of the amount invested in the business in order to earn that profit. The higher the rate, the more effectively the capital is being employed.

■ **Formula**

$$\frac{\text{Net profit}}{\text{Capital employed}} \times \frac{100}{1}$$

■ **Example**

Using the final accounts of Daniel's business, and taking capital employed to be the total of the capital owned and the long-term liabilities on 31 March 20–2:

$$\frac{\$10\,000}{\$80\,000} \times \frac{100}{1} = 12.5\%$$

Gross profit as a percentage of sales

This is sometimes known as **gross profit as a percentage of turnover**. Turnover is the net sales (the sales less sales returns). This measures the gross profit for every $100 of sales. It indicates how profitable the sales were. This varies between businesses in different industries or trades. Within one business, the gross profit percentage may be similar from year to year. Generally, the higher the rate the more profitable the business. However, a price-cutting policy may reduce the *rate* but produce a greater *amount* of profit.

Any significant reduction from previous years should be investigated. Possible causes include –
(a) selling goods at cut prices
(b) holding seasonal 'sales'
(c) offering trade discounts to customers buying in bulk
(d) not passing on increased costs to customers.

The gross profit percentage may be improved by such measures as –
(a) looking for cheaper suppliers
(b) increasing selling prices
(c) increasing advertising and sales promotions
(d) changing the proportions of the different types of goods sold.

These measures may improve the gross profit percentage, but can have other effects, e.g. increasing selling prices may result in loss of customers.

■ **Formula**

$$\frac{\text{Gross profit}}{\text{Net sales}} \times \frac{100}{1}$$

■ **Example**

Using the final accounts of Daniel's business –

$$\frac{\$30\,000}{\$100\,000} \times \frac{100}{1} = 30\%$$

Net profit as a percentage of sales

This measures the net profit for every $100 of sales. It indicates how well a business is able to control its operating expenses. The higher the rate, the more profitable the business.

Within one business, the net profit percentage may be similar from year to year, but hopefully it will increase (showing that the expenses are being kept under control). The percentage is influenced by the different types of expense. Some expenses vary according to the amount of sales, e.g. salespeople's commission, whereas other expenses are fixed and remain the same whatever the sales, e.g. rent. The expenses should be reduced wherever possible. Any improvement in the gross profit percentage will also affect the net profit percentage.

■ **Formula**

$$\frac{\text{Net profit}}{\text{Sales}} \times \frac{100}{1}$$

■ **Example**

Using the final accounts of Daniel's business –

$$\frac{\$10\,000}{\$100\,000} \times \frac{100}{1} = 10\%$$

Liquidity ratios

The term 'liquidity' means the ease and speed with which assets can be turned into cash.

Current ratio

This is sometimes known as the **working capital ratio**. It compares the assets which will become liquid within 12 months with the liabilities due for payment in that time. This is a measure of the business's ability to meet existing current liabilities as they fall due. Anything between 1.5 : 1 and 2 : 1 may generally be regarded as satisfactory, but much depends on the type and size of the business. A ratio of over 2 : 1 may imply poor management of current assets.

There must be sufficient working capital to finance the day-to-day trading of the business. The consequences of not having enough working capital include –
(a) problems in meeting debts as they fall due
(b) inability to take advantage of cash discounts
(c) difficulties in obtaining further supplies
(d) inability to take advantage of business opportunities as they arise.

Ways of improving the working capital include –
(a) introduction of further capital
(b) obtaining long-term loans
(c) reducing owner's drawings
(d) selling surplus fixed assets.

The actual **cash** position may be improved by such policies as increasing the proportion of cash sales, reducing the debtors collection period and taking longer to pay creditors. Whilst these measures will improve the cash position they may have other effects, e.g. taking longer to pay creditors could result in refusal of further supplies.

■ **Formula**   Current assets : Current liabilities

■ **Example**   Using the final accounts of Daniel's business –

$30 000 : $12 000 = 2.5 : 1

Quick ratio

This is sometimes known as the **acid test ratio**. It compares the assets which are in money form, or which will convert into money quickly, with the liabilities due for payment in the near future. This calculation excludes stock, which is **not** regarded as a liquid asset. Stock is two steps away from being money – firstly it has to be sold, and secondly the money has to be collected from the debtors. In addition, some of the stock may be unsaleable for various reasons. The quick ratio shows whether a business would have any surplus liquid funds if all the current liabilities were paid immediately from the liquid assets.

A ratio of 1 : 1 is usually regarded as satisfactory. This indicates that liquid assets match the current liabilities. With a ratio of 1 : 1, the current liabilities can be paid without the need to sell stock immediately (probably at reduced prices), and without fixed assets having to be sold. As with the current ratio, the quick ratio required depends on the type and size of the business. A ratio of more than 1 : 1 may indicate poor management of liquid assets, e.g. too high a bank balance indicates that funds are not being used to the best advantage.

■ **Formula**   Current assets – stock : Current liabilities

■ **Example**   Using the final accounts of Daniel's business –

($30 000 – $9 000) : $12 000 = 1.75 : 1

Rate of stock turnover

This is sometimes known as **stockturn**. It is the number of times a business sells and replaces its stock in a given period of time. The quicker the stock is turned over, the greater the gross profit (provided the profit margin remains the same). Within one business, the rate of stock turnover may be similar from year to year. If it increases, it may indicate efficiency is improving: if it reduces, it may mean that the business has too much stock, or that the sales are slowing down.

The rate of stock turnover depends on the type of business. A business selling relatively low-value 'everyday' requirements, such as newspapers, will have a very high rate of turnover, whereas a business selling high-value luxury goods, such as expensive jewellery, will have a very low rate of turnover.

■ **Formula**   The rate of stock turnover can be calculated in two ways –

(a) $\dfrac{\text{Cost of goods sold}}{\text{Average stock}}$ to give the number of **times** stock is sold and replaced in the period

(b) $\dfrac{\text{Average stock}}{\text{Cost of goods sold}} \times \dfrac{365}{1}$ to give the number of **days**, on average, the stock is held before being sold

■ **Example**   Using the final accounts of Daniel's business –

(a) $\dfrac{\$70\ 000}{(\$7\ 000 + \$9\ 000) \div 2} = \dfrac{\$70\ 000}{\$8\ 000} = 8.75$ times

(b) $\dfrac{\$8\ 000}{\$70\ 000} \times \dfrac{365}{1} = 41.71$ days

Collection period for debtors

This is sometimes known as the **debtors/sales ratio**. It is the average amount of time that debtors take to pay their accounts. The quicker the debtors pay, the better it is, as the money can then be used elsewhere in the business. Within one business, the collection period may be similar from year to year. If it decreases, it may indicate that the business has a more efficient credit control policy. If it increases, it may indicate an inefficient credit control policy, or that the business is having to allow longer credit terms in order to maintain sales.

It is useful to compare this *actual* collection period for debtors with the terms of credit *allowed* when the goods were sold. The older a debt is allowed to become, the greater the risk of it becoming a bad debt. Ways of improving the collection period for debtors include –
(a) offer cash discounts for early settlement of debts
(b) charge interest on overdue debts
(c) refuse further supplies until the outstanding balance is paid
(d) improve credit control (send regular Statements of Account, 'chase' overdue debts, etc.)
(e) consider invoice discounting and debt factoring*

*The services provided by a factor include maintaining the sales ledger, collecting the debts and advancing money against the debts. A discounter makes advances against certain debts, but does not maintain the sales ledger. The trader is charged a fee by the factor or the discounter for the services provided.

■ **Formula**

$$\frac{\text{Debtors}}{\text{Credit sales}} \times \frac{365}{1}$$

(or $\times \frac{52}{1}$ to give an answer in weeks

or $\times \frac{12}{1}$ to give an answer in months)

■ **Example**

Using the final accounts of Daniel's business –

$$\frac{\$8\,000}{\$100\,000} \times \frac{365}{1} = 29.2 \text{ days}$$

Payment period for creditors

This is sometimes known as the **creditors/purchases ratio**. It is the average amount of time the business takes to pay its creditors. Within one business, the payment period may be similar from year to year. If it decreases, it indicates that the business is paying its creditors more quickly. If it increases, it may indicate that the business is short of liquid funds and is finding it more difficult to pay. Taking extended credit benefits the liquidity position as the business is able to use the money for other purposes for a longer period. The drawbacks to delays in paying creditors are the loss of any cash discounts which may be available, and the damage to the relationship with the suppliers.

■ **Formula**

$$\frac{\text{Creditors}}{\text{Credit purchases}} \times \frac{365}{1}$$

(or $\times \frac{52}{1}$ to give an answer in weeks

or $\times \frac{12}{1}$ to give an answer in months)

■ **Example**

Using the final accounts of Daniel's business –

$$\frac{\$12\,000}{\$72\,000} \times \frac{365}{1} = 60.83 \text{ days}$$

Inter-firm comparison

The accounting ratios of a business can be compared with those of previous years in order to assess the business's performance. It is also useful to compare the accounting ratios of one business with those of a similar business.

■ **Example**

Daniel Duval has been in business for several years. Two years ago his sister, Daisy Duval, opened a similar business in a different town. The following information is available:

	Daniel $	Daisy $
For the year ended 31 March 20–2 –		
Sales – cash	–	60 000
credit	100 000	30 000
Cost of sales	70 000	64 400
Purchases – credit	72 000	61 400
Expenses	20 000	14 350
At 1 April 20–1–		
Stock	7 000	8 000
At 31 March 20–2 –		
Stock	9 000	5 000
Debtors	8 000	2 500
Bank	13 000	3 700
Creditors	12 000	7 200
Capital employed	80 000	68 000

(a) For each business calculate –
Rate of return on capital employed
Gross profit as a percentage of sales
Net profit as a percentage of sales
Current ratio
Quick ratio
Rate of stock turnover
Collection period for debtors
Payment period for creditors

(b) Using each of the ratios, compare the performances of the two businesses.

(a) The detailed calculations are only shown for Daisy's business, as those for Daniel's business have already been shown.

	Daniel Duval	Daisy Duval
Rate of return on capital employed	12.5%	$\dfrac{\$11\ 250}{\$68\ 000} \times \dfrac{100}{1} = 16.54\%$
Gross profit as percentage of sales	30%	$\dfrac{\$25\ 600}{\$90\ 000} \times \dfrac{100}{1} = 28.44\%$
Net profit as percentage of sales	10%	$\dfrac{\$11\ 250}{\$90\ 000} \times \dfrac{100}{1} = 12.5\%$
Current ratio	2.5 : 1	$\$11\ 200 : \$7\ 200 = 1.56 : 1$
Quick ratio	1.75 : 1	$\$6\ 200 : \$7\ 200 = 0.86 : 1$
Rate of stock turnover	8.75 times	$\dfrac{\$64\ 400}{\$6\ 500} = 9.91$ times
Collection period for debtors	29.2 days	$\dfrac{\$2\ 500}{\$30\ 000} \times \dfrac{365}{1} = 30.42$ days
Payment period for creditors	60.83 days	$\dfrac{\$7\ 200}{\$61\ 400} \times \dfrac{365}{1} = 42.80$ days

(b) Comparison of the businesses:
Profitability:
Daniel's gross profit as a percentage on sales was slightly better than Daisy's. Despite this, Daisy earned a better net profit as a percentage of sales, which may indicate that Daniel is not controlling his expenses as well as Daisy. The return on capital employed in Daisy's business was better than Daniel's, which may indicate that Daniel is not making the most effective use of the capital.

Liquidity:
The working capital in each business is satisfactory, as the current assets cover the current liabilities. Daniel also has a satisfactory quick ratio, but Daisy may find it difficult to meet the current liabilities when they fall due. (See page 233 for ways in which liquidity may be improved.) Daisy has reduced her stock during the year, and has turned her stock over more quickly than Daniel. It may be that Daniel should consider reducing his stock, and try to increase his rate of turnover by advertising and possibly reducing his profit margin slightly.

All Daniel's sales were on credit terms, whereas only one third of Daisy's sales were made on credit. The collection period for debtors is very similar in each business. Daniel is taking an average of 60.83 days to pay the creditors, whereas Daisy is taking only 42.80 days on average. This may be linked to the fact that Daisy has a quicker rate of turnover and a large proportion of cash sales.

Problems of inter-firm comparison

It is important to remember that every business is different and has different requirements and different accounting policies. A comparison with the accounting ratios of other businesses is useful, but should be undertaken with caution.

To give meaningful results, the comparison should be made with a business of the same type, in the same trade, and of approximately the same size. A comparison of the accounts of a sole trader who has a small general store with annual sales of $100 000, with the accounts of a limited company that has engineering factories in several countries, and annual sales of $10 million, would not provide any useful information. Even a comparison of businesses of the same type, of a similar size, and in the same trade, can give misleading results. Points to bear in mind when comparing the accounting ratios of two businesses include –

(a) The accounts may be for one year only, which will not show business trends, and, in addition, that year may not be a typical year.
(b) The financial years may end on different dates, and the period covered by the accounts may be different.
(c) The businesses may operate different accounting policies, e.g. one business may use the straight line method of depreciation, and the other business may use the reducing balance method.
(d) There may be differences which affect the profitability and the items on the Balance Sheet, e.g. one business may own premises, and the other business may rent premises; one business may be financed entirely by the owner's capital, and the other business may be financed partly from long-term loans.
(e) The accounts do not show non-monetary items, but these can play an important part in the success of the business, e.g. the quality of management and the reputation of the business.

(f) The accounts are based on historic costs, which do not indicate the effects of inflation.

(g) It is not always possible to obtain all the information required about another business in order to make a true comparison.

Users of accounting statements

There are two groups of people who may be interested in analysing and interpreting the accounting statements of an organisation. One group, who either own, or are employed by the organisation, may be described as **internal users**. Anyone else with an interest in the accounting statements is regarded as an **external user**.

The **owner(s)** and the **manager(s)** of a business will be interested in the profitability and the liquidity. They use ratio analysis to assess past performance, to plan for the future, and to identify any areas where corrective action is required. Any **investors** in a business are also interested in the profitability and future prospects of the business.

A **bank manager**, who is asked by a business to authorise a bank loan or overdraft, will study the accounting statements. She will be interested in whether interest can be paid when due, whether the loan or overdraft can be repaid when due, and whether there is sufficient security to cover the amount of the loan or overdraft. These matters are also of interest to any other **lenders**. **Creditors** are interested in the liquidity position and how long the business normally takes to pay for goods bought on credit. A creditor will take these into account when deciding the credit limit and the length of credit allowed. The future prospects of the business are also important to creditors. Creditors may not have access to the accounts of sole traders and partnerships, as these forms of businesses are not required to publish their accounts.

The **members** of a non-trading organisation, such as a club, will be interested in the financial position of the club as this can affect whether subscriptions will be increased, whether there is enough money to provide new facilities, and so on. Members will also be concerned if the organisation made a deficit, and will want to know what is being done to prevent this in future.

Limitations of accounting statements

Accounting statements provide valuable information about a business's performance. It is important to remember, however, that they do have limitations, and do not provide all the relevant information about a business. A business's final accounts, and consequently the ratios prepared from these accounts, reflect what has happened in the past. Certain significant events may take place between the end of the financial year and the date when the final accounts are analysed. New fixed assets may be purchased, stock levels may have altered significantly, the liquidity position may have changed for the better (or the worse), and so on.

The accounts record transactions at their actual, or **historic**, cost. This is the only way to establish a definite amount at which to record transactions. In times of inflation, however, it becomes difficult, if not impossible, to make meaningful comparisons of transactions occurring at different times. When a country has high inflation, $10 000 spent on equipment in 20–8 will not purchase the same amount of equipment as $10 000 spent in 20–2.

Accounting ratios can be used to compare the results of a business for one year with the results of previous years, and with the results of other businesses. Such a comparison can be useful, but only if a comparison of 'like with like' is made. The problems of inter-firm comparison have already been explained. All businesses should apply the accounting concepts of **prudence** and **consistency**, but they may use different accounting methods (e.g. different methods of depreciating fixed assets), which make it impossible to make a meaningful comparison of certain ratios. There is also the problem of different businesses using different definitions. Earlier in this chapter, capital employed was defined as the total of capital owned plus the long-term liabilities at the end of the financial year. This is only one of the accepted definitions of capital employed. Inter-firm comparison of the return on capital employed is only meaningful if the same definition of capital employed is applied.

Applying the **money measurement** concept, the accounts of a business only record information that can be expressed in monetary terms. There are many factors which affect the future performance of a business that do not appear in the accounting statements. Despite the fact that some of these are outside the business itself, such as government policy, competition, new technology, and so on, they can have a significant effect on the future performance of the business. Such things as the quality of management, the skill and reliability of the workforce, the age and condition of the fixed assets, the ability to adapt to changing market conditions, and so on, also influence the performance of the business. All these are within the control of the business itself, even though they do not appear in the accounting statements.

Despite their limitations, bookkeeping and accounting are invaluable tools in recording the financial transactions and assessing the performance of a business.

Review questions

1. (a) State how the capital employed in a sole trader's business is calculated.
    [IGCSE 2000]
   (b) State what is meant by the working capital of a business.
    [IGCSE 1997]
   (c) Name **one** accounting ratio that measures a business's profitability.
    [IGCSE 1999]

(d) Suggest **one** example of an accounting ratio that measures the efficiency of a business.

[IGCSE 1997]

(e) Explain the difference between the current ratio and the quick ratio.

[IGCSE 1996]

(f) (i) What is meant by the rate of stock turnover?
(ii) Suggest **one** reason why the rate of stock turnover of a business may vary from year to year.

[IGCSE 1996]

(g) The gross profit of a business for the year ended 31 March 1997 was $120 000 and the expenses were $80 000.
(i) Calculate the net profit for the year.
(ii) The sales of the business for the year were $200 000. Calculate the net profit as a percentage of the sales.

[IGCSE 1997]

2. Rik Nemo's trading results for the year ended 31 March 1998 were as follows –

	$
Stock of goods: 1 April 1997	4 000
31 March 1998	16 000
Purchases	112 000
Sales	160 000

(a) Calculate, for the year ended 31 March 1998, showing your workings:
(i) Rik's cost of sales
(ii) Rik's average stock
(iii) Rik's rate of stock turnover.

(b) State and explain why it is an advantage for Rik to know his rate of stock turnover.

(c) Calculate, for the year ended 31 March 1998, showing your workings:
(i) Rik's gross profit
(ii) Rik's gross profit as a percentage of sales.

(d) Suggest **two** reasons why the gross profit percentage of a business may vary from year to year.

[IGCSE 1998]

3. (a) The following balances were included in the books of Jeri Mander, a sole trader, on 31 March 1998:

	$
Debtors	3 000
Creditors	6 000
Stock	9 000
Accrued expenses	1 500
Cash at bank	2 500
Cash in hand	200
Insurance paid in advance	300

Calculate Jeri's working capital at 31 March 1998. Show your workings.
(b) Calculate, showing your workings:
  (i) Jeri's current ratio
  (ii) Jeri's quick ratio.
(c) State and explain **two** reasons why it is important for a business to have enough working capital.

[IGCSE 1998]

4. Cato is a trader. Cato's brother also owns a business. The following information is taken from the accounts of both businesses:

	Cato's business	His brother's business
Gross profit as a percentage of sales	20%	45%
Rate of stock turnover	50 times	3 times
Debtors at end of year	$100	$4 000

One business sells food. The other sells electrical goods.

(a) State whether Cato owns the food business or the electrical goods business.
(b) Explain **two** reasons for your answer to (a).

[IGCSE 1997]

5. Joey is in business as a sole trader. His Trading and Profit and Loss Account for the year to 31 March 1997 and his Balance Sheet at that date were as follows –

Trading and Profit and Loss Account for the year to 31 March 1997

	$	$
Sales (all on credit)		120 000
Less Cost of sales		
Stock at 1 April 1996	14 000	
Purchases	72 000	
	86 000	
Stock at 31 March 1997	16 000	70 000
Gross Profit		50 000
Less Overheads –		
Selling and administration expenses		35 600
Net Profit		14 400

Balance Sheet as at 31 March 1997

	$	$
Fixed assets at net book value		82 185
Current assets		
Stock	16 000	
Trade debtors	20 000	
Bank	3 415	
	39 415	
Current liabilities		
Trade creditors	25 600	13 815
		96 000
Financed by:		
Capital at 1 April 1996		99 100
Profit for the year		14 400
		113 500
Drawings		17 500
		96 000

(a) Calculate the following accounting ratios for Joey's business:
  (i)   net profit as a percentage of capital employed
  (ii)   percentage of net profit to sales
  (iii)   percentage of gross profit to sales
  (iv)   current ratio
  (v)   quick ratio
  (vi)   rate of stock turnover
  (vii)   collection period for debtors.

(b) Joey compared some of the accounting ratios for his business with the ratios for other similar businesses. These were:

percentage of net profit to sales	15%
percentage of gross profit to sales	35%
quick ratio	1 : 1
rate of stock turnover	6 times

  (i)   State whether each of Joey's four ratios is better or worse than that of the other similar businesses.
  (ii)   Give a reason for each of your answers to (b) (i)
  (iii)   State whether or not you think Joey should be satisfied with the ratios for his business.

[IGCSE 1997]

*6. Seng and Poh are traders dealing in the same range of goods. Their summarised Balance Sheets at 31 March 1998 are given below.

	Seng $000	Seng $000	Poh $000	Poh $000
Fixed assets		100		125
Stock		28		30
Debtors		32		40
Balance at bank		10		–
		170		195
Creditors	35		35	
Bank overdraft	–	35	15	50
		135		145
Capital		100		110
Net profit for the year		35		35
		135		145

The following further information relates to the year ended 31 March 1998:

	$000	$000
Sales	350	400
Cost of sales	210	272

(a) Using the information given above, calculate for Seng **and** Poh:
 (i) percentage of gross profit to sales
 (ii) percentage of net profit to sales
 (iii) net profit as a percentage of the capital employed at 31 March 1998
 (iv) the rate of stock turnover (stocks at 1 April 1997 were: Seng $14 000, Poh $38 000)
 (v) the collection period for debtors.
(b) Using each of the ratios you have calculated in (a), compare the performances of the two businesses.
(c) State **three** ways in which the collection period of debtors may be improved.

[IGCSE 1998]

7. The following is a summary of information extracted from the accounts of a sole trader for two years:

	1998 $	1999 $
Sales	65 000	82 000
Cost of sales	26 000	36 000
All other expenses	19 000	26 000
Opening stock	10 000	8 000
Closing stock	8 000	12 000
Debtors	4 000	7 000
Bank	1 500	2 800
Creditors	5 000	11 000
Capital at year end	100 000	120 000

(a) For each of the two years calculate:
   (i) gross profit as a percentage of sales
   (ii) net profit as a percentage of capital employed
   (iii) current ratio
   (iv) quick ratio
   (v) collection period for debtors
   (vi) payment period of creditors
Make your calculations to one place of decimals.

(b) Use your answers to (a) to compare the performance of the business in 1999 with its performance in 1998.

(c) The owner of this business has obtained the accounts of another, different type of business for 1997. State **five** reasons why he should not use the other business's accounts to compare with his own accounts.

[IGCSE 1999]

8. Charlie Brown is a sole trader whose Balance Sheets are shown below.

Balance Sheet as at 30 September

	1995 $	1996 $		1995 $	1996 $
Capital	43 000	50 000	Fixed Assets	35 000	40 000
Creditors	7 000	10 000	Stock	8 000	16 000
			Debtors	5 000	3 500
			Bank	2 000	500
	50 000	60 000		50 000	60 000

You are given the following additional information:
1. For the year ended 30 September 1996 Charlie's sales were $300 000. His gross profit was 20% of sales and his net profit was 8% of sales.

2. Charlie did not introduce any new capital into the business during the year.

(a) For the year ended 30 September 1996, calculate Charlie's:
 (i) cost of sales
 (ii) purchases
 (iii) expenses
 (iv) drawings
(b) (i) Calculate the rate of stock turnover for Charlie's business for the year ended 30 September 1996.
 (ii) Explain why it is important for the owner of a business to know its rate of stock turnover.
(c) Charlie tells you three facts about his business.
 1. He is expecting a large seasonal increase in sales in the last three months of 1996.
 2. He has been successful in collecting debts.
 3. He has persuaded his suppliers to give him a longer time to pay them.

Suggest how **each** of these three facts is shown in the Balance Sheet.

[IGCSE 1996]

9. Brock decided to purchase Kamil's business. Kamil's assets and liabilities at 1 October 1997 were as follows –

	$
Fixtures and fittings	10 000
Delivery van	8 000
Office equipment	4 800
Stock	11 000
Trade debtors	3 750
Prepaid expenses	816
Bank overdraft	2 741
Trade creditors	2 980
Expenses owing	300

Brock purchased Kamil's business on 1 October 1997, taking over all the assets and liabilities at the values shown above. Brock paid Kamil $36 000 for the business including Goodwill.

(a) Prepare the Balance Sheet of the business as it appeared on 1 October 1997 immediately after Brock had purchased it.
(b) Calculate for the business –
   (i) the current ratio
   (ii) the quick ratio
(c) Brock hopes to earn 15% return on his capital. Calculate the profit he must earn.

[IGCSE 1997]

Answers to review questions

Chapter 1   Question 2

Farad

Balance Sheet as at 31 March 20–6

Assets	$	Liabilities	$
Machinery	34 000	Capital	65 000
Fixtures and fittings	22 000	Loan from bank	20 000
Stock	28 400	Creditors	15 400
Debtors	13 400		
Cash	2 600		
	100 400		100 400

Chapter 2   Question 4

Bandara Bargains

Bank account   Page 1

Date	Details	Folio	$	Date	Details	Folio	$
20–5				20–5			
Aug 1	Capital	2	25 000	Aug 2	Rent	3	400
				5	Purchases	4	1 850
				28	J. Kamati	5	2 460
				29	Drawings	11	100
				31	Balance	c/d	20 190
			25 000				25 000
20–5							
Sept 1	Balance	b/d	20 190				

248 Accounting: IGCSE

B. Bandara Capital account — Page 2

Date	Details	Folio	$	Date	Details	Folio	$
				20–5 Aug 1	Bank	1	25 000

Rent account — Page 3

Date	Details	Folio	$	Date	Details	Folio	$
20–5 Aug 2	Bank	1	400				

Purchases account — Page 4

Date	Details	Folio	$	Date	Details	Folio	$
20–5 Aug 5	Bank	1	1 850				
9	J. Kamati	5	2 600				

J. Kamati account — Page 5

Date	Details	Folio	$	Date	Details	Folio	$
20–5 Aug 18	Purchases returns	8	140	20–5 Aug 9	Purchases	4	2 600
28	Bank	1	2 460				
			2 600				2 600

Sales account — Page 6

Date	Details	Folio	$	Date	Details	Folio	$
				20–5 Aug 13	Cash	7	260

Cash account — Page 7

Date	Details	Folio	$	Date	Details	Folio	$
20–5				20–5			
Aug 13	Sales	6	260	Aug 21	Advertising	9	90
Aug 25	Commission received	10	50	31	Balance	c/d	220
			310				310
20–5							
Sept 1	Balance	c/d	220				

Purchases Returns account — Page 8

Date	Details	Folio	$	Date	Details	Folio	$
				20–5			
				Aug 18	J. Kamati	5	140

Advertising account — Page 9

Date	Details	Folio	$	Date	Details	Folio	$
20–5							
Aug 21	Cash	1	90				

Commission Received account — Page 10

Date	Details	Folio	$	Date	Details	Folio	$
				20–5			
				Aug 25	Cash	7	50

Drawings account — Page 11

Date	Details	Folio	$	Date	Details	Folio	$
20–5							
Aug 29	Bank	1	100				

Chapter 3   Question 2

Joe Kover
Trial Balance as at 30 June 1998

(a)

	Debit $	Credit $
Stock 1 July 1997	14 000	
Purchases	70 000	
Trade creditors		10 000
Sales		90 000
Trade debtors	6 000	
Rent paid	3 000	
Balance at bank	5 000	
Fixtures and fittings	22 000	
*Capital		20 000
	120 000	120 000

*Capital is inserted as the balancing figure.

(b) See Chapter 2.

Chapter 4   Question 4

(a)   Josiah Mangombe – Cash Book

Date	Details	Folio	Discount Allowed $	Cash $	Bank $	Date	Details	Folio	Discount Received $	Cash $	Bank $
1996						1996					
Sept 1	Balance	b/d		400		Sept 1	Balance	b/d			1 800
3	A. Brown		5		95	12	J. Smith		12.5		487.5
7	Sales				300		C. Jones		5		195
12	Capital				5 000	15	Wages			200	
15	Sales			176		21	Salaries				650
23	Sales			307			Motor				
25	AZ Ltd.		20		780		expenses			210	
						30	Drawings				800
							Balance	c/d		473	2 242.5
			25	883	6 175				17.5	883	6 175
Oct 1	Balance	b/d	NL1	473	2 242.5				NL2		

(b)

Josiah Mangombe – Nominal Ledger

Discount Allowed account   Page 1

Date	Details	Fo	$	Date	Details	Fo	$
1996 Sept 30	Total for month	CB	25				

Discount Received account   Page 2

Date	Details	Fo	$	Date	Details	Fo	$
				1996 Sept 30	Total for month	CB	17.5

(c) Entering only the monthly total of discount received and discount allowed in the respective discount accounts saves time and greatly reduces the number of entries in these accounts.

Chapter 5   Question 2

Katie

(a) & (b)   **Josiah Mangombe – Cash Book**   Page 1

Date	Details	Folio	Total Received	Date	Details	Vo	Total Paid	Stationery	Postages	Wages	Ledger accounts
			$				$	$	$	$	$
20–6 May 1	Balance	b/d	90	20–6 May 3	L. James	1	15				15
				9	Postage stamps	2	4		4		
				15	Stationery	3	7	7			
				21	T. Giles	4	9				9
				24	Postage stamps	5	2		2		
				29	Wages	6	40			40	
							77	7	6	40	24
				31	Balance	c/d	13	NL1	NL2	NL3	
			90				90				
June 1	Balance	b/d	13								
	Cash		77								

252 Accounting: IGCSE

(c)

Katie

Nominal Ledger

Stationery account — Page 1

Date	Details	Folio	$	Date	Details	Folio	$
20–6 May 31	Petty cash	PCB1	7				

Postages account — Page 2

Date	Details	Folio	$	Date	Details	Folio	$
20–6 May 31	Petty cash	PCB1	6				

Wages account — Page 3

Date	Details	Folio	$	Date	Details	Folio	$
20–6 May 31	Petty cash	PCB1	40				

Purchases Ledger

L. James account — Page 1

Date	Details	Folio	$	Date	Details	Folio	$
20–6 May 3	Petty cash	PCB1	15				

T. Giles account — Page 2

Date	Details	Folio	$	Date	Details	Folio	$
20–6 May 21	Petty cash	PCB1	9				

Chapter 6   Question 4

(a) Kuomi International
(b) (i) 4 × $50 = $200
    (ii) $200 + $240 = $440
(c) (i) Sales journal
    (ii) Purchases journal
(d) Credit Note
(e) Invoice total $440
    Less goods returned (2 × $50)   100
    Amount owing   340
(f) Debtor

Chapter 7   Question 6

Al Haffar Stores

Profit and Loss Account for the year ended 31 October 20–1

	$	$
Gross Profit		67 500
Add Commission received		7 500
		75 000
Less Salaries and wages	27 100	
Packing and postage	1 850	
Rent and rates	7 510	
Loan interest	1 000	
Insurance	1 430	
Motor expenses	10 110	49 000
Net Profit		26 000

Balance Sheet as at 31 October 20–1

	$	$
Fixed assets		
Buildings		29 000
Machinery		11 000
Motor vehicles		16 100
		56 100
Current assets		
Stock	21 140	
Debtors	8 200	
Bank	14 100	
Cash	260	
	43 700	
Less Current liabilities		
Creditors	15 100	
Working capital		28 600
		84 700
Less Long-term liabilities		
Loan – Finance Co.		10 000
		74 700
Financed by		
Capital		
Opening balance		64 000
Plus Net Profit		26 000
		90 000
Less Drawings		15 300
		74 700

Chapter 8   Question 3

(a) (i) & (ii) See Chapter 8
(b) (i)   Capital expenditure – purchase of a fixed asset
   (ii) Revenue expenditure – maintaining a fixed asset
   (iii) Revenue expenditure – day-to-day running expense
   (iv) Capital expenditure – cost of a fixed asset
   (v) Revenue expenditure – day-to-day running expense
(c) (i)   In the Profit and Loss Account the expenses are understated by $2 000, so the net profit is overstated by $2 000.
   (ii) In the Balance Sheet the fixed assets are overstated by $2 000, and the capital account balance is overstated as the net profit is overstated by $2 000.

Chapter 9   Question 5

Van Wyk & Co.
Trading and Profit and Loss Account for the year ended 31 May 20–4

	$	$	$
Sales		60 900	
Less Sales returns		300	60 600
Less Cost of goods sold –			
Opening stock		6 300	
Purchases	46 500		
Less Purchases returns	200		
	46 300		
Carriage inwards	200	46 500	
		52 800	
Less Closing stock		6 800	46 000
Gross Profit			14 600
Add Commission received			
(1 900 + 200)			2 100
			16 700
Less Repairs		550	
Motor vehicle expenses			
(680 + 120)		800	
Insurance (280 – 20)		260	
Wages		4 630	
Office expenses (470 – 10)		460	6 700
Net Profit			10 000

Chapter 10   Question 5

Cosey, Fann and Tootie

(a) Machinery account

Date	Details	Folio	$	Date	Details	Folio	$
1998				1998			
May 1	Balance	b/d	108 000	Oct 8	Disposals	b/d	11 000
June 6	Bank		20 000	1999			
Dec 12	Largo Alfactum		14 000	Jan 7	Disposals		7 000
				Apr 30	Balance	c/d	124 000
			142 000				142 000
1999							
May 1	Balance	b/d	124 000				

(b) **Provision for Depreciation of Machinery account**

Date	Details	Folio	$	Date	Details	Folio	$
1998				1998			
Oct 8	Disposals			May 1	Balance	b/d	42 000
	(3 yrs × 25%			1999			
	× $11 000)		8 250	Apr 30	Profit & Loss		
1999					(25% × $124 000)		31 000
Jan 7	Disposals						
	(2 yrs × 25%						
	× $7 000)		3 500				
Apr 30	Balance	c/d	61 250				
			73 000				73 000
				1999			
				May 1	Balance	b/d	61 250

(c) **Disposal of Machinery account**

Date	Details	Folio	$	Date	Details	Folio	$
1998				1998			
Oct 8	Machinery		11 000	Oct 8	Provision for		
1998					depreciation		8 250
Jan 7	Machinery		7 000		Bank		4 000
				1999			
				Jan 7	Provision for		
					depreciation		3 500
				Apr 30	Profit & Loss		2 250
					(Loss of $3 500 –		
					Profit of $1 250)		
			18 000				18 000

Chapter 11   Question 8

John Mafule

(a)   Profit and Loss Account for the year ended 30 June 20–6

	$	$
Gross Profit		32 400
Add Discount received		1 800
		34 200
Less Discount allowed	1 600	
Bad debts	210	
Increase in provision for doubtful debts	30	
Rent (10 500 – 500)	10 000	
Wages	21 600	
General expenses (4 120 + 150)	4 270	
Loan interest	350	
Depreciation of fixtures and equipment	2 900	40 960
Net Loss		6 760

(b) **Balance Sheet as at 30 June 20–6**

		$	$	$
Fixed assets		Cost	Depreciation to date	Net book value
Fixtures and equipment		29 000	11 600	17 400
Current assets				
Stock			16 200	
Debtors		6 200		
Less Provision for doubtful debts		310	5 890	
Prepayment			500	
			22 590	
Less Current liabilities				
Creditors		8 400		
Accrual		150		
Bank overdraft		2 000	10 550	
Working capital				12 040
				29 440
Less Long-term liabilities				
Loan				5 000
				24 440
Financed by				
Capital				
Opening balance				39 600
Less Net Loss			6 760	
Drawings			8 400	15 160
				24 440

Chapter 12   Question 2

(a) **Cash Book (bank columns only)**

Date	Details	Folio	$	Date	Details	Folio	$
1998				1998			
Oct 1	Balance	b/d	6 035	Oct 1	Bank charges		200
					Bank interest		84
					Balance	c/d	5 751
			6 035				6 035
1998							
Oct 1	Balance	c/d	5 751				

(b)   **Bank reconciliation statement as at 30 September 1999**

		$	$
Balance as per bank statement			5 996
Add amounts not yet credited – Enni & Co.			627
			6 623
Less cheques not yet presented – Brite Lite			
	Electrical Co.	772	
	Ojay Containers	100	872
Balance as per cash book			5 751

(c) (i) Any three from –
Unsigned, or signature differs from specimen signature
Undated, or bears a future date
Out of date (over 6 months old)
Words and figures do not agree
Insufficient funds in Cosi Bros.' bank account

(ii) Debit Cosi Bros.' account with $42
Credit Bank account with $42

(d) See Chapter 12.

Chapter 13   Question 6

(a) Explanation of one from –
Correction of errors
Opening entries
Recording items that do not pass through another book of prime entry
Recording unusual transaction

Millie Plainfeather

(b)   Journal

Date	Details	Folio	Debit $	Credit $
1996 June 1	Motor vehicles Star Garage Motor vehicle bought on credit		10 000	10 000
June 5	Electricity Rent Error in posting electricity to rent account, now corrected		300	300

(c) **Statement of Corrected Net Profit for the year ended 20 June 1996**

	$	$
Net Profit from Profit and Loss Account		26 800
Less Provision for doubtful debts	900	
Depreciation of office equipment	400	
Motor expenses	500	1 800
Correct Net Profit		25 000

Chapter 14   Question 3

David

(a) **Purchases Ledger Control account**

Date	Details	Folio	$	Date	Details	Folio	$
20–4				20–4			
Sept 1	Balances	b/d	40	Sept 1	Balances	b/d	2 800
	Purchases			Sept 30	Purchases		6 300
	returns		1 100		Cash		10
	Bank		5 750		Balances	c/d	30
	Discount						
	received		110				
	Balances	c/d	2 140				
			9 140				9 140
20–4				20–4			
Oct 1	Balances	b/d	30	Oct 1	Balances	b/d	2 140

(b) Until the error is corrected, the credit balance on the purchases ledger control account will be overstated by $100.

Chapter 15   Question 6

Maria

(a) **Cash book (bank columns only)**

Date	Details	Folio	$	Date	Details	Folio	$
1997				1998			
May 1	Balance		6 025	Apr 30	Creditors		3 660
1998					Wages		2 200
Apr 30	Cash sales		19 000		Rent		6 000
	Debtors		5 640		Rates		5 100
	Balance	c/d	910		Electricity		615
					Drawings		14 000
			31 575				31 575
				1998			
				May 1	Balance	b/d	910

262 Accounting: IGCSE

(b) **Trading and Profit and Loss Account for the year ended 30 April 1998**

	$	$
Sales		24 760
Less Cost of goods sold		
Opening stock	4 000	
Purchases	3 840	
	7 840	
Less Closing stock	5 000	2 840
Gross Profit		21 920
Less Wages	2 200	
Rent (6 000 – 400)	5 600	
Rates (5 100 + 140 – 180)	5 060	
Electricity	615	
Depreciation of fixtures & fittings	2 000	15 475
Net Profit		6 445

Calculations

1. Sales

Total Debtors account

Date	Details	Folio	$	Date	Details	Folio	$
1997				1998			
May 1	Balance		600	Apr 30	Bank		5 640
1998					Balance	c/d	720
Apr 30	Sales		5 760				
			6 360				6 360
1998							
May 1	Balance	b/d	720				

	$
Total sales for the year were –	
Credit sales	5 760
Cash sales	19 000
	24 760

2. Purchases

Total Creditors account

Date	Details	Folio	$	Date	Details	Folio	$
1998 Apr 30	Bank Balance	c/d	3 660 300 ───── 3 960	1997 May 1 1998 Apr 30	Balance Purchases		120 3 840 ───── 3 960
				1998 May 1	Balance	b/d	300

(c) Maria's drawings have exceeded the money in the bank, resulting in a bank overdraft. Her drawings have also exceeded the net profit for the year, resulting in a reduction of her capital. Consequently, it would be advisable for the drawings to be considerably reduced in the following year.

Chapter 16   Question 5

Newport Social Club

(a) (i)   Bar Trading Account for the year ended 31 August 1996

	$	$
Sales		83 400
Less Cost of sales		
Opening stock	5 200	
Purchases	37 200	
	42 400	
Less Closing stock	6 000	
Cost of goods sold	36 400	
Wages of bar staff	12 500	48 900
Profit on bar (transferred to Income and Expenditure Account)		34 500

264 Accounting: IGCSE

(ii) **Income and Expenditure Account for the year ended 31 August 1996**

		$	$
Income			
	Subscriptions (17 000 + 700)		17 700
	Profit on bar		34 500
	Profit on social events		3 750
			55 950
Expenditure			
	Wages (29 250 – 12 500)	16 750	
	Treasurer's salary	5 000	
	Secretarial expenses	3 100	
	General expenses	2 500	
	Rates and insurance	4 250	
	Depreciation of sports equipment	1 000	32 600
	Surplus for the year		23 350

(b) **Balance Sheet as at 31 August 1996**

	$	$	$
Fixed assets	Opening book value	Depreciation for year	Closing book value
Land and buildings	50 000	–	50 000
Sports equipment	10 000	1 000	9 000
	60 000	1 000	59 000
Current assets			
Stock in bar		6 000	
Subscriptions owing by members		700	
Bank		4 550	
Cash		1 750	13 000
			72 000
Financed by			
Accumulated Fund			
Opening balance			48 650
Plus Surplus for year			23 350
			72 000

Chapter 17   Question 6

A B & C

(a) Capital accounts

Date	Details	Folio	A $	B $	C $	Date	Details	Folio	A $	B $	C $
1997 Apr 1	Balance	c/d	21 000	16 000	8 000	1997 Apr 1	Balance	b/d	15 000	10 000	
							Bank				8 000
							Goodwill		6 000	6 000	
			21 000	16 000	8 000				21 000	16 000	8 000
						1997 Apr 2	Balance	b/d	21 000	16 000	8 000

(b) (i) **Profit and Loss Appropriation Account for the year ending 31 March 1998**

		$	$	$
Net Profit				81 000
Less Interest on capital –	A	2 100		
	B	1 600		
	C	800	4 500	
Partner's salary –	B		12 000	16 500
				64 500
Profit shares –	A		21 500	
	B		21 500	
	C		21 500	64 500

266 Accounting: IGCSE

(ii) Current accounts

			A	B	C				A	B	C
Date	Details	Folio	$	$	$	Date	Details	Folio	$	$	$
1998 Mar 31	Drawings Balance	c/d	16 000 7 600	17 000 18 100	15 000 7 300	1998 Mar 31	Interest on capital Salary Profit share		2 100 21 500	1 600 12 000 21 500	800 21 500
			23 600	35 100	22 300				23 600	35 100	22 300
						1998 Apr 1	Balance	b/d	7 600	18 100	7 300

Chapter 18   Question 3

The X Company

(a) Manufacturing Account for the year ended 31 March 1999

	$	$
Cost of material consumed		
Opening stock of raw material	13 000	
Purchases of raw material	94 000	
Carriage inwards	4 400	
	111 400	
Less Closing stock of raw material	15 000	96 400
Direct wages		36 000
Prime Cost		132 400
Factory overheads		
Indirect wages	15 000	
Fuel and power	20 000	
Rent	9 000	
Depreciation of machinery	18 000	62 000
Production cost of goods completed		194 400

Answers to review questions 267

(b) **Trading and Profit and Loss Account for the year ending 31 March 1999**

	$	$
Sales		240 000
Less Cost of goods sold		
Opening stock of finished goods	11 000	
Production cost of goods completed	194 400	
	205 400	
Less Closing stock of finished goods	16 000	189 400
Gross Profit		50 600
Less Office salaries	16 000	
General expenses	7 600	
Depreciation of office equipment	2 000	25 600
Net Profit		25 000

Chapter 19   Question 3

Sharon Scarlett

(a) **Departmental Trading and Profit and Loss Account for the year ended 30 April 2000**

	Department A		Department B	
	$	$	$	$
Sales		80 000		40 000
Less Cost of goods sold				
Opening stock	5 500		4 900	
Purchases	48 200		31 400	
	53 700		36 300	
Less Closing stock	5 700	48 000	6 300	30 000
Gross Profit		32 000		10 000
Less Salaries	12 000		8 000	
Rates and insurance	1 000		1 000	
Administration	2 000		2 000	
Advertising	1 000		500	
Carriage outwards	400		200	
Depreciation of fixtures	500	16 900	500	12 200
Net Profit (Net Loss)		15 100		(2 200)

(b) See Chapter 19.
(c) Explanation of any three from –
Department B is making a loss.
Department B's gross profit to sales ratio is only 25% compared to 40% for Department A.
If Department B is closed, all the expenses allocated to it will not necessarily disappear.
If Department B is closed, the sales of Department A may be affected.
If Department B is closed, staff morale and the confidence of customers and suppliers may be affected.
Space presently occupied by Department B could be used for some other purpose.

Chapter 20   Question 6

(a)   Seng and Poh

Ratio	Seng	Poh
i. Percentage of gross profit to sales	$\frac{\$140}{\$350} \times \frac{100}{1} = 40\%$	$\frac{\$128}{\$400} \times \frac{100}{1} = 32\%$
ii. Percentage of net profit to sales	$\frac{\$35}{\$350} \times \frac{100}{1} = 10\%$	$\frac{\$35}{\$400} \times \frac{100}{1} = 8.75\%$
iii. Net profit as a percentage of capital employed on 31 March 1998	$\frac{\$35}{\$135} \times \frac{100}{1} = 25.93\%$	$\frac{\$35}{\$145} \times \frac{100}{1} = 24.14\%$
iv. Rate of stock turnover	$\frac{\$210}{\$21} = 10$ times	$\frac{\$272}{\$34} = 8$ times
v. Collection period for debtors	$\frac{\$32}{\$350} \times \frac{365}{1} = 33.37$ days	$\frac{\$40}{\$400} \times \frac{365}{1} = 36.5$ days

(b) Both businesses earned the same amount of net profit. Seng earned the better net profit as a percentage of sales, as he earned the same net profit as Poh on a lower amount of sales. The expenses as a percentage of sales is the difference between the gross profit percentage and the net profit percentage. Poh controlled his expenses better, as he has the lower percentage of expenses to sales. Seng had the higher percentage of gross profit to sales. It may be that Seng was able to buy cheaper goods than Poh, or that he did not pass on price increases to his customers. Seng had a slightly better return on the capital employed, so he used the capital a little more effectively.

Seng had a quicker rate of stock turnover than Poh, which would have helped increase Seng's gross profit. It may be that Poh's sales are slowing down or that more extensive advertising is required. Seng had a slightly shorter collection period for debtors than that of Poh. This may indicate that Poh's credit control policy was not as effective as Seng's, or that Poh allowed longer credit in order to maintain sales.

(c) See Chapter 20.

Cambridge International Examinations

IGCSE ACCOUNTING

Specimen Paper 1 – Multiple choice

Time allowed – 1 hour

There are 40 questions in this paper. Answer **all** questions. For each question there are four possible answers: A, B, C, and D. Choose the **one** you consider correct. Each correct answer will score 1 mark.

1. Why does a business owner measure profit?
   A to compare actual results with expected results
   B to find the amount of his bank balance
   C to find the amount of his capital
   D to know how much he can spend on assets

2. In which order are current assets shown in the Balance Sheet?
   A bank, cash, stock, debtors
   B cash, bank, debtors, stock
   C debtors, stock, cash, bank
   D stock, debtors, bank, cash

3. Why is a balance sheet prepared?
   A to show cash payments and receipts for a year
   B to show debtors and creditors at a certain date
   C to show the financial position of a business at a certain date
   D to show the income and expenditure for a year

4. A capital account shows the amount owed by a business to its owner. Of which concept is this an example?
   A business entity
   B consistency
   C matching
   D prudence

5. When is revenue earned?
   A when goods are ordered by the customer
   B when an invoice is sent to the customer
   C when the customer pays for the goods
   D when the customer gains ownership of the goods

6. A business always uses the same basis for valuing stock from one period to the next. Which accounting concept applies?
   A consistency
   B money measurement
   C prudence
   D realisation

7. A prepayment is deducted from the relevant expense and treated as a current asset. Which accounting concept applies?
   A duality
   B matching
   C money measurement
   D prudence

8. What is an example of the prudence concept?
   A Accrued expenses are treated as a liability.
   B An owner's drawings are deducted from capital.
   C Only items with a monetary value are included in accounting.
   D Profit is not overstated.

9. B. Lilly sold goods on credit to S. Farr. Some of the goods are damaged and Farr returns them to Lilly. Which document is sent by Lilly to Farr?
   A advice note
   B credit note
   C debit note
   D invoice

10. Ralph & Co. allows Jill trade discount of 25% and cash discount of 5% if invoices are paid within 30 days.
    Jill buys goods with a list price of $1 600 from Ralph & Co.
    Which amount will be entered in Jill's purchases journal?
    A $1 120
    B $1 140
    C $1 200
    D $1 600

11. Which book of prime entry is part of the double entry system?
    A cash book
    B journal
    C purchases journal
    D sales journal

12. X returns damaged goods to Y, the supplier. In which book of prime entry does Y record this transaction?
    A journal
    B purchases returns journal
    C sales journal
    D sales returns journal

13. A trader buys television sets for re-sale from Astra on credit. Which entries record the transaction in the trader's ledger?

	Account debited	Account credited
A	Astra	Purchases
B	Astra	Television sets
C	Purchases	Astra
D	Television sets	Astra

14. A debit entry in the cash account is matched by a credit entry in T. Leonie's account. What do these entries record?
    A goods sold to T. Leonie for cash
    B payment of cash to T. Leonie
    C purchase of goods from T. Leonie for cash
    D receipt of cash from T. Leonie

15. Where are the expense accounts, revenue accounts and purchases account found?

	Sales ledger	Purchases ledger	Nominal ledger
A	√		
B		√	
C			√
D	√	√	√

16. Why does a business prepare a trial balance?
    A to provide a list of all its assets and liabilities
    B to calculate its profit or loss
    C to check the accuracy of its ledger entries
    D to check its bank balance

Cambridge International Examinations 273

17. The totals of a trial balance do not agree. Which type of error causes this?
    A a compensating error
    B an error of addition
    C an error of commission
    D an error of principle

18. A purchase on credit of $500 from Mitchell was credited in error to Mitchison's ledger account. Which journal entries correct this error?
    A debit Mitchison, credit Mitchell $500
    B debit Mitchell, credit Mitchison $500
    C debit Suspense, credit Mitchell $500
    D debit Mitchison, credit Suspense $500

19. A difference on a trial balance was entered in a suspense account. It was later found that:
    rent paid $1 500 was entered on the credit side of the rent account
    a payment of $840 for telephone was debited in the telephone account as $940
    What is the trial balance difference in the suspense account?
    A $1 400 credit
    B $2 340 debit
    C $2 900 debit
    D $3 840 credit

20. Why is a bank reconciliation statement prepared?
    A to calculate the bank balance for the balance sheet
    B to check the amount owing from debtors
    C to show how much has been paid to creditors
    D to show the amount of petty cash in hand

21. A cash book balance was $1 790 (Dr.). When compared with the bank statement, unpresented cheques were $1 040 and deposits not credited were $820. What was the balance on the bank statement?
    A $70 debit
    B $1 570 credit
    C $2 010 credit
    D $3 650 credit

22. A truck costs $10 000. The price included $50 for petrol. The total payment of $10 000 was debited in the trucks account. What is the effect on the Profit and Loss Account and Balance Sheet?

	Profit and Loss Account	Balance Sheet
A	Profit overstated by $50	Fixed assets overstated by $50
B	Profit overstated by $50	Fixed assets understated by $50
C	Profit understated by $50	Fixed assets overstated by $50
D	Profit understated by $50	Fixed assets understated by $50

23. What is the reason for charging depreciation?
    A to provide money to replace an asset
    B to reduce the cost of repairing an asset
    C to show an asset's market value
    D to spread an asset's cost over its useful life

24. Which item is capital expenditure?
    A fuel for vehicle
    B insurance for vehicle
    C purchase of vehicle
    D repairs to vehicle

25. A machine cost $12 000 on 1 January 2000. Its scrap value after four years will be nil. If it is depreciated by the straight line method, what is the machine's book value on 31 December 2001?
    A $12 000
    B $9 000
    C $6 000
    D $3 000

26. What is the advantage of using the reducing balance method of depreciation?
    A It allows for increasing cost of repairs.
    B It is easy to calculate.
    C It is a quicker way of writing off assets.
    D It shows assets at realisable values in a balance sheet.

27. The table shows balances in the books of a business.

	$
Accrued expenditure	700
Bank overdraft	1 300
Creditors	2 500
Debtors	3 600
Prepayments	400
Stock	?

The current ratio is 2 : 1
What is the value of the stock?
A $1 100
B $3 700
C $4 300
D $5 000

28. What is the correct treatment of 'carriage inwards' in the accounts of a sole trader?
    A Add it to carriage outwards in the Profit and Loss Account.
    B Add it to purchases in the Trading Account.
    C Deduct it from carriage outwards in the Profit and Loss Account.
    D Show it separately as an expense in the Profit and Loss Account.

29. A partner makes a loan of $10 000 to the business. Interest is 10% per annum. What is the correct treatment of the interest on the loan in the partnership's accounts?
    A credit Profit and Loss Account $1 000
    B debit Profit and Loss Account $1 000
    C credit Profit and Loss Appropriation Account $1 000
    D debit Profit and Loss Appropriation Account $1 000

30. Which item appears in the Profit and Loss Appropriation Account of a partnership?
    A goods taken by a partner for own use
    B interest on a partner's loan
    C partners' drawings
    D partners' salaries

31. What is **not** considered when profit is calculated from incomplete records?
    A depreciation of fixed assets
    B interest on a loan to the business
    C the owner's winnings in a competition
    D wages paid to owner's wife for working in the business

32. On 1 January, Roy paid $50 000 into a bank account to start his business. On 31 December, the following information was available:

	$
Fixed assets	45 000
Current assets (including balance at bank)	35 000
Creditors	15 000

A year's depreciation on fixed assets, $8 000, was also to be provided. During the year, Roy withdrew $12 000 from the business for his own use. What was Roy's profit for the year?

A $7 000
B $15 000
C $19 000
D $27 000

33. What does the capital of a business equal?

A fixed assets + current assets + current liabilities
B fixed assets + current assets – current liabilities
C fixed assets – current liabilities – current assets
D fixed assets + current liabilities – current assets

34. The table shows balances in the books of a business:

	$
Balance at bank	1 100
Creditors	1 500
Debtors	3 000
Stock	4 000

What is the net working capital?

A $3 600
B $6 600
C $8 100
D $9 600

35. The working capital of a business is shown.

	$
Stock	15 000
Debtors	16 000
Bank	4 000
Cash	1 000
	36 000
Creditors	9 000
	27 000

What is the current ratio?

A 1.3 : 1
B 2.3 : 1
C 3 : 1
D 4 : 1

36. The working capital of a business is shown.

	$
Stock	8 000
Debtors	12 000
Bank	6 000
Cash	500
	26 500
Creditors	5 000
	21 500

What is the quick ratio?
A 1.3 : 1
B 3.7 : 1
C 4.3 : 1
D 5.3 : 1

37. A Trading Account for the year ended 31 December 2000 is given.

	$	$
Sales		300 000
Less Cost of sales		
Stock 1 January 2000	30 000	
Purchases	200 000	
	230 000	
Less Stock 31 December 2000	20 000	210 000
		90 000

The rate of stock turnover is calculated using average stock held. What is the rate of stock turnover?
A 4.2 times
B 6 times
C 8.4 times
D 12 times

38. What is found by deducting expenses from gross profit?
A balance at bank
B capital
C cost of sales
D net profit

39. What does a trader discover when he compares his net profit with his gross profit?
A cost of sales
B expenses of carrying on the business
C the total of his payments
D why the business has made a loss

40. What should the owner of a business do to find if there has been an improvement in the financial position of his business?
  A Compare this year's Balance Sheet with last year's Balance Sheet.
  B Compare this year's Profit and Loss Account with last year's Profit and Loss Account.
  C Compare this year's Balance Sheet with that of a similar business.
  D Compare this year's Profit and Loss Account with that of a similar business.

Cambridge International Examinations

IGCSE ACOUNTING

Paper 2 May/June 2001

Time allowed – 1 hour 30 minutes

Answer all questions.

1. (a) State the effect on gross profit if closing stock is undervalued.
    [1]

   (b) State how the capital employed in a sole trader's business is calculated.
    [2]

   (c) Smith returns some goods bought on credit from Brown.
      (i) Name the document that Brown issued to Smith.
    [1]

      (ii) Name the book of prime (original) entry in which the return of the goods is recorded –
          1. in Smith's books
          2. in Brown's books.
    [2]

   (d) Complete the following sentence:
       'A credit balance on a ledger account shows either a … or … of the business'.
    [2]

   (e) In a three column cash book, state what is meant by a 'contra entry'.
    [1]

   (f) (i) State **one** reason why a supplier gives trade discount to a customer.
    [1]

      (ii) On 1 April Jones bought goods on credit from Green, $2 000. Green allows 25% trade discount and a cash discount of 2% for payment within one month.
          Jones paid Green on 25 April. How much did he pay? Show your workings.
    [4]

   (g) (i) Give **one** example of a fixed asset.
    [1]

(ii) A business provides annually for the depreciation of its fixed assets. State how this depreciation is shown –
1. in the Profit and Loss Account
2. in the Balance Sheet.

[2]

(h) (i) The purchase of a new vehicle was wrongly entered in the purchases account. Name this type of error.

[1]

(ii) For **each** of the three items place one tick (✓) in the correct box.

	Capital expenditure	Revenue expenditure
1. Purchase of new premises		
2. Repairs to old building		
3. Legal fees paid in connection with factory extension		

[3]

(iii) State and explain what is meant by the accounting concept of duality.

[2]

2. Sam Panne owns a furniture store. His Trading Account for his last financial year is shown below. Some words and figures are missing.
(a) In each of the boxes (i) to (v), enter the missing word(s) or figure.

[5]

Sam Panne

Trading Account for the year ended 31 December 2000

	$	$		$	$
(i) [ ] 1 January 2000		10 000	Sales	(ii) [ ]	
Purchases	36 000		Less Returns	3 000	60 000
Less Returns	(iii) [ ]				
	34 000				
	44 000				
Stock 31 December 2000	(iv) [ ]				
(v) [ ]	36 000				
Gross Profit	24 000				
	60 000				

Cambridge International Examinations 281

(b) Calculate Sam's gross profit as a percentage of his sales for the year. Show your workings.

[2]

(c) (i) Calculate Sam's rate of stock turnover. Show your workings.

[4]

(ii) Suggest **one** way in which Sam might use the information in (i) regarding his rate of stock turnover.

[2]

3. Jason's cash book for March 2001 showed the following entries:

Cash Book (bank columns only)

2001			$	2001			$
March	1 Balance	b/d	2 400	March	16 Cheque, I. Dolittle		760
	6 Cash & cheques		510		12 Cheque, F. Francisco		580
	18 Cheque, A. Foley		300		30 Cheque, J. Zapata		190
	29 Cheque, M. Jackson		450		31 Balance	c/d	2 130
			3 660				3 660
April	1 Balance	b/d	2 130				

Jason received the bank statement shown below on 2 April 2001.

2001		Dr. $	Cr. $	Balance $
March 1	Balance			2 400 Cr.
8	Cash and cheques		510	2 910 Cr.
9	Cheque, Dolittle	760		2 150 Cr.
15	Cheque, Francisco	580		1 570 Cr.
21	Cheque		300	1 870 Cr.

(a) Prepare a statement reconciling the balances shown in Jason's cash book and bank statement on 31 March 2001.

[9]

(b) Jason's financial year ends on 31 March. In his Balance Sheet as at 31 March 2001 –
  (i) Under what heading will 'Bank' be shown?

[2]

  (ii) What amount will be entered for 'Bank'?

[1]

(c) Certain items shown on a bank statement may not yet be entered in the customer's cash book, e.g. a direct debit paid by the bank. Name **one** other item of this type.

[1]

282 Accounting: IGCSE

4. Wayne Shorter makes up his annual accounts to 30 April. His trial balance at 30 April 2001 showed a shortage on the debit side of $220. The difference was posted to a suspense account. The following errors were later discovered:
1. The sales journal had been over-cast by $500.
2. The purchase of additional office furniture costing $1 000 had been entered in the purchases account.
3. The wages account had been under-cast by $200.
4. Discount received of $240 had been incorrectly posted to the debit side of the discounts allowed account. No entry had been made in the discounts received account.

(a) Prepare the entries in Wayne's journal, with narratives, to correct the above errors.

[14]

(b) Write up the suspense account to show the required amendments. Start with the balance arising from the difference on the trial balance.

[6]

(c) If capital expenditure is incorrectly treated as revenue expenditure, explain how this affects –
  (i) the net profit shown in the Profit and Loss Account;

[2]

  (ii) the fixed assets shown in the Balance Sheet.

[2]

5. Jodie Tharp is a sole trader whose financial year ends on 31 March. On 1 April 2000, balances in Jodie's ledger included the following:

	Dr. $	Cr. $
Electricity		400

During the year ended 31 March 2001, Jodie made the following payments for electricity by cheque:

	$
15 April 2000	400
10 July 2000	310
18 October 2000	650
9 January 2001	540

At 31 March 2001, the amount owing for electricity was $590.

(a) Record the above transactions in the electricity account. Start with the balance on 1 April 2000. Balance the account at 31 March 2001. Show the amount transferred to the Profit and Loss Account for the year ended 31 March 2001.

[11]

(b) Complete the following sentence for Jodie's Balance Sheet as at 31 March 2001:

The balance on the electricity account is shown as a… in Jodie's Balance Sheet as at 31 March 2001.

[2]

(c) (i) State and explain what is meant by the accounting concept of matching.

[2]

(ii) Explain how the matching concept is observed by the adjustments made in **(a)** in the electricity account.

[2]

Cambridge International Examinations

IGCSE ACCOUNTING

Paper 3 May/June 2001

Time allowed – 1 hour 45 minutes

Answer all questions

1. Mohammed is an office trainee who has recently joined the staff of F. Amato and Son. You have been asked to explain to him how the accounting records are maintained.

   (a) State **two** reasons why a business uses a Sales Journal. [2]

   (b) The books of original entry show the following transactions for March 2001:

Sales Journal		
Mar 11 M Ali		
Goods		165
24 Z. Hussain		
Goods	400	
Trade Discount	80	320

Journal		
Mar 31 Bad debts	65	
M. Ali		65

Sales Returns Journal		
Mar 30 Z. Hussain		
Goods	50	
Trade discount	10	40

Cash Book (debit side)	Discount Allowed	Bank
Mar 8 Z. Hussain	6	194
19 M. Ali	11	429
31 M. Ali		100

On 1 March 2001 Z. Hussain had a debit balance of $200 and M. Ali had a debit balance of $440.

Write up the ledger accounts of Z. Hussain and M. Ali as they would appear in F. Amato and Son's sales ledger for the month of March 2001.

[11]

(c) Mohammed looks at the nominal ledger and asks you to explain the entries in the insurance account. The account shows –

Insurance account

2000		$	2000			$
Jan 1 Balance b/d		150	Dec 31 Profit & Loss			330
July 1 Bank		360	Balance	c/d		180
		510				510
2001						
Jan 1 Balance b/d		180				

You first show him the alternative presentation for the account as follows –

Insurance account

	Dr. $	Cr. $	Balance $
2000			
Jan 1 Balance b/d	150		150
July 1 Bank	360		510
Dec 31 Profit & Loss		330	180

Explain **each** entry in the Insurance account as it appears in the nominal ledger.

[8]

2. The balances in the books of Sprinters Athletic Club on 1 February 2000 were –

	$
Bank	640
Equipment	1 500 (original cost $2 500)
Insurance prepaid	120
Subscriptions owed by members	200
Accumulated fund	2 460

The treasurer produced the following information for the year ended 31 January 2001:

Receipts	$	Payments	$
Balance 1 February 2000 b/d	640	Athletic association fee	150
Subscriptions	3 450	Expenses of annual party	1 890
Sale of tickets for annual party	2 160	Rent of stadium	1 350
		Insurance	370
		Purchase of new equipment	1 600
		Travelling expenses	475
		General expenses	195
		Balance 31 January 2001 c/d	220
	6 250		6 250
Balance 1 February 2001 b/d	220		

Additional notes

1. At 31 January 2001 subscriptions prepaid by members amounted to $300; insurance prepaid amounted to $175.
2. Equipment is depreciated using the straight line (equal instalment) method at 20% p.a. on the total cost of equipment held at the end of the year.

(a) Prepare the Income and Expenditure Account for the year ended 31 January 2001.

[12]

(b) Prepare the Balance Sheet as at 31 January 2001.

[8]

3. (a) Zani maintains a purchases ledger and a sales ledger and prepares control accounts at the end of each month.
On 1 April 2001 the balances brought down on the control accounts were –

	$
Purchases ledger control account	2 400 credit
Sales ledger control account	2 900 debit

Totals of the journals for April 2001 were –

Purchases journal	3 630
Sales journal	5 940
Purchases returns journal	40
Sales returns journal	70

The cash book for April 2001 showed –

	$
Cheques paid to creditors	3 260
Cheques received from debtors	4 850
One of the cheques received was later dishonoured	130
Cash received from a creditor in respect of an over-payment	20
Discount allowed	120
Discount received	85

The journal entries for April 2001 showed –

Bad debts written off	45

Prepare the Purchases Ledger Control account and the Sales Ledger Control account for the month of April 2001. Bring down the balances on 1 May 2001.

[17]

(b) On 30 April 2001 the balances on the Sales Ledger Control account disagreed with the list of balances in the sales ledger by $45. It is found that bad debts written off have not been recorded in the personal accounts.

What is the total of the list of balances in the sales ledger?

[1]

4. Robina and Sabena are in partnership, sharing profits and losses equally. On 1 April 2000 the balances on their capital and current accounts were –

	Robina	Sabena
	$	$
Capital account	20 000	15 000
Current account	5 000 credit	2 000 debit

During the year ended 31 March 2001 partners' drawings were –

	$
Robina	3 000
Sabena	6 000

The Profit and Loss Appropriation Account for the year ended 31 March 2001 showed –

			$	$	$
Net Profit					12 800
Interest on drawings	Robina			180	
	Sabena			360	540
					13 340
Interest on capital	Robina		1 400		
	Sabena		1 050	2 400	
Partner's salary	Sabena			3 500	5 950
					7 390
Profit shares	Robina			3 695	
	Sabena			3 695	7 390

(a) Prepare the partners' Current accounts as they would appear in the ledger for the year ended 31 March 2001. Bring down the balances on 1 April 2001.

[9]

(b) On 1 April 2001 Robina and Sabena decided to admit Fatima to the partnership. She paid $15 000 into the firm's bank account on that date.

It was agreed that profits and losses of the new partnership would be shared:

Robina 2/5   Sabena 3/5   Fatima 1/5

Goodwill was valued at $8 000 on 1 April 2001. The capital accounts of Robina and Sabena were adjusted for Goodwill on the admission of Fatima but a Goodwill account is not maintained.

Prepare the Capital accounts of Robina, Sabena and Fatima as they would appear in the ledger immediately after Fatima was made a partner. Bring down the balances on 2 April 2001.

[14]

5. Steven Enonga's results for the year ended 31 December 2000 show –

	$
Sales	58 000
Cost of sales	36 000
Expenses	11 500

All his purchases and sales are made on credit terms. Purchases for the year amounted to $42 000.

His Balance Sheet at 31 December 2000 shows –

	$
Fixed assets	112 000
Stock	8 000
Debtors	7 000
Creditors	6 500
Bank overdraft	4 500

Steven is pleased with his results but thinks they will be even better in 2001. He has purchased new equipment and is building up his stock in preparation for an expected increase in trade.

He decided to compare his results for 2000 with those of other similar businesses for the same period and obtained some average ratios from his trade association.

Ratio	Average for the trade	Column (a)
Gross profit as a percentage of sales	33.33%	37.93%
Net profit as a percentage of sales	16.75%	
Net profit as a percentage of capital employed	10.44%	
Current ratio	2.2 : 1	
Quick ratio	1.09 : 1	
Collection period for debtors	62 days	
Payment period for creditors	45 days	

(a) Complete column (a) in the table above to show the ratios for Steven's business. Calculations should be correct to **two** decimal places. The first item has been completed as an example.

[6]

(b) For **each** of the following ratios suggest one possible reason for the difference between Steven's ratio and the average ratio. The first one has been completed as an example.

Gross profit as a percentage of sales –
It may be that Steven is able to purchase goods more cheaply than other firms in the industry.

Net profit as a percentage of sales
Current ratio
Quick ratio
Collection period for debtors
Payment period for creditors

[12]

INDEX

A
Accrued expenses	86–87
income	90–91
Assets, current	71
fixed	70–71

B
Bad debts, recovered	120–121
writing off	120
reducing possibility of	127
Balance Sheet	70–74
Balance Sheet equation	2
Bank overdraft	33
Business entity, concept of	80

C
Capital employed	229
expenditure	83
owned	229
receipt	83
Carriage inwards	16
outwards	16
Cash book, two-column	29–33
three-column	33–37
Commission, error of	24
Compensating errors	24
Concepts	80
Consistency, concept of	82
Contra entries	30
Conventions	80
Correction of errors, effect	
on profit	152–153
on Balance Sheet	153–154
Credit Note	50–51
Creditors payment period	235–236
Current ratio	232–233

D
Debit Note	49–50
Debtors collection period	234–235
Depreciation, causes of	104
methods of	104–107
Direct material	213
labour	213
expenses	213
Discount, cash	33–34
trade	48
Dishonoured cheque	34
Drawings	16
Duality, concept of	81

E
Errors not revealed by trial balance	24–25
revealed by trial balance	23

G
Going concern, concept of	81
Goodwill, on admission of new partner	205–208
Gross profit percentage	230–231

I
Income & Expenditure Account	187–190
Inter–firm comparison	236–239
Invoice	48–49

L
Ledger, division of	29
Liabilities, current	71
long term	71
Limitations of accounting statements	239–240

M
Margin	178
Mark–up	178
Matching, concept of	82
Money measurement, concept of	81

N
Net profit percentage	232

O
Omission, error of	24
Original entry, error of	24
Overheads, factory	214

P
Partners' capital accounts	201–203
current accounts	201–203
Partnership, admission of new partner	205–208
agreement	198–199
Appropriation Account	199–201
Prepaid expenses	88–89
income	92–93
Prime cost	214
Principle, error of	24
Production, cost of	213–214
Profit & Loss Account	67–68
Prudence, concept of	82
Purchases journal	55–57
returns journal	55–57

Q
Quick ratio	233–234

R
Realisation, concept of	81
Receipts & Payments Account	184–185
Return on capital employed	231
Revenue expenditure	83
receipt	83
Reversal, error of	25
Running balance accounts	16–17

S
Sales journal	53 55
returns journal	53–55
Statement of account	51–52
Statement of Affairs	167
Stock, finished goods	217, 219
rate of turnover	179, 234
raw material	213, 219
valuation	83–84
work in progress	216, 219
Subscriptions	192–193
Suspense account	149–151

T
'T' accounts	16
Trading Account	64–66
Turnover	231

U
Users of accounting statements	239

W
Working capital	229, 233